THE PARENTS' MANUAL

THE
PARENTS' MANUAL

A Guide to the
Emotional Development of
Young Children

ANNA W. M. WOLF

Second, revised edition

FREDERICK UNGAR PUBLISHING CO.
NEW YORK

TO THE MEMBERS OF THE STAFF

PAST AND PRESENT

of

THE CHILD STUDY ASSOCIATION OF AMERICA

in acknowledgment

TABLE OF CONTENTS

INTRODUCTION   xi

CHAPTER ONE

BRINGING HOME THE BABY   3

The right start. Breast feeding. Bottle feeding. Weaning.
Foundations of a sound nervous system. The Great God
Routine. Grandmothers. A daily schedule. The Beginnings
of Discipline. Habits and what not to do about them. Thumb
Sucking. What you can do about it. Crying. A good foundation—what is it? Help for Mother. Father's role. Troubling
habits.

CHAPTER TWO

WHAT SHOULD WE EXPECT OF OUR
    CHILDREN?   34

Sleep and Sleep Routines. The Child Eats. Offer—don't urge.
Mistakes at Mealtime. Success at Mealtime. Make Allowances.
Overeating. Do they like what's good for them? Bladder and
Bowel Training. How early can a baby learn? Wet or dry?
Don't force it. What parents forget. Other Good Habits. Is
it natural to be neat? Manners Do Matter. Cultivating the
spirit. Honesty. Imagination? Stealing. Make haste slowly.

CONTENTS

CHAPTER THREE

DISCIPLINE   70

Routine—the Basis of Discipline. "My Day." Good management equals good discipline. Good and bad behavior. Conscience. Counterfeit Love. Managing children. Rewards and
Punishments. Show that you know how he feels. These things
count most. A Case History: The Story of Two Brothers.

CHAPTER FOUR

BROTHERS AND SISTERS   96

How to Prepare Your First Baby for Your Second. Jealousy.
Handling Jealousy. How to Help Your Most Troublesome
Child. Look beneath the surface. A physical illness from
emotional causes. Family Friction—Values and Abuses. No
Two Alike. Middle and youngest children. The only boy and
the only girl. The Problem of the "Only" Child. Only means
lonely. How to help. Parents—Meet your. Children! "To
each according to his needs."

CHAPTER FIVE

THE CHILD AND HIS FRIENDS   126

Sociability Starts Early. How optimism begins. Playing together. How One Parent Cured One Bully. Primitive Ego in
the Nursery. We learned slowly, too. They shouldn't be too
good. Children Are All Different. Helping the Shy Child.
Help them find skills. Play Group or Nursery School. Choose
a good one. Parents and teachers. Friendships.

CHAPTER SIX

SEXUALITY IN CHILDHOOD   154

Infantile bodily pleasures. Bowel Training and Sex. Is
pleasure bad? The Child and His Body. Facts and feel-

ings. They are more worried than you think. Giving Information and Limiting Experience. Sleeping with parents. The right word is the best word. Nudity. Father's role. Your child and your neighbor's child. Sex Play Among Children. The Child Who "Never Asks." All children are interested in sex. Don't start with bees. Masturbation. What not to do. The parent's role. Ask yourself questions. Revaluation of Goals.

CHAPTER SEVEN

THINGS TO MAKE AND DO 186

What Toys Shall I Buy My Children? Play—Many Meanings and Many Uses. Playing Hard and Working Hard. Learning to play alone. "My child won't stick to anything." Keeping interest alive. Hobbies. Getting out. Books and Learning to Read. Tell them a story. Some Hopes. Just for fun. Holidays. Birthdays. Christmas.

CHAPTER EIGHT

THE FORGOTTEN FATHER 216

Old Homes and New. Dominant women. "What does your father do?" Any Wife to Any Husband—and Vice Versa. Try getting together first. Father's Companionship. The Importance of Being Father. The tired businessman. The maternal instinct in fathers. "A Man About the House." Building masculine men. And womanly women.

CHAPTER NINE

PSYCHOLOGICAL GROWING PAINS 240

Foundations of Mental Health. "Will he outgrow it?" Take it easy. Two important principles. Some Common Problems. When thumb sucking persists. The bitten nail. "Physical" ailments. The wet bed. Speech defects. The stuttering child. Negativism. Anger and aggression. Destructiveness. Fears—

their meaning and management. The timid child. How Serious Is a Child's Problem? Common sense can be overrated. How to tell a passing problem from a serious one. Who and where are the "experts"?

CHAPTER TEN

PROBLEM PARENTS 278

Teamwork is fundamental. Getting Away from Mother. Apron strings cause trouble. One way or another. They must be cut. Are you a "strong personality"? Leave them—sometimes. When Parents Fail—and Why. Mixed feelings. The intangible barrier. When parents need psychiatrists. Children and Divorce. Helping them know the truth. Mental hygiene of the broken home. Women in Conflict. Out of a job. Complications. Conflicts—external and internal. Personal Opinions.

CHAPTER ELEVEN

WHAT IS CHARACTER EDUCATION? 316

SUGGESTED READING 327

INDEX 333

INTRODUCTION

THE MOST VALUABLE THING parents can do for their children is enjoy them. This is essential, though it may not be easy, nor all that is needed. Childhood is not always as happy as it is supposed to be. It is a lighthearted time, but it is also a time of complex emotional changes, sometimes filled with confusion and anxiety. Parents, to be helpful, need both knowledge and good will. One is not enough without the other.

A child must be a source of good, solid, simple satisfaction to the adults with whom he lives. If he is not, neither the most perfect care nor the most scientific management can ever make up for it. Even the youngest infant is aware of the drawn brow and tense hands of an anxious mother. "Smile," orders the two-year-old, as his fingers try to push up the corners of his mother's mouth. To him the matter is simple. A smiling mother is a mother who is happy to have him around. She loves him. He knows that he is good and knows the pleasure of the self-satisfaction that is as necessary to him as milk. A child who grows up feeling that he never pleases his mother will probably go through life feeling that he can never amount to much. This feeling will influence him even as an adult, though he may have acquired both virtues and success.

Real enjoyment of children, however, can come only from interest in them through all their moods and phases. Laughter at their cuteness and ecstasies over their charms do not give any real indication of what goes on in the deeper layers of adult feelings. Children are not a free show for grownups' entertainment.

Real enjoyment means liking to do things with them and for them. It means pleasure in their society and interest in the things that interest them. It means trying to understand what they are feeling, even when they are most exasperating and not at all attractive. For children are not always happy. Even when they are reasonably and lovingly treated, sometimes they respond with anger and hostility.

Enjoyment is a matter of feeling and mood and cannot be simply willed into existence. It is much harder, therefore, to tell parents how to achieve it than to tell them how to deal with the specific problems—puzzling, vexing, exasperating, and humorous—that arise in every family. It is natural enough for parents to hope for a book that will offer rules of procedure, for it is comparatively easy to learn rules and follow them. Unfortunately, however, there are no rules that will always work in the management of children, as parents and others soon discover. There are, of course, certain principles, and this book will refer to them from time to time. But they are principles that apply largely to sound living. And what parents want, quite justifiably, is help in applying principles to a particular child in a particular situation.

"Of course," most parents say, "we wanted our children. We expected to enjoy them."

"But," they add—if they are honest—"it's hard to enjoy them when John is always making his sister cry because he snatches her toys, or hits her, or teases her. How can we enjoy Mary when she is rude to her grandmother and sulks before our friends? Tell us how to prevent these things. Then we can enjoy our children. Until then, we have to admit that much of the time we feel both irritation and real anxiety."

A great many books intended to answer these questions have already been written. Nearly all of them hold out the hope that children will be happy, independent, and courteous, if only parents will take their job seriously from the moment the child is born—if only they will conscientiously train him to "form habits" of happiness, independence, and courtesy. This habit-training school of child psychology has been very busy and seems to have done a good deal of harm. It has given the impression that the inevitable difficulties arise only because parents have not nipped bad habits in the bud or have not found ways to encourage good ones.

This is true only in a very limited sense, if at all. Many so-called bad habits which make children hard to live with are not in any way due to faulty training. They are normal phases of growth that may be inherent in the very nature of childhood. They are an essential part of development. On the other hand, some "bad habits" are more threatening to sound development and cannot be understood or corrected without closer study of the individual child.

This does not mean in either case that parents should merely stand by and do nothing. It does mean, though, that any action they take should be based on a thorough knowledge of some of the underlying mental mechanisms of childhood.

Habit training, to be sure, has a place. Children do need a chance to practice and to enjoy the right way of doing things. They need a guiding hand—often a restraining hand. But the success or failure of parents does not depend on the mechanical perfection of their training, but on their understanding of the deeper meanings of "good" behavior or "bad" behavior. It depends even more on the effective sympathy that exists between them and their children. Most parents do not need techniques for management as much as they need experiences that create warm affection and mutual enjoyment. Only on such a basis can techniques begin to work.

People differ in their natural ability to get along with children. Nearly everybody takes pleasure in a charming and friendly child, but there are many people who become instantly antagonistic when they are disturbed by a more heedless and less attractive one. In theory, no doubt, they respect the rights of such a child, but they prefer to do so at a distance, leaving the practical routines to someone else. On the other hand, there are people who really love children, who know how to feel as they feel and live with them from moment to moment as they live. These people are drawn quite naturally to children of all kinds and rarely have difficulties with little children. They are the born parents and teachers.

Some of them, however, have trouble with children in the growing-up stage. They find it hard to follow the youngster's half-baked and awkward fumblings with the adult world. Another mother, who was never able to play comfortably in the sand pile and who never really learned to love alligators in the bathtub, may then begin to come into her own. She feels at ease with the almost-adult child, whose thoughts and feelings are similar to hers.

Although the ability to enjoy children comes more naturally to some than to others, it can be developed. Objective study of all that science has to offer on the subject of child development does not guarantee success, but it can help. Knowledge makes for a certain sureness of touch in all that one does; parents need this if they are to proceed quietly through the barrage of opinions which may assail them from friends and relatives and from books. Parents are entitled to know that they can and will make plenty of mistakes in handling their children's emotional problems without ruining the children for life. But they are not entitled to live in a fool's paradise or to pooh-pooh real danger signals. Many psychological growing pains may best be left alone, in the belief that children will "grow out of" them, but not all behavior difficulties can be dismissed so easily.

Much has been said lately about the importance of common sense in getting along with children. Either you have it or haven't it, apparently—and all parents, of course, think that *they* have it. Perhaps common sense in the handling of children has become so uncommon that it is in need of a thorough reawakening. Certainly many a child has been rescued from an abyss of unhappiness and brattishness by the application of simple, sensible principles. Indeed, I hope that this book will offer its own brand. But it is foolish to pretend that common sense can cover all situations and solve all problems. There are times when special knowledge and techniques, also, must be brought to bear and when parents need expert counsel for their children's emotional ailments, just as they may need them for physical ailments. Child psychology and psychiatry contain a technical body of knowledge too vast to lay before even intelligent laymen in a book of this scope. Nevertheless, parents do need a general guide to the problems their children may be struggling with from time to time. They need to know when and how they can best help their children, as well as when and where to go for professional advice when they cannot.

In the course of this book we will be driven again and again to the conclusion that it is not so much what parents *do* as what they *are* that counts most in the management of children. In other words, there are certain steps toward maturity that parents themselves should take before they can be in a position to give the best to their children. Right here we confront a dilemma, for it is often as futile to exhort parents and tell them what *they* should be as it is to expect old-fashioned moral preachments to influence children. In many cases the parent is quite aware of his weaknesses and would like to be different—but cannot. In other words, there are problem parents, and they will probably need help in straightening out their own personal difficulties as adults before they can go much further in helping their children. Nevertheless, the majority of fathers and mothers will eagerly learn from any source. They turn to their own experience and their widening knowledge of human development; they read and study; they apply the lessons of day-to-day living with children in a trial and error fashion.

Most young parents—even psychologically sound ones, even those well endowed with common sense—make many mistakes from lack of knowledge. They give in to needless anxieties, or, on the other hand, fail to recognize when a child suffers from real emotional distress. Perhaps all any book on childhood can do is offer some short cuts, make suggestions, and give some warnings; and hope that, although some parents will not profit, others will.

To keep our zest and pleasure in the job of being a parent and yet remain responsible and watchful—this seems to be the task. To accomplish this parents must first know that life, with or without children, is unlikely to offer complete and perfect solutions. Along with the satisfactions there will be periods of irritation, anxiety, and even of anger and despair. Life with children is much like married life. It is carried on always in a state of unstable equilibrium, held upright by the belief that something wholly satisfactory lies just around the corner. Despite the illusion in both cases, the important thing will always be the mood that emerges and gives family life its essential coloring. There will be some genuinely black days. There will be some permanent disappointments that must be accepted, but there will also be many hours each day that make us sure that the game is worth the candle.

In the belief that parents really can increase the number of those hours, this book is offered. It will be concerned largely with the emotional forces in that period from birth to the age of six or seven, when the child is closely bound to his parents by ties that lay the foundations for all that is most significant for his emerging personality.

THE PARENTS' MANUAL

CHAPTER ONE

BRINGING HOME
THE BABY

THE FIRST YEAR can be a joy if the baby is well and if his father and mother are in a mood to relish him. In spite of the adjustments called for and the uncertainties of today, babies will continue to be born alike to the cautious and the incautious members of the population. Some may ask "Is it right to bring children into such a threatened and hazardous world? Is it not an act of pure selfishness?" Yet having asked, they will disregard their own answers and go right on founding families. This lack of logic is altogether healthy; the very existence of the human race depends on it.

Children don't need the warmly feathered nest and the years of calm security nearly as much as we think they do. A baby can be born into conditions of poverty and war, can

[3]

suffer dozens of other upheavals, and can weather them all—provided his parents somehow manage to welcome him and to face their problems with realism and courage. Children need security, of course, but what they need is an inner security of the affections, not external comforts.

They also need parents who have a sense of proportion. There may be real mountains, but there should not be imaginary ones, built on molehills. To be frightened because a baby is sick is one thing; but it is quite another to be anxious all the time because he might be sick or because he begins to show a "bad habit." On questions of health a doctor can always give advice; on questions of "bad habits" it is hoped that this book may show that many of them are only a normal part of infancy and should be understood as such. Maternal fussing is the very worst thing that can happen to a baby. Some of it, perhaps, can be forgiven in the case of a first child, when the mother is inexperienced and unsure of herself. But too many people fuss just because they are fussy.

The only cure for this is self-knowledge and growth on the part of the mother. There is rarely a good substitute for a mother, even an inexperienced mother, and a poor makeshift gets everyone off to a bad start. Babies need their mothers, for reasons that should become clear in the course of these chapters; and though baby nurses and helpers may have a real place, they should not assume command. A great deal, too, depends on the parents' inner readiness for a baby. Sometimes this is absent at first and grows only as the baby grows, but the *capacity* must exist—the capacity for taking the next step in a maturing partnership and assuming heavier responsibilities. With the coming of a baby it will be necessary for parents to live both more dangerously and less egotistically; to expend themselves emotionally, and to run risks which are deeper than mere financial risks. Whoever brings children into the world has given hostages to fortune.

THE RIGHT START

Every baby should be under the care of a doctor who should see him first, if possible, before he leaves the hospital. Here the doctor who is about to take over the case can consult with the physicians who have been in charge, so that he may profit by what they already know about the diet and other needs of the baby. The doctor should be someone whom the mother likes and trusts and is not afraid to bother, even with foolish questions. Even a well baby should be seen by the doctor at regular intervals, to suggest changes in diet or medication and give immunizing shots. Good books and pamphlets on child care are available at low cost and are reassuring and helpful—useful guides in the matter of everyday routines and basic handling.

A room that lets in direct sunlight is highly desirable—usually more desirable, if a choice must be made, than a very quiet room. Except for sudden sharp sounds, babies and young children are not so disturbed by noise as grownups think they are.

[5]

Many can learn to sleep soundly and peacefully through traffic noises, dish clatterings, radio music, and voices. For the first few months it may be convenient to have the baby's crib near the parents' bed at night. But six months should be long enough, and after the baby is a year old he should certainly sleep elsewhere. Married couples need privacy, and children are not always asleep when we think they are. When space is limited and there is only one bedroom it is often more practical to give it to the baby and his paraphernalia and to have a day bed in the living room for the parents. Or additional space may be gained by sacrificing the dining room and serving meals on a folding table in the living room. This may make it necessary to dispose of the dining-room suite which is often a white elephant in the modern home, anyway.

Breast Feeding

The question of whether to nurse a baby or not should never, except in case of disease, be settled ahead of time. Since artificial feeding has become so successful as a scientific substitute for breast milk it is surprising how many women, especially young ones, say that since it is "just as good" for the baby they need not bother to nurse him. Some women have the erroneous impression that it will make their breasts sag. Others just have a feeling, for which they have no clear reason, that they would rather not. Or they feel that it confines them too closely to the house. Many women in their first pregnancy are not always aware of what they really want and often decide to wait until the latter part of their pregnancy before making up their minds one way or the other. Often, too, they may leave the decision to the doctor.

Bottle Feeding

We don't know yet whether or not artificial feeding is really "just as good" for the baby. Certainly for women who live in homes without good refrigeration or the facilities for sterilizing utensils, an ever-ready supply of clean, fresh breast milk is much safer. But even when every facility for scientific cleanliness is available we still have the question of the difference, both measurable and more subtle, between the health of the breast-fed baby and the bottle baby.

In any case, experienced pediatricians increasingly favor breast feeding if it is possible. In many cases it is the obstetrician who pooh-poohs the importance of breast feeding—possibly because it's easier to prepare a formula than help a new mother establish her milk supply. Or it may be that either consciously or unconsciously he seeks popularity with his patients. Sometimes there has been strong resentment between these two groups of practitioners. The pediatrician or family doctor takes over the baby after he has been weaned, or when the mother has already decided against nursing. There is nothing left for him to do but take the best possible care of his small patient, prudently keeping his mouth shut.

Whatever effect it may have on the baby's physical health, there is another important angle to the nursing question. This is the effect of nursing on the mother herself and on the whole mother-child relationship. It is interesting that many women who have previously been indifferent find that they

[7]

want to nurse their babies once they are born. It also seems to be true that a woman who has decided in advance against nursing her first baby finds that she is most anxious to nurse her later ones. The truth seems to be that all our attitudes toward the major physical experiences of life—menstruation, sex relations, pregnancy, nursing, menopause, death—are never purely rational. It is unsafe to predict just what our emotions and desires concerning them will be. Therefore, it seems worth while to suggest that there is something in the nursing experience that tends to deepen the relationship between mother and child and to mature the mother's capacity for giving the best that she has. But this is not always true. Many maternal women prefer to bottle feed, and there is no reasoning with oneself about it. Perhaps women who can accept themselves unreservedly as women do take special pleasure in a performance as definitely female as nursing, but this hundred per cent female scarcely exists in modern civilization. At any rate, there are many ways for a mother to show affection for her baby; breast feeding may be one of the best ways, but it is not the only one.

Nevertheless, many mothers keenly desire to nurse their babies. Once in a while, however, there may be some difficulties. Some physicians claim that the cause of such failure lies in the fact that such women do not really want to; or that the modern world has made it impossible for them to lead the placid life which might make them good cows. But while these accusations may apply in some cases they certainly do not apply in others, and any rubber-stamp opinion like this does injustice to the large numbers of women who are willing

[8]

to make any sacrifice in order to nurse their babies and yet cannot do so. The most usual reason is that the doctors and nurses who tend the mother in the early weeks do not take the time or trouble to make it possible. Occasionally there may be some physical reasons, too, such as inverted nipples. Though generalizations are dangerous, this much can be said: scientifically supervised artificial feeding can, apparently, produce perfectly sound children. This is especially true when the mother realizes that her inability to nurse her baby may mean something of value lost for him as well as for her and tries to make it up to him as best she can. Knowing this, she should make each bottle feeding as warm and personal an experience as possible, holding the baby in her arms while feeding, so that he may have all the comfort that bodily contact can give.

Weaning

The whole nursing process and the pleasure of getting nourishment are the infant's first and fundamental experience of loving and being loved, and giving it up is among his earliest and severest disappointments. Some take the experience harder than others, but it is always of great importance that weaning—whether from breast to bottle or from bottle to cup —should not be hurried. No arbitrary date should be set to begin the process; the baby's own willingness to change should be the cue. Mothers should avoid forcing the matter over violent resistance. It is always better to make the transition slowly, so that the baby may become quite accustomed to sucking water or some of his milk from a bottle before he is expected to give up the breast. Similarly, in making the transition from bottle to cup it must be expected that the baby may object. Sucking is a pleasure not lightly relinquished.

In most instances, children who have been nursed can start tentatively with a bottle a day at the age of about five months; those who have been bottle fed before this time may be ready to accept the cup at about ten months. But children vary greatly, and neither matter should ever be forced. A premature baby or one who has been ill or subjected to strains of any kind will need more time to make the change than a more robust child. It is important also not to make too many demands at once. The day after a loved grandmother has left is no time to expect a child to give up his bottle, nor should he be expected to at any other time when there is stress or change in routine. The mother, in other words, should be guided constantly by what the child shows he is ready for. She should understand that the manner in which she introduces him to each new step in his development, or asks him to forgo some pleasure, may vitally affect his future emotional stability.

Foundations of a Sound Nervous System

Someday much more will be known about the mental and emotional life of the infant, but until such knowledge is available we shall do well to base many of our actions on the accumulated experience of the human race. It is the besetting sin of the educated young mother to rely too completely on rules and "science" and to overintellectualize her human relationships. Her own instincts, if she knew where to find them, would in many cases be a wiser guide than any half-baked knowledge she may have acquired. Scientific procedure should be observed with infants just as far as positive facts will take us. Millions of lives have been saved by modern knowledge of nutrition, bacteria, immunization, and the careful observance of hygienic routine. But this is not all, and we should stop pretending that it is all. In the whole region of personality development science has only recently begun its explorations and is only beginning to give us hints. Yet it is in this very sphere of the emotions that every mother must make decisions daily. The false notion that a baby's life is little more than vegetative is fast giving way to the view that much happens during the first weeks and months that will be of vast importance for future character and temperament. The conditions under which a child's simplest instinctive needs are gratified or denied are of great importance. The foundation of future troubles may be laid during these months by discomforts and disappointments—whether acute or protracted—and by long frustration of desire.

Modern psychiatry tends to the view that a strong sense of peace and physical pleasure makes a better foundation for a sound personality than premature exposures to discipline and denial. Discipline and denial must inevitably come and the child must learn to meet them, but he is far better equipped to do this after a period in which genuine dependence and the privileges of infancy have run their full course. During this period he should, if possible, grow to think of his mother as the unfailing source of all pleasure, satisfaction, and love. Only in the later months should he also see her as someone who must exact denials.

Fortunately, most people need no proof of the close relation between love and health, both physical and mental. The conduct of their own daily lives as adults makes them realize this. Literature today, as well as science, fully recognizes this fact. But still there are some who are surprised that this connection applies equally to the youngest infant and who therefore ignore its prime importance during the months in which the foundations of health are being built.

In a certain babies' hospital a group of infants were living under conditions which were considered the best possible for health and well-being. They were isolated as much as was practical to spare them the possibility of exposure to germs. They were handled by the nurses only when absolutely necessary for bathing and feeding and changing. Their diet, of course, was the best that could be devised for each individual; and their defects, if they had any, were carefully considered and corrected wherever possible. Yet, for reasons which baffled the chief of staff, these babies weighed less and were inferior in general robustness to the babies who lived at home and were brought to the clinic for occasional checkups. The home-grown babies, brought up under haphazard conditions —some even in tenement districts reckoned positively undesirable—showed a greater mental alertness and a definite physical superiority which puzzled the physicians. They finally decided to experiment with the one thing that the home babies had and the hospital babies had not. Soon there appeared on each hospital baby's order chart the following item: "One hour of loving a day." During this hour the babies were to be handled, talked to, and smiled at. The nurses were to relax and become human; so were the babies. After a brief period of this treatment the all-round improvement of the babies was a matter of record.

THE GREAT GOD ROUTINE

Nothing, then, is better for the baby than that his mother should enjoy him. Armed with the Great God Routine she bathes, feeds, naps, airs, and dresses her baby in such a way that she has plenty of time and inclination just to sit and watch him kick, and to laugh at his antics. A practical routine is a necessity for the household. More important, it helps to build in the child the comforting knowledge that his wants are inevitably provided for.

There is danger, however, when routine becomes sacrosanct. When this occurs, anything that happens to disturb it may cause a young mother to be thrown off her balance, to become anxious or almost panicky. One of the first things she has to learn is that, if necessary, the baby's bath hour *can* be changed, his daily airing *may* be omitted. Laws are good, but they do not suffer if they are occasionally broken.

Grandmothers

Among the greatest disturbers of routine, at least in the mother's mind, are visitors and relatives; especially, to put it frankly, her husband's relatives. Take grandparents, for example. Foolish, meddlesome, or omnipresent grandparents can do much to unhinge a mother who, with her first baby, is struggling to gain self-confidence and to discover the best way in which she, as an individual, can manage.

The most troublesome grandparents are those who have never learned to show restraint in the matter of dropping in and remarking that the baby is looking pale and that they are sure he needs such and such. They will get along better if they are not too touchy about criticism and will try to remain open to suggestions and to maintain an attitude of curiosity and open-mindedness about new "theories," instead of taking a patronizing "I-raised-five-children-myself-dear" attitude toward everything modern. On the other hand, a really grandmotherly grandmother who can bring humor, experience, and tact into the home when she comes, who is willing to fill in and be useful in emergencies, who manages to settle down and shed a little peace and composure at the right times—that grandmother is an asset that should be carefully cultivated and highly valued.

What part a grandmother will play in the life of a child is not wholly a matter of fate. A mother who has imaginative sympathy for the stake that an older woman has in her grandchild can do a great deal to further the relationship. Often, however, the mother tends to be cool or suspicious from the beginning and regards grandparents as mere nuisances to be suffered as best one can. She is too insistent that things be done *exactly* her way or not at all and attaches undue importance to the technical details of her routines. Actually, while the grandmother may do things differently and perhaps not quite according to the most improved modern method, she may still

[14]

be equally successful with the baby. Mothers who lack self-confidence in what they are doing for the baby and who distrust their own ability for independent judgment and decisions in their households are likely to make either one of these mistakes: they may let the grandmother dictate to them unendingly and upset their own plans at a moment's notice, or they may be *over*assertive about their own right to complete authority, jealously rejecting every suggestion that the grandmother offers, interpreting everything as the wish to interfere. A great many young mothers have not yet grown up or are only half grown up. They are still struggling to demonstrate their independence, and in this struggle a baby is made to serve as a convenient weapon. By using every excuse to keep the baby all for herself and to limit the grandmother's contacts with him, this type of immature mother can go on pretending that she is more self-reliant than she actually is. Needless to say, this process, even when carried on unconsciously, cheats the baby as well as the grandmother out of a relationship which should have great values.

Of course, the mother and not the grandmother must have the final authority. Routine has its own demands. Babies should not be roused from their sleep, interrupted while eating, snatched up when they are playing, or tickled and gurgled over till they are too excited—but neither should they be severely isolated and put on view only on alternate Sundays from four to five. There is a spirit here which can make or break something very worth having, for a loving grandmother can be one of life's good gifts to a child, as both fairy tales and reality testify again and again. While maintaining her own control, the mother should encourage the grandmother to bathe and care for the baby and should even pay her the compliment of going out occasionally and leaving her completely in charge. Even the mother who does all her own work can sometimes arrange a "day off" in this way. Things do not have to be done the same way at all times. The best way to deal with foolish grandmothers—who, after all, are no more foolish as a class than mothers—is to give them real responsibility and talk over old ways as compared with new. The balance of wisdom is not always in favor of the new.

A Daily Schedule

Here is a reasonable daily schedule for a baby from approximately six to twelve months of age. Many items apply as well to a younger baby; many to an older one. It is subject to modification at all points.

7 A. M. (or whenever he wakes and calls) Baby changed to dry diapers; dry bed; may stay alone in crib with toys; may munch on graham crackers or teething biscuit.

8 A. M. Breakfast with the family, propped in his own chair; or crawling about the floor, playing with spoons or envelopes.

9 A. M. Bath. (Not necessary every day.)

9:45 A. M. Out in carriage or playpen; may sleep until 12; then be changed and given water. (Remember that not all days are alike for a mother, and though it is good for a baby to get outside 2 or 3 hours daily, he need not be taken outdoors every morning and every afternoon.)

12 to 12: 30. On floor of room; free to crawl.

12: 30 P. M. Luncheon.

1: 30 to 4 P. M. Outdoors. In winter, sits up and plays in carriage; in summer, plays in pen. Windy days, plays in pen indoors. If it is inconvenient to take him out, baby may be
dressed for outdoors and placed in pen near open window
in sunlight and in a place free from wind. May sleep part of
this period.

4 to 5: 30 P. M. Changed; given orange juice. Plays on bed
with or without clothes. Can be left outdoors longer in
pleasant summer weather.

5: 30 P. M. Sponge bath in summer.

6 P. M. Playtime with father; supper.

7 P. M. Bedtime. If no nap in the afternoon, this may be at 6 or
6: 30 P. M.

Please note that part of the time the baby is encouraged to
crawl on the floor. He needs this activity and the chance to
exercise his body against a hard surface, and it is great fun for
him to navigate about the rug and explore the world from the
underside of tables and chairs. Later he will pull himself up
and reach for various household objects—they are sure to be
much more fascinating than the toys inside his pen. While
all this presupposes that the floors are kept reasonably clean, it
is not a good idea to make a fetish of this cleanliness and move
around in front of the baby with a mop and a bottle of disin-

fectant. He will probably pick things up from time to time and put them in his mouth and must be watched in case some should be pins or needles, but anyone who has a horror of dirt and is given to the kind of fanatical cleanliness that is no longer considered godliness might be better off without children. Children and dirt have an affinity for one another, and strong prejudices must be overcome sooner or later. Before meals, of course, the baby should be cleaned up; and during this crawling age—and thereafter—the bath may be more conveniently given at the end of the day. Frequently, two baths are necessary.

THE BEGINNINGS OF DISCIPLINE

As early as the age of about three months a problem will arise which is destined to remain with parents as long as their children are growing up and which will be referred to again and again in the course of this book. This is the ever-recurrent question of how often a child should have his own way and how often he should be made to conform to ours. How can we tell when we are giving a child his just dues as an immature and dependent creature, with needs essentially different from ours, and when we are simply giving in and "spoiling"? In the end, nobody likes a spoiled child, not even the child himself.

However, a great deal of the antispoiling counsel offered to young parents is based on the assumption that a baby should never be allowed to get the upper hand for a moment and that if parents once lose control they have lost it forever. In the name of this fallacious doctrine some parents have decided that from the moment a baby opens his eyes he must be taught to refrain from everything that does not conform to the order of a civilized household. They want conformity at once and no nonsense. Therefore they adopt drastic measures of "training." They establish rigid regularity with regard to eating, sleeping, and staying alone; and soon they expect it in habits of bowel and bladder control as well. They do not pause to inquire into the nature and needs of an infant. They do not observe what he *is,* but are inclined to see only what he *should become.* This attitude makes for haste and pressure and often for premature severity which, although it may be well intentioned, runs counter to the infant's paramount need for peace and comfort. In rearing a child, every point in his development calls for a skillful balance—ensuring satisfactions with one hand and imposing demands with the other. During the first months of life the balance should be *heavily* on the satisfaction side. The resulting sense of well-being and good nature, far from spoiling the child, is likely to make him much more willing to accept denials when the time comes. Only when our satisfactions have been firmly grounded in the physical experiences of infancy are we likely to grow strong enough to tolerate the frustrations which inevitably come in later life.

During the first year, the ordinary demands of a child's routine constitute "discipline" of a very real kind. The baby has to meet a cold, strange world, quite different from the safe, warm, fluid universe to which he was accustomed before birth. Birth itself is an ordeal. His whole organism—lungs, stomach, and nervous system—has been violently revolutionized. Added to this, he is often expected to eat and sleep only at specified times; to be bathed, dressed, and subjected to all the outrages of civilized living. Sooner or later all these troubles are necessary. This is discipline enough; further demands can well wait until the child is thoroughly accustomed to the rhythm of daily life and until he feels secure and compensated by the pleasures offered through his mother's love.

HABITS AND WHAT NOT TO DO ABOUT THEM

There are several so-called "bad habits" of infancy and early childhood that are very perplexing, especially when parents do not know whether or not they may lead to something serious. For example, children between the ages of one and three, or thereabouts, may be given to curious addictions. Head bumping, wool picking, blanket sucking, and rocking (usually on all fours in an automatic rhythmic way) are among the ways in which an ingenious infant may harass his parents and even the neighbors.

Troubling Habits

One two-year-old used to spend the early-morning hours rocking in his crib so violently that the head of the crib banged constantly against the wall between his room and the next apartment. The tenants on the same floor, as might be imagined, protested at the disturbance to their morning sleep. Even with the crib set out in the middle of the room his rocking eventually worked it up against the wall again. Finally his mother removed the casters from the crib so that it could not move, whereupon he took to bumping his head noisily against the sides. She then devised a neat quilted cap that fit down low over the baby's forehead. This she put on him before he went to bed, encouraging him to find it pretty and letting him admire himself in the mirror. After this, when he started banging his head, the noise it used to make and the particular sensation it gave him were no longer there. Without his knowing why, the pleasure had lost its flavor. He gave it up in disgust and found other things to do.

Yet such behavior often resists any attempt to thwart it. Punishments are useless. Such habits, though inconvenient, rarely cause physical injury to the child and usually disappear of their own accord. Prevent practical inconveniences, such as has just been described, and ignore the rest. Scientifically, such behavior has great interest; and if understood, might help to fill many gaps in our knowledge of childhood. Meanwhile, we suggest that whenever a child starts bumping or rocking, someone should pick him up, cuddle and soothe him, or play with him for a few moments.

Parents should remember always that the mere fact that certain behavior disappears does not always mean that it has been permanently disposed of. The observant mother watches to see whether or not her child merely transfers the impulse to something else—bed-wetting, night terrors, or just general irritability. She will have no right to congratulate herself because the original misbehavior has been cured if it has only taken on a new and equally undesirable form. Frequently, however, children give up even an urgent need for eccentric behavior in some quite wholesome way, and development can then proceed undisturbed. But the cautious mother holds the facts in her memory for future reference; she does not dismiss them as having no possible importance or meaning.

Meanwhile the first course of action is to help the child find so many absorbing interests and so many other things to do that such peculiar pleasures will be supplanted. This is not always easy, but time is working on the mother's side. Just the fact that the child grows older usually helps. Since a great many of these annoying practices occur while the baby is in bed—either at night or at naptime—it may be necessary to break the usual rules and routine and keep the child busy doing something less objectionable at these times. It *may* be something as simple as cuddling a favorite toy or sucking on a discarded rattle; he *may* go off to sleep quietly in a sleeping bag fastened by tapes to the crib, or accept other gentle restraints without much protest. But if he is really a hardened addict none of these devices will be effective. He will defeat them all. If he does, the mother may have to break another rule and sit with him after he has been put to bed, and with conversation or other pardonable trickery get him off to sleep before he knows it. This, of course, may also fail, or it may result in the child's shifting the time for his particular addiction to the early-morning hours. In this case the mother will do well to be philosophical, consoling herself with the knowledge that the child will probably deal with the problem best if let alone. About all she can do after that is to take what steps she can to prevent annoyance to other people and go off to sleep herself.

Face picking, or similar practices which threaten some injury or real disfigurement, may require medical advice and some sort of bandage to prevent possible infections. But severe punishments or mechanical restraints that drive the child. into a frenzy of rage or terror should always be avoided. It is far better to let the habit go on than to interfere too ruthlessly with something for which the child, temporarily at least, feels a compelling need. Experience shows that children do work out of these distressing phases in their own way and in their own time.

Thumb Sucking

Thumb sucking is another practice extremely common during the first and even second year. It is a matter about which people, especially when uninformed, may feel strongly. A great deal of ill-considered advice may be handed around among parents. Dire consequences are predicted. Grandmothers fret, mothers frown, fathers have visions of orthodontists' bills running into astronomical figures. Because nobody really stops to ask questions about either the causes or the consequences of the habit, prejudices flourish.

"I just can't bear to see him do that," we hear people say of a thumb-sucking baby. "He looks so *horrid!*"

Certain careful scientific research has been done, not only on the question of thumb sucking in infants, but on the wider question of the sucking instinct in all young mammals. There is no doubt that *sucking for its own sake* represents a most powerful drive in the very young. When we know how deep the need to suck really is we can no longer regard it merely as a bad habit to be repressed ruthlessly as soon as possible. Mounting evidence shows that this sort of thoughtless repression may produce other undesirable developments and general discontent. Many authorities feel that forcible restraints may even tend to prolong the habit. Certainly it seems clear that throughout the first year of life one of the child's main sources of pleasure is sucking. In carrying things to the lips, to bite and to chew, he reveals the fact that the lips are more than a means of satisfying hunger; they are a genuine pleasure zone. Even children who have never sucked their thumbs or fingers appear to have an overwhelmingly strong urge to suck their toys, blankets, diapers, the sides of their cribs, their own tongues, or anything handy. Any mother knows how hard it is to keep a child from doing this, and wise mothers learn to be pretty easygoing about it. They keep toys reasonably clean and then pretend not to notice. They have learned, too, that as the infant grows older he puts away infantile things. After a year or two the mouth area normally begins to fade as a primary pleasure zone; the child turns to many other things for his pleasures and presently gives up excessive sucking of his own accord.

In other words, sucking is not just a "bad habit." While children show wide differences in the intensity of the need, it is in some measure an appropriate and necessary activity during the first year or so of life. Far from trying to prevent it, it is important to see that the infant is supplied with all that he, as an individual, needs; just as we offer him all the foods he needs. What we should like to do, however, if we knew how, is to provide him with enough sucking to satisfy him *during the feeding process itself,* so that he does not need to supplement it by sucking his thumb or anything else. It has been claimed also that the amount of thumb and finger sucking is closely related to the amount of sucking *time* that a child has at breast or bottle and that breast fed babies are less apt to suck their thumbs. A mother often gives her baby indefinite time at the breast because she is never sure how much he is getting. But she tends to remove the bottle as soon as it has been emptied.

What You Can Do About It

The lessons to be derived from this seem clear:

1. Try to *prevent* your baby from sucking his thumb by giving him plenty of sucking time while feeding. If he shows a tendency to want his thumb, perhaps *for him* more frequent meals are indicated, as well as longer sucking time at each meal.

2. Never hurry a baby away from the breast or bottle. Wait until he is all through mouthing and toying with the nipple. Give him all the chance he needs to enjoy the lip sensations involved. No meal, whether for young or old, should be

strictly business. A meal should be enjoyed in a cozy, friendly relation with another person. This is better, both for the digestion and for a general sense of well-being.

3. Do not attempt to wean a baby from breast or bottle too soon. He may still not be ready to give up sucking. He can drink from a cup all the rest of his life. Eight or ten months is not too early for some children, but it is for others. The process should be gradual. Don't force him; don't hurry. Be guided always by the signs the child may give you, showing that he is ready for the next step with a bit of cajoling from you. In most cases a child should have accepted the cup by the time he is two.

4. Sometimes the milk flows so rapidly from the bottle that a child's hunger is gratified and he falls asleep before he has had time enough for sucking. If a child cannot be induced to suck long enough at his meals (a lack of sufficient sucking time while feeding will be indicated by a strong tendency to suck at other times whatever is handy), the flow of milk may be reduced by getting new nipples on which he must work harder and suck longer for the same amount of food.

5. If these measures do not seem to diminish the child's eagerness for his thumb, the old-fashioned pacifier (which will horrify your mother and delight your grandmother) has often proved to be the better of two evils—if you can call it evil. This much-maligned object is easy to keep clean, and if made of solid rubber does not cause stomach-ache through

the swallowing of air. Its advantage lies in the fact that it is not a part of the child—and so is not always available and does not constitute an ever-ready temptation. The fact is that the child seems to find it easier to give up the pacifier than to give up his thumb. In addition, the pacifier causes less injurious pressure against the jaw and palate.

6. Most important of all—don't let the child share your anxiety. If none of these measures succeeds, it is far better to let him do as he likes than to harass him and yourself with mechanical restraints that give rise to battles of wills, tantrums, and sleepless nights. Approximately one child out of every three or four sucks his thumb at some time and to some degree. An overwhelming majority get over the habit gradually after the first or second year, without corrections or deliberate restraining, since at this time the pleasure derived from mouth stimulation begins to fade out, having had its day in the course of normal development. It should be added that most of these children continue to suck their thumbs at bedtime, or when they are tired, shy, ill, or emotionally disturbed, for quite a time after the habit has otherwise disappeared.

Experts differ on the question of whether thumb sucking injures the mouth and nasal passages and changes the position of the permanent teeth. Severe dental malocclusion and malformed jaws are unhygienic and unsightly and cannot be lightly dismissed if they actually do result from thumb sucking. Some dental research shows that injury *occasionally* results from certain types of thumb sucking. Some authorities have maintained that these malformations right themselves unless the sucking is continued after the permanent teeth appear in the fifth or sixth year, but more recent investigations have tended to demonstrate that the injury, even when the habit is confined to the earlier years, *may* be permanent. It seems safe to say, however, that these cases are extremely few as compared with the total number of thumb suckers. A great deal of dental malocclusion has nothing whatever to do with thumb sucking, and the majority of thumb suckers have probably incurred no jaw injury whatever. Before jumping to the conclusion that a thumb-sucking child is doomed to dental trouble we must consider many things—his age, the intensity and type of sucking, and the actual condition of his mouth.

Crying

Another matter which causes sharp disagreement is the parents' attitude toward crying.

"Shall we let the baby cry it out?" asks the mother. "When we have seen that he is dry and comfortable and that no pins are sticking him, should we just close the door and go away even when he screams for hours?" Simple answers are at hand, glibly offered in reply to a problem which is by no means simple. The dogma states: "Certainly you should let him cry. He must learn that crying cannot get him what he wants. If you go to him you are actually teaching him to cry." But is this the whole answer? Even after we have eliminated wet diapers, stomach-aches, and safety pins, we still do not know what deeper discomforts and anxieties a child may be suffering when he is denied human company or asked to forgo the warmth of his mother's body or her comforting pat as he is turned over her shoulder.

In spite of this, it is certainly true that the baby must learn eventually to accept regulations. During the early weeks of life, a crying baby needs prompt attention, a change of position, a bit of rocking, or perhaps feeding. But after 2 or 3 months, he can stand *some* "frustration." Suppose, then, we let him cry—perhaps ten minutes more or less, to see if he will settle down and accept his loneliness. If his woe is not too great it may expend itself in this time. But let us hope that the day is over for the Spartan mother who listens while her baby screams for hours on end, suppressing her own doubt and anguish.

Hard and fast rules are dangerous because they do not consider individual needs. Premature babies, babies who have been sick, and babies who appear unusually sensitive and highly strung probably should not, during the early months, be subjected to as much denial as others. Differences must all be considered and experiments made; often the best way is only arrived at by trial and error. If a mother must go to the baby in the night it is definitely not a sign that she has failed in her duty or that the baby is going to be an incorrigible. Some of it is sure to happen; to a certain extent it is expected along with wetting, teething, and the other trials of being (and having) a baby.

One does, however, lay the *foundations* of discipline in these early months. This discipline, as has already been suggested, will for a long time consist of nothing but the daily routine and the process of introducing the baby into the ways of eating, bathing, dressing, and going to bed. Like all discipline, it should be both flexible and firm and should be administered by people who know when to make exceptions and how to laugh and relax.

Help for Mother

It calls, moreover, for the leadership of the mother herself. There is no such thing as successfully "turning the baby over to an expert," while the mother stands around helplessly or appears occasionally in the nursery to play with the baby when everything is going nicely. Whoever helps with the children, whether grandmother, temporary nurse, houseworker, or permanent nurse (now largely an extinct species), should be an assistant to the mother, not a know-it-all nursery tyrant. A houseworker, or a practical nurse who will do part of the housework, who is willing to do things your way and is agreeable to have around, usually is best. Of course, the most invaluable help, if he is willing, can be the father during the hours when he is at home.

Definitely, however, there is a place for some sort of helper to the mother and for someone whom the baby learns to accept and love as an occasional substitute. This person—whoever she may be—should be happy in her own life, and willing and eager to learn. She should be affectionate and tolerant, yet have a good head on her shoulders. She should understand the importance of maintaining the mother's place in the child's life. A child should realize from the beginning that no matter who else does things for him or takes care of him, his mother comes first, that he is her baby and no one else's, and that his destinies are controlled by his mother's love and his mother's authority. This will mean that, in general, she should take charge of the bathing, dressing, feeding and physical routines whenever she can. It is through these things that one learns to know a baby. It is important also that the baby discovers, as he grows into a child, that his mother knows what she is about and is able to get things done. No paid person should ever be regarded as a permanent fixture in a child's life. Hired help comes and goes, but mothers should go on forever; and a child's sense of security depends on the firm establishment of this knowledge. Otherwise the loss of an outsider on whom he learns to depend may be as severe a shock to a child as the loss of a mother.

Father's Role

A word about the baby's father, who has so far been mentioned only parenthetically. This is not fair, for one of the injustices done a man in a house with a baby is just this tendency to treat him parenthetically. Sooner or later he will probably resent this household which revolves around a baby and slink off, if he is lucky, to his workshop in the basement, while the women go on talking about formulas and weight charts.

It may be argued with some justice that the father counts most as the child grows older, and a discussion of his special contribution is therefore reserved for a later chapter. Nevertheless, the arrival of a first baby is likely to mark a critical period in the relation of husband and wife. Responsibilities have begun in real earnest; and adjustment to the new routine often causes much fatigue and irritability. Rearing children is an acid test of unselfishness in both parents.

For the father, during the first months at least, it often seems doubtful whether the pleasures of having a family outweigh the hardships. He may have wanted children in theory, but he has probably never realized what it would be like when this strange, demanding creature actually arrived and took over the house. But many fathers respond to a young baby with the same fascination as the mother and can be almost as interested in the minutiae of baby tending. Babies often seem to take readily to the larger, firmer hands and low voice of the father, who therefore may sometimes have a quite calming influence over a fretful baby. To many a man, however, it must often appear that his home has been transformed into a woman's world where he counts for little. He may be as delighted as his wife by the baby's antics and by the daily signs of growth. Pride and astonishment at his offspring go hand in hand. He may even assist in practical care and learn the techniques of bathing and diapering. But his pleasure in these rites will be short-lived if his wife pushes him aside and does the job better.

Many young couples, if the wife is also a busy worker, or has a job outside the home too, have agreed to share equally in household demands. They have discovered, however, that while fifty-fifty sharing in these matters may work as a makeshift, it rarely succeeds as a permanent way of life. A mother's responsibility for her child somehow persists in remaining more urgent, more personal, and more detailed than a father's. In the same way the father feels essentially responsible for the breadwinning. Although a man needs a home, part of him at least rebels if he suspects that this intense domesticity is to be all there is to marriage and to living. He is jealous of his freedom and needs the outside world and its chance for conquests as few women do; in his children he looks primarily for companions and allies. He looks too for vicarious fulfillment of his own half-realized, sometimes wholly defeated, hopes. The result is that many fathers have to wait longer than mothers for pleasure in their children, and attempts to force matters usually do not help.

The arrival of a baby should be a challenge to men and women to make a deliberate effort to keep their interest in one another and in the outside world more actively alive than ever. For a woman, the experience of becoming a mother must never be allowed to degenerate into complete absorption in physical details and nursery anecdotes, in problems of housekeeping and neighborhood gossip, with a consequent forgetfulness of everything else that might have meant her fuller growth. Whatever the demands of the physical side of child rearing—and there are many—she should remain aware that her children have minds and personalities and that a hard world awaits them, for which they may or may not be prepared. In the wider problems of a child's equipment to meet real living the father is likely to be genuinely and intensely interested, as the mother will soon discover. Moreover, his realistic appreciation of all that is involved in the demands of the outside world may be much keener than hers, and his contributions to the task of preparing the child for life can be quite indispensable.

CHAPTER TWO

WHAT SHOULD WE EXPECT
OF OUR CHILDREN?

IN ATTEMPTING to give parents some help in deciding what they should expect of their children and at what ages they may expect it there is always the danger of inviting an interpretation that will be either too literal or too careless. Parents, like other people with special predispositions, tend to find nourishment for their own biases wherever they look.

"The book says that a baby should be absolutely dry by the time he is twenty months old or something is drastically wrong," says the rigid and anxious type of parent.

"The book says that you should simply let the child wet as long as he wants and pay no attention to him," says the careless parent, quoting the same book.

There is no way of making any counsel completely foolproof and there is no way to prevent certain parents from finding apparently good reasons for doing what they please —which usually means that they will act as their particular temperaments prompt them to, quoting some authority to show that it is all right. Nevertheless, the majority of parents are essentially well balanced and are quite able to profit by a knowledge of sensible procedures. They have a right to know and they will want to know what performances they may expect at various ages, but they will also need to be reminded that there are wide variations in children's growth and that no generalizations can ever take the place of knowledge of an individual child.

SLEEP AND SLEEP ROUTINES

The very young baby sleeps most of the time and usually is awake only when being bathed, dressed, and fed. As children grow older their waking hours lengthen, and at the same time it becomes clear that some need much more sleep than others.

The following table may be helpful in estimating the approximate amount of sleep necessary for healthy children in twenty-four hours, but as always each child's needs may vary.

Birth to one year—from fifteen to twenty hours

One to two years—from fourteen to sixteen hours

Two to three years—from thirteen to fourteen hours

Three to five years—from twelve to thirteen hours

Five to six years—eleven hours

[35]

Until the child is about a year old a mid-morning nap as well as a longer afternoon nap is advisable, but this can gradually be given up after the first birthday—the exact age varying, of course, with the needs of the individual. The afternoon nap, from 12:30 or 1 to 2 or 3 o'clock, should, however, be kept as part of the schedule for as long as it is practical and the child clearly seems to need it. While some children of these ages sleep solidly for a couple of hours, others refuse to sleep at all. Even in this case, a rest period in the crib is well worth preserving as a definite part of the day's routine. It is a boon to mother as well as to the child. *Forcing* inactivity upon a child, however, often merely increases restlessness, and when this happens the child is better off if he is allowed to play in his crib with toys or books than making futile attempts to lie quietly. Very occasionally it will be necessary to stay with a child to keep him quiet and contented. This may be merely the better of two evils—and can usually be avoided by good management.

This good management consists largely in getting the child to accept sleep as the next part of his day's schedule. Avoid argument and health talks on the benefit of sleep. A child should not be required to sleep, but only to lie down in his bed. Quiet must be induced by the parent's own quiet and confidence; it cannot be forced. Strenuous "roughhouse" just before bedtime is a great temptation to fathers, since this is often the only time of day when they can be with their children. Also, most children tend to high spirits during these hours. In individual cases, it may have no effect on the child's willingness to quiet down later. The parents should watch to see if this is so and then regulate the child's activities accordingly.

Even more objectionable than strenuous physical play is a type of nervous hurry and pressure to get through routines at bedtime. If the person putting the child to bed is in this state of mind, it is difficult for the child to relax. A mother should always arrange her own time so that she can waste a little with her child at bedtime. If a story or conversation is customary after lights are out, she should not rush through it; and she need not feel that she is instilling "bad habits" if she realizes that on some nights, and at some times of his life, her child needs more of her time. But it is also her responsibility to make the child feel that sooner or later he must accept the fact that she will leave him alone. Here the child's attitude will vary and is always influenced by the emotional upheavals in his inner life. Sometimes it is easy to call a halt when a three-year-old is demanding a glass of water, or the toilet, or using any of the other obvious tricks to get his mother back; sometimes, however, these tricks mark real anxiety and fears. If a child is going through a difficult phase, or if he is unhappy or angry, it may interfere with his sleep. When this is the case, proper habits are less important than help for the child in his whole adjustment to life.

THE CHILD EATS

It is an astonishing fact that eating, on which life itself depends, should be an ever-recurrent problem of childhood.

Some children, it is true, appear to be hearty and omniverous eaters from the day they are born, and today's parents seem much less fussy and worrisome about their children's eating. The majority of children show variations in their habits and preferences—sometimes so slight they are hardly noticed, but sometimes more extreme. To a large extent, children's eating habits are a product of the mother's wisdom—or lack of it. But not always. A child may be a hearty eater up to a certain age and then swing over into indifference or even dislike of food. The reverse of this is also common. He may have strong prejudices and preferences for certain foods on the basis of color, consistency, or other factors that have nothing to do with food value. He may eat gluttonously without being really hungry, or show indifference or distaste at mealtime when he really needs the food. Evidently food comes to have emotional meanings for the child, often highly capricious, which cannot be explained wholly on the basis of physical needs.

Most doctors today have come to recognize the fact that children show strong individual differences, both to amounts and kinds of foods, and mothers are warned that consideration must be given to these variations and preferences. Forcible feeding, often called "training the child to eat everything put before him," now gives way to the sounder view that even a very young child is much more than a mere digestive apparatus. Indeed, to insist in the name of a "balanced diet" that all foods offered be eaten, whether the child wants them or not, may only strengthen his resistance. Long experience and the most careful studies of food behavior in young children constantly affirm that it is wiser to have more tolerance for the child's own choices and to allow him a certain leeway in his fads and fancies. The parent's best course is to *offer* the child whatever the doctor orders, making mealtime as pleasant as possible—always avoiding entreaties, insistence, punishments, and "scenes" of all kinds. Instead, attention should be turned to featuring preferred foods and preferred times for eating.

Offer—Don't Urge

Foods that are rejected when first offered should not be forced. They can be presented again some other time. Some thought should also be given to cooking and serving foods in ways that might be more palatable to a particular child. This is not pampering; it is actually the best way to cultivate a robust appetite. If the mother can stand it when the child will not eat a conventional meal, the child will gradually learn to accept what is customary—though this will take far longer for some children than for others. Remember always that the goal is not to "get food in" but to foster whatever leads to pleasure in eating.

One hears much of the "starvation method" for treating noneaters. If a child won't eat, we are told, give him his chance three times a day and, if he refuses, let him go without. He will soon feel the pangs of hunger and call for his supper. This method works with many children, but for others it may act as a challenge, resulting in a stubborn, unhappy struggle between mother and child. Everything depends on the spirit in which such a plan is carried out. If the mother sets her teeth, so will the child. On the other hand, a genuine willingness to let the child decide will usually lead to his eating enough. It must also be remembered that while some children refuse food simply because they want to torment their mothers, others may do it because they have developed fears and aversions that are beyond their control. The mother must learn to judge which situation it is that she is coping with. If it is the former, forget about strong-arm methods and try to win back the child's confidence. Even if the child's refusals are largely motivated by a will to power—as they often are—remember that children do better when won away from such attitudes by a friendly approach, instead of being forced to accept the domination of an adult.

Mistakes at Mealtime

Here are some common mistakes made by many mothers with regard to their children's eating:

1. Being the kind of person who is naturally anxious and fussy about health routines. A child soon discovers it if his mother is easily disturbed when things don't go according to schedule and is consequently tempted to try his power and produce a sensation by dawdling or refusing to eat.

2. Giving portions which are too large or demanding that the *entire* meal be eaten.

3. Refusing to consider the child's taste and demanding that he "eat everything that is put before him."

4. Engaging in too much conversation and distracting "games" with the child at mealtime and feeding him every mouthful.

5. Going to the other extreme of rigid isolation for the child, with no conversation, no play, and no help permitted when the child gets tired.

6. Demanding that table manners be more perfect than it is reasonable to expect at the child's age, instead of endorsing hearty appetite and pleasure at mealtime.

Success at Mealtime

In the majority of cases the best policy is to offer the proper food, give some encouragement—even help if necessary—and then let the child's own appetite decide. If he refuses to eat in a reasonable length of time—twenty minutes for breakfast and a half-hour, perhaps, for dinner and supper—the meal should be removed. But in removing the meal it is very important that the attitude of the mother should be one of friendly indifference. The accent here is on *both* the friendliness and the indifference. A simple comment, "I guess you're not very hungry today," or anything else that is neutral and unconcerned is all that is necessary. Whisking the tray away in stony silence or with an irritated gesture is worse than nothing, for it tells the child just what he shouldn't know—that, weak and helpless as he feels himself to be, he has found a way in which he can successfully disturb his all-powerful mother. As is well known, a taste of power goes to the head of even the very young.

Children usually begin to feed themselves at the age of about a year and a half or two years. A good plan is for the mother to guide the child's hand to his mouth as he holds the spoon.

If she herself is armed with another spoon she can easily scoop up the food that misses its mark or slips from the corners of his mouth. It will be a messy performance, but it can also be fun for both mother and child as progress is made. At two a child may be able to feed himself quite adequately, but, by three or four, he may have tired of an exciting, new accomplishment and may want help again. In general, there seems to be no reason why children should not have some assistance as long as they make steady progress in the direction of self-help. This is a good rule, and it applies to many other things besides eating. But as soon as children begin to abuse their mother's willingness to help, and use mealtime as an occasion for "putting on an act," a halt should be called and the meal should be over, even though practically nothing has been eaten.

Usually when a mother says that her child "eats positively nothing" we find that he has had half a glass of milk, has nibbled at a piece of bread, and has eaten his dessert; from the point of view of nutrition this is far from nothing. For some reason, in the minds of most mothers vegetables have become the most highly valued of all foods, perhaps because they contain that magical substance, vitamins, regarded as especially essential to health and a balanced diet. A child, however, does not need a balanced diet at every meal—or even every day—and even a meal completely missed rarely does harm. Usually it will be found that a mother who declares that her child is a food problem will admit on questioning that the doctor finds him physically sound and in no way undernourished. Perhaps he is not as plump as other children, and a little extra fat would help; even in this case, however, you do nothing but harm when you *insist* that food be taken.

It is extremely rare for a genuinely undernourished child to refuse to eat, but when this happens the problem must be solved under careful medical supervision, perhaps even with psychiatric study and guidance.

Food fussiness, as we have already seen, is common. Children will eat this and not that; they will not eat meat if the spinach has touched it; they will not eat food unless it is of a certain consistency. Or perhaps they find fats repulsive. These things happen. They cannot always be attributed to bad training or example. Plenty of children who have had no encouragement to be finicky or hypersensitive and whose parents are hearty eaters go through these phases, anyway.

Make Allowances

Even when we cannot be sure just how these aversions are built up, we can shorten their duration by being tolerant of them—at least for the time being. A child who will eat no vegetables except raw carrots and canned peas, for example, may get along very well with just these for several months. Later on the same child may forget that he hates strings beans and beets and discover that they are what he likes above everything else. In trying to teach children to like all foods by forcing them to "eat everything," even against strong resistance, we often forget that we may in reality be teaching them to hate them more, to dread mealtime, and to build up resentments against the authorities who do the forcing. What we want is a well-nourished child who enjoys mealtime. This is the best insurance for good eating habits. In the end, the child who has been able to eat what he wants will probably like a wider variety of food than the child who has stored up unhappy associations with eating.

Don't force a child to eat against strong resistance.
Don't bribe him to eat or punish him for not eating.
Let him take his time, but end the meal if he makes a scene or dawdles interminably.

Other things being equal, dessert comes last. Children can be taught that this is customary. Desserts are sweet—if taken before meals, they may diminish the appetite. Also, it is usually more customary to sit down while eating. But if a child really eats better if he starts with dessert and ends with soup, or if he seems more comfortable, as some children do, if he stands while eating, it is well to remember that there is no harm in these things. The same applies to eating between meals. There is no objection to it if the child still wants to eat at mealtime. In other words, although customary, routinized practices in eating are desirable and practical, they should be allowed to develop slowly.

Overeating

Children who eat too much or too fast are less common than children who refuse to eat, and parents tend to be more indulgent toward these things. Though it may be necessary to keep some children, for special reasons, from eating too much of certain foods, any consistent attempt to check a child's appetite should be undertaken only in consultation with the doctor. Overweight is only rarely due to a glandular condition, but when it is, it will not help to limit the diet—other forms of treatment are indicated. Gobbling and hasty eating are considered bad table manners and often cause parents to protest that indigestion will surely be the result. As it happens, this is unlikely; and it is not a good idea to predict dire consequences that do not happen. When older children overeat continually, and when it becomes almost an obsession, as is sometimes the case, the causes must be sought in some emotional maladjustment. Merely limiting the food will not help.

Do They Like What's Good for Them?

Dr. Clara Davis, a pediatrician in a Cleveland, Ohio, hospital, made an experiment several years ago to determine whether very young children, if given altogether free choice, would select for themselves the right kind of food in the right quantities. When the children were taken into the hospital to be under her supervision they were all under a year and had all been breast-fed by their mothers and had received no other food. The procedure was as follows:

At mealtime, a nurse presented each baby with a tray containing many types of food, some raw, some simply cooked, but all unseasoned and unmixed. For example, there was no custard, but its ingredients—sugar, egg, milk, and salt—would each appear in separate dishes. There were also finely cut cereals, meats, fish, bone marrow, fruit, vegetables, and such, so that at each meal the infant was presented with all the pos-

[45]

sibilities for a balanced diet and then left to make his own choice. He could take whatever he wanted, in any quantity. The nurse was provided with two spoons—one to be used by her, the other for the child to use if he wanted to. The nurse did not spoon anything out for the baby until he himself had made a move toward one of the dishes—sometimes trying to drink from it, sometimes helping himself with his hands, sometimes just pointing. Then she gave him whatever he wanted for as long as he wanted it. All the children ate eagerly and heartily and evidently looked forward to their meals with pleasure. Sometimes they chose a varied diet, sometimes they went on special "jags" for a period. Dr. Davis says in her report: "It proved impossible to predict what would be eaten at a given meal. An infant might eat from one to seven eggs, or none; or from one to four bananas." (It is also of interest that one child who came into the hospital with evidences of rickets helped himself freely to cod-liver oil.)

Most important, however, is the fact that all the children loved to eat and were free of digestive disturbances, and that at the end of the experimental period (six months to one year) they were in excellent health and spirits, normal as to bone structure and general physical development. They were also rapidly learning to feed themselves.

Certainly this experiment has definite lessons for parents. It is not offered here as conclusive proof that infants are best reared by such a method, or that parents can try the whole of such a procedure in their own homes. But it does strongly suggest that most children, unless there are special circumstances, are far more likely to develop satisfactory food habits if they are left to their own devices and not driven to eat even when they don't want to. Furthermore, it suggests that they can generally be trusted, if presented regularly with a variety of foods, to make their own selections as to what they want and how much they need.

BLADDER AND BOWEL TRAINING

The child's training for bladder and bowel control is another matter about which storms often rage. The emotion raised by this is likely to be particularly intense, because for most people the idea of filth and bowel functioning is closely associated. Moreover, cleanliness has been elevated to a major virtue, with the result that the whole matter of bladder and bowel control has taken on a highly moralistic coloring. This makes the mother feel that there is need for haste in getting the child trained, out of all relation to the merely practical inconvenience of soiled diapers. Mothers are too likely to feel that a "clean" baby is somehow a better baby. Nurses usually feel particularly strongly on this subject and if left to themselves will try to train a child too soon and too severely— especially old fashioned trained nurses, whose hospital training has fostered far too high an opinion of cleanliness.

How Early Can a Baby Learn?

Fortunately, the pendulum is definitely swinging away from the emphasis on early training which was the fashion a generation ago. Most specialists today are willing to let babies be babies for a good many months before demanding that they give up their own will and their own habits for ours. Nevertheless, there is still some anxiety and impatience. It is natural for a mother to want to discard diapers, human to want to see a child take the next step forward. A baby's nervous system at this age is too immature in the early months for any rigorous course of training, and whatever success such training achieves, it is of extremely questionable value. Mothers hope for results before they can reasonably expect them. Along with the hope goes disappointment; with disappointment, pressure for success begins. The baby responds to pressure by being stubborn, and in this way a vicious circle is established, with many unwholesome consequences in nervous tension and resistance.

Today most specialists, having in mind the emotional requirements of children as well as their physical health, advise mothers to wait until the child is in his second year before even starting bowel training. More important than the age, however, are the child's own signals of his readiness to respond to training. He flushes, wiggles, grasps his genital. He may then *go to,* preferably not be *put on,* a toilet seat or "chair," with his feet resting on the ground, and is probably beginning to be old enough to understand what his mother means by her grunts and other suggestions. But he may not comply at once. The mother must have patience and she must take care not to show that she considers this too important. If she obviously cares too much the child may begin to take pleasure in thwarting her, or, on the other hand, he may become too dependent on her praise. When resistance is clearly indicated it is best to postpone the training altogether and try again in a few weeks. The use of suppositories is inadvisable, since this tends to train only the sphincter muscle, not the child's attitude.

It is well to notice when the child usually moves his bowels and to choose this time to put him on the toilet. In most cases this is right after a meal, but there are individual differences, and the mother should note them and adapt her plan of training to them. Children may show wide variation in becoming reliable in the matter of their bowels. For many months after a child *seems* reliable there may be occasional lapses, and the mother should be able to regard them as regrettable but not calamitous. "That's too bad," she may say quite seriously, "because you don't *have* to do it in your pants any more. You're a big enough boy to tell me when you have to go to the toilet." Then she should change his pants and say no more about it.

Wet or Dry?

In general, the same principles apply to training for bladder control, and it must be understood that the ability to control this function is a complex and difficult one which requires tolerance. Fifteen to eighteen months is time enough to make a serious attempt to start, and transferring the *responsibility* for using the toilet from mother to child comes even later during the second or third year. Hope and persuade, but do not nag, browbeat, or threaten. Do not, in your impatience, shorten the intervals if there are accidents, but lengthen them when the child shows that he can control himself longer. At first, accept lapses with equanimity; later, when the child demonstrates more capacity for control, with disappointment. But your attitude must be one of reassurance and encouragement.

A child is likely to be wet at naptime and at night for quite a while after he has learned to keep dry in the daytime. He may be three or even four years old before he can really be relied on at night—and boys take longer than girls. After the child is three or four years old, it may help to withhold fluids after 5 P.M., or to take him to the toilet just before you go to bed. In this case his sleep should be disturbed as little as possible during this process, since he is likely to urinate when he feels the pressure of the seat against him, even if he does not seem to be aware of what is going on. Sometimes, a child seems to learn, even while asleep, that this and this only is the time to urinate. But some authorities doubt that this helps.

Don't Force It

If, however, he refuses to comply and is angry and irritated at being taken up, it is best to postpone the attempt and try again in a month or so. In general, it does no good to continue with any of these training procedures against violent resistance; it is better to wait until the child is a little older. Time usually comes to the rescue if we are patient.

Like other types of learning, bladder and bowel control *can* be effected earlier than is here recommended. But, as we have seen in other instances, the process is a difficult one, and sometimes even apparent success comes at the cost of emotional injury. It is not at all uncommon for children trained too early to develop fears in connection with the toilet, or to revert to wetting and soiling later on, when they are old enough to be completely trained.

This is illustrated by the case of a child whose mother, a naturally fussy and exaggeratedly cleanly person, took great pride in the fact that her baby "never soiled a diaper after eleven months." When the child was about three years old, however, she began to show gradually increasing fears in going to the toilet, and by the time she was four she was quite unable to move her bowels naturally. Every movement was accompanied by protests, screams, and finally an enforced enema.

Study of the factors in the child's training that led to this condition revealed several points of interest. First, the mother had been extremely zealous in the child's bowel training and had branded every lapse as "bad," "disgusting," and "filthy." Second, the same attitude was expressed whenever the child showed any interest in excretory matters. If she watched a dog move its bowels on the street, she was hastily pulled away. Looking at her baby sister's stools in her diaper was equally taboo. Finally, it appeared that the family had owned a puppy which behaved after the manner of most puppies and that the mother, disgusted and impatient with the task of training, had finally sent it away, telling the child it was too dirty to keep at home. At this point the child's toilet fears began in real earnest. She was not "naturally" clean at all. She had the same interests that all children have, but she had unfortunately learned to conceal them because of fear of disapproval or punishment. The fate of the dog made her feel that everything connected with the bowel function must be bad and that she would be punished or perhaps, like the little dog, even lose her home. Control in her case became over-control and fear.

Training is likely to go forward rapidly after the end of the first year, but sometimes even after a long period of apparently complete control young children will revert again to a phase of wetting and even soiling. This is not only true of children trained too young; it may also arise when fatigue, illness, disappointment, frustration, or other crises have placed a child under special nervous tension. It is extremely common after the birth of another baby in the family, and may express the older child's wish to be a baby again. These lapses do *not* indicate that the parents should redouble their training efforts. Rather, they should discover the cause of the child's emotional problems, and, if possible, eliminate it. This will be discussed more fully later.

By the age of four or five, control should be practically complete. After this, if frequent lapses occur, the parents should first consult a physician and then, if necessary, a child-guidance specialist.

What Parents Forget

Parents, since they do not expect it, are usually quite shocked when they discover that many children, far from being disgusted with their excrements, seem to take actual pleasure in them and want to talk and laugh about them and sometimes touch and play with them. Many a mother on entering the two-year-old's room after his nap makes the discovery that he has not only moved his bowels—he has smeared himself, his crib, and the walls above it with the products. Unfortunately, our own memories play us tricks; there are many things in our own childhoods which we cannot be expected to remember. This forgetfulness makes it hard for our children. Since we cannot remember doing these things ourselves we are likely to think of children who do them as unnatural little beasts who must be controlled at once, when we should, instead, realize that they are passing through a wholly normal phase of childhood. Yet it is highly important that we realize this; the parent's attitude in the matter of the child's excretory habits has lasting consequences. The fact that the sex organs and the excretory organs lie so closely together makes for complications of both functions. Because of their proximity it is likely that the attitude which an individual forms toward one function will carry over to the other as well.

The mother who berates her two-year-old with cries of "disgusting," "horrid," "filthy," and "bad," when she catches him indulging in typically infantile pleasures in connection with his bowel functions, is likely to give him the idea that anything associated with these organs and these bodily regions is also "bad." This interferes not only with sound sexual functioning in later life, but also with the healthy development of the whole personality.

If a strong interest in the excretory function is treated with understanding it will run its course and subside of its own accord far more certainly and soundly than if the child is frightened and shamed into pretending that he has no such interest. With tolerance, however, must go patient but steady guidance, leading the child on to the next step—which parents must always be ready for. In other words, this tolerance should not be complete tolerance for an indefinite period. The parents' job is still to help the child grow up. Eventually he must become civilized. For most two-year-olds, simple distractions from excessive "toilet play" are enough. Cries of "Naughty, naughty," slaps, and exclamations of disgust are positively harmful. But at four, five, or eight (these interests often die hard) we can begin to give a child the feeling that he can now find better things to do and that his parents have had enough of continuous toilet play and toilet jokes.

OTHER GOOD HABITS

Parents should not be surprised to find that clean clothing, bathing, and clean hands and faces do not particularly appeal to children. While they may be willing to conform to our demands and should be expected, within limits, to do so, a really spontaneous interest in cleanliness is not due much before adolescence. No matter what nurses say, a child who is "a perfect little lady," who shudders at dirt and fusses at a spot, is not as normal as the child who does not mind these things. Adults who make cleanliness a fetish should take care not to impose their peculiarities on children. This does not mean that they should not see to it that a child washes his hands before meals. This is certainly an esthetic measure, as well as a sanitary one. A child between two and six, however, will frequently have to be led to the washbasin and supervised in the process. A child between six and twelve should go when told; but even at this period parents may expect to give many reminders.

"But, Mother, my hands *are* clean!"

"Sorry, Pete, they're all grimy between the fingers, and there's a black shadow from the wrist up which I have an idea will disappear with soap and water."

Not until after the age of twelve or thereabouts do children —girls possibly earlier than boys—actually begin to care for cleanliness. Of course, washing behind the ears and clean fingernails come last of all, and it is as hard to persuade many children to get into a bathtub as it is to persuade the same ones to get out. All in all, we must accept the fact that our children do not live by quite the same standards we do. When, for example, we see our youngster run his hands along the window sill in a railroad car and then put his fingers in his mouth, possibly the best thing we can do is learn to look the other way.

Of course, hygiene has its claims. We cannot permit a child to rescue a fallen candy from the city pavement and eat it, but we should not be shocked because he wants to. Most adults claim that hygiene is the reason for all sorts of prohibitions which in reality are determined either by their own standards of esthetics or by more deeply determined but no more rational feelings of what is right and wrong. Children do not share these feelings, though in the course of time they gradually acquire them.

Before children are six years old there is not much reason

for telling them about germs. After that, they may learn about them as they learn about other natural facts of the world they live in. Germs should not be used to frighten children or to persuade them to be clean. The younger child should be told that "We wash our hands before we eat because it is nicer"— not because there is a germ on dirty hands which will give us a dreadful disease if we don't. An older child may certainly be told that Johnny is not in school today because he has a cold, and a cold means that he has germs in his nose and throat which could be coughed or sneezed onto the other children and give them colds. Keep children away from the movies or public playgrounds during a serious epidemic, and tell them why. But try to treat the subject of disease rationally and quietly and, if it comes, try to relieve, by the use of self-control and common sense, whatever mounting anxiety a child may feel. There are dangers, and children should know about them; there are methods for avoiding dangers—polio shots, for example—and these should be explained. The parents' attitude in this counts for everything. An anxiety-ridden parent can work havoc with a certain type of child.

Is It Natural to Be Neat?

Neatness is akin to cleanliness and usually is not learned early. It is commonly supposed to be the result of early training. "She never *had* to pick up her clothes," we hear people say. Actually, however, many of our habits have their roots in matters far more complex than mere training and, until science tells us more, many peculiarities are perhaps best written off under the general heading of "temperament." This, of course, is no explanation. While it is dangerous for parents to accept every fault or tendency as temperamental, there are, nevertheless, certain differences which, for practical purposes, they had better learn to accept. Every mother knows that while Jane, the eldest, quickly learned to put away her toys and hang up her clothes, Kate could never be taught to care and was always messy. While neatness is certainly a desirable trait and saves times and confusion, it must be admitted that some of the most useful adults have *never* learned to be neat. It is wise, of course, to teach children systematic and orderly ways of doing things, but the most important factor will always be the parents' own standards in these respects. Usually, though not always, a home that is reasonably neat and orderly produces children who value these standards.

Be ready to give help to the younger child, as it is needed— until he is eight, perhaps, or older. "I'll hang up your dress while you put your underwear in the hamper," or, "I bet I can put these blocks away faster than you can get your trains into the box in the closet." Gradually more and more responsibility can be shifted to the child. Someday he should know that it's his job, and his alone, to do certain chores. Put on a little pressure, but not so much that irritability and stubbornness result and you defeat your purpose. Time and again you will have to acknowledge that this particular child is not ready, after all, to be wholly relied upon. For a long time there will have to be reminders; exceptions must be made and help given for many years to come. Growth toward responsibility, the most important and the most inclusive of all character traits, comes slowly.

Training in punctuality conforms to many of the same principles as training in neatness. First of all, its virtues should not be overrated by parents. Of course, give some instruction and "training." Be fairly punctual yourself. Remind children occasionally of the passage of time and show that you value orderly living. But be ready also to give help at many points —and don't nag. As in the case of neatness, some of the best people never achieve perfection in this respect. Fortunately, most parents recognize that a young child's sense of time is imperfect and do not make many demands before he goes to kindergarten or school. After this, however, they are likely to be perturbed by dawdling, and "hurry" is the most common and most repeated of all household words around 8 A. M. Even at the age of six many children still need help. And help is not nagging; it is mainly the presence of a mother to say, "Here are your shoes. Put them on while I get your clean shirt." By the time a child is eight or nine there should be less of this, and if he still persists in dawdling and daydreaming the best thing to do is let him be late for school and take the consequences. However, it would be wise to talk this plan over with the teacher ahead of time and ask her help. By the time a child is ten he should be punctual most of the time under his own compulsion, but there are wide temperamental variations as well as other special reasons for giving some help even then.

MANNERS DO MATTER

It seems as though manners were perhaps a field in which parents, at least so-called "modern" ones, had reversed their usual tendency and were not demanding enough of their youngsters. Inconsiderateness from children is often tolerated unnecessarily and with unpleasant consequences, in the name of "freedom." Bad-mannered children end by being as disgusted with themselves as the grownups are.

"His mother shouldn't *allow* him to act that way," said a child of six to her own mother, while watching a contemporary put on a particularly obnoxious display. Often it is far easier to make definite demands and impose certain standards than to abide by a parental policy of complete indifference. It is easier not only for the parent but for the child, too.

This does not mean that a four-year-old must be put through all the paces which pass for good manners in adults. From the beginning the emphasis should be placed where it really belongs and where the child can understand it. "Manners" are arbitrary, but "friendliness" is a familiar and warm idea to a child. It makes sense. A child can be told that it is a friendly act to take off one's hat, to say please and thank you, how do you do and good-by, and to leave the best chair or the best piece of chicken for the other fellow. He can be told that there are special reasons for being friendly to older people. Sometimes, when "reasons" are beyond the understanding of a young child, it is best to fall back on what is "customary," at least until he is older. It is customary to let ladies go first and to give one's seat to an elderly woman in the bus. But even though the reasons are not wholly clear it is wise for parents to see that the value of these practices is acknowledged in some way—not with nagging, public rebukes, and threats, but with the detaining hand and the word of reminder.

Cultivating the Spirit

In most cases, the spirit of an act should be accepted for what it is, even when the letter is violated. A child who exclaims, "Oh, boy, that sure is *neat!*" is certainly being friendly and should not be called to order, even though he has omitted the customary thank-you for a gift. Conversely, a child who goes through the proper motions of compliance and courtesy, but does so with a sullen spirit, should not be allowed to feel that his behavior has been satisfactory. Most important of all, however, are the manners that children see in their daily life. No instructions concerning good manners can ever be a substitute for experience. If children are to become courteous to others, they must themselves be treated with habitual courtesy. This does not mean formality and set rituals—it means friendliness, respect, and consideration.

Many children are shy and self-conscious. They are often seized with panic when confronted with a social situation and find it difficult to be courteous. With them, as with the younger children, the best plan is to say for them the words they cannot speak.

"Thank you, Mrs. Brown. It was a lovely party," says a

mother to her child's hostess, while she leaves unrebuked the child who stands silent, with downcast eyes, beside her.

This seems a much better way than, "Say thank you to Mrs. Brown and tell her what a good time you had," or to insist on compliance from a child who is unable at the moment to bring forth a word. Humiliating children in front of others weakens or angers them and increases their already poor opinion of themselves. Criticism or punishments, if any, should wait until later. Meanwhile, an obstreperous child can be removed from the room as fast and as quietly as possible. Guests—or even just the family at mealtimes—resent being treated to scenes.

Sometimes children amuse or embarrass us, as the case may be, by apparently naïve but tactless remarks.

"You can take it back to the store, because I have a Teddy bear just like that," a child may say to a friend who has brought him a gift. Or he may ask his grandmother, "Why do you have that funny pink wart on your chin?"

Parents love to recount these tales as after-dinner conversation, seeing them as proof that their children are still wholly honest, untrammeled by the hypocrisies of adult society. But, while some of these childish remarks *may* be quite inadvertent, children are often not so naïve as they seem. Somewhere and somehow they have learned that they can get away with something that amuses or shocks the grownups and at the same time rids them of a few of their own animosities. Perhaps it is the grownups who are naïve in seeing nothing more in these situations than an embarrassing moment and in failing to realize that children are not always so innocent as they may appear.

"But this is an extra-lovely bear!" the mother may say, "and I'm sure your teddy would like a little brother." This may suffice for the moment. Later the child (if he's three or over) may be shown how sorry Mrs. So-and-so must have been because he wasn't pleased with the bear. Her trip to the store can be described, with the suggestion that we do thank people for wanting to please us, as well as for actually doing so. It will be easier to make this view of the matter clear if the children themselves have had experience in giving presents or in helping their parents plan and select them.

HONESTY

Many small children and some older ones go through periods of lying and stealing on the long road to honesty. Probably no one has a perfect record in this respect. Yet we regard honesty as an essential character trait above all other things, and a breach of it in our children fills us with alarm. Instantly our imagination runs riot. What if this child of ours should fail to mend his ways? We picture all the shady individuals we know or know about and wonder whether our children are destined to add to their number. In our anxiety we are likely to lose all perspective, so that we misjudge the seriousness of the behavior.

The first thing to remember is that honesty has a slow growth; nobody is born honest. Conscience, while it starts to develop at an early age, develops irregularly and slowly. A child of two and a half who screams, "Naughty boy, naughty boy!" in a loud agony of guilt when he wets his bed may have hazier ideas of right and wrong in other respects. One small boy, for example, eying a dish of plums but knowing he was not allowed to have any, took his mother by the hand to lead her from the room. "You go 'way," he explained. It seemed quite logical to him. When he sent his mother out of the room he sent his conscience also and so was free to help himself to the forbidden fruit.

These early dishonesties are no indication whatever of a naturally deceitful nature. They mark a stage of growth. For the little child, the parents' sanction and taboo are the whole moral world. Right is what his mother makes him do; wrong is what she forbids him, and he learns very gradually to prefer right because it earns him the smiles and approval that come to mean more to him than following his own whims. It is another step, of course, to the birth of a real conscience—an inner need to choose the right even when it hurts—yet eventually this does come about, and the parents' standards make themselves heard even when the parents themselves are not there. It is extraordinary how commanding the parents' standards are and how the imprint of them is almost all there is to an adult conscience. Right and wrong, for many grownups, still remains about what their parents taught them, and nothing else.

Honesty is not acquired by strict training on a mechanical reward-and-punishment basis. It is true that the mother's approval of honesty can be a reward, just as her disapproval can be punishment, and that much will therefore depend on whether the parent-child relationship is one in which hostility and defiance, or the reverse, have been fostered. Honesty is a complex attitude of mind which develops through association with people of whose love one is sure and who are honest themselves and admire honesty. A deceitful child may be punished time and again for dishonesty or made to "practice" honesty, but if his mood is antagonistic and resentful he will learn nothing. Parents, also, must be scrupulous in their dealings with children and all others. Nine tenths of even the social lies that parents tell could be avoided, and if we must let children know that there are times when we withhold some of the truth in order to be kind, we should explain to them our reasons for doing this.

Children of two or three years of age often lie quite freely. The wish is father to the thought. When they are caught doing something they should not, they momentarily wish it undone and hope they may make it so by saying it is so. Punishments usually have the effect of driving the deceit farther underground—the child merely learns that he must be more careful, instead of learning to value the truth.

When a parent discovers a very young child in an untruth, the best plan is just to make a correction.

"You took the candy. See, you have some chocolate still on your fingers. You must always say what is true."

After that, the matter may be dropped until the next time. It is important, however, not to treat these lapses as funny or cute. Don't smile about them. "True" is a very important

[64]

word, and children should learn as soon as possible of the great importance we attach to it.

Imagination

For children in their early years the border line between fact and fancy is very hazy, and the telling of tall stories is extremely common. Once launched on a good tale, children quickly begin to believe in the truth of their own creations.

"That's a wonderful story," the mother can say, after she has been told about the magnificent fleet of ten white automobiles that Tommy's father is buying for him. "Tomorrow you can tell me some more. But, of course, we know they aren't *really* true, they're like fairy stories."

An older child may make up stories that sound entirely plausible. When he continues to tell these after he is old enough to be able to tell fact from fancy—five or six, perhaps —they probably represent a deep-felt wish or perhaps reflect anxiety. It is common for a timid boy, struggling with the problem of his own fears of bigger and rougher boys, to tell a tall story of meeting other fellows on the way home and dealing out black eyes all round, so that they all ran home crying. One only child who felt decidedly out of things when all her friends discussed their brothers and sisters created a large family for herself, with the individual characteristics of each member so well described that she fooled everybody who did not know the facts.

Such incidents should not pass unnoticed. Children should know that we are not fooled and that we object to these stories because they are not true. We can make it very clear that we regard this sort of thing as something they should learn to pass beyond. But often a dose of good-humored kidding may prove to be more effective than a moral lecture. Moreover, parents should pay attention to the information these fabrications may give them. Often they furnish a clue to a child's inner problems. Timid boys, for example, need patient encouragement to help them build better relations with other children. In some cases, home relationships need reconstruction, too. Although in the case of the little girl who was an only child it was impossible to supply the brothers and sisters (whose arrival she perhaps feared as much as desired), there were certain other things that could be done: more young friends could be invited to visit for a night, a week end, or a longer period during vacations, so that she could at least have some of the fun which she imagined her friends to be having.

Stealing

Petty pilfering is also common in early childhood. After a child is six or seven it may begin to have more serious implications, but the small thefts of the early years can usually be counted among the irregularities of normal growth. To the child of three or four we may simply explain that this thing which he has appropriated belongs to someone else and must therefore be returned. When he is a little older he should begin to realize that he knows it belongs to someone else, that it is *wrong* to take it, and that he must now take it back. If the parents treat the whole matter seriously and firmly it is likely to be just as effective, for reasons already given, as out-and-out punishment. If lying and stealing continue into the later years, however, and if no real improvement occurs over a long period of time, we must suspect that inner forces are driving the child in this sort of behavior. Then we must call in expert professional advice and find out where the roots of the trouble lie and how the child can be helped.

Make Haste Slowly

Whether in matters of nursery cleanliness, or of courtesy, kindliness, and honesty, or those later traits closely bound up with responsible ways of living, young parents often fail to realize that children cannot be won immediately to civilized and reasonable ways of doing things. Conscience develops slowly and irregularly. Children at first do what pleases them, and this is often diametrically opposed to what pleases adults. Adults are made miserable, for example, by a loud noise close to their ears, but children rejoice in it; adults love quiet and repose, but children are pleasantly stimulated by confusion. To an adult, dawdling and delay are violent irritants, but a child just can't see why. Adults hate dirt; children positively seem to love it. To an adult the living-room couch is a place to recline and rest; to a child it may be a hide-out that must be defended from gangster raids. And *how* they love to use beds as springboards for jumping, and how it messes up our beautiful bedspreads!

All these differences are real. Unless they are understood and places are provided and regulations made for children's needs as well as adults', living with children deteriorates into irritation and conflict. With irritation and conflict a child is stimulated to resistance all along the line. Even the so-called force of good example and the most consistent training for "good habits" will do no good if the parents' relation to their child breaks down, for it is largely the friendly feeling which children have for their parents that first prompts them to consent to give up purely egoistic goals and to accept co-operative ones.

"Aw shucks, my hair looks O.K., but if Dad wants me to brush it again I might as well do it," says the ten-year-old to himself.

And the daughter of fourteen who gets the family breakfast on Sunday morning does it, not because she has been methodically trained to, but because it's more fun to bask in the warmth of the all-round pleasure that results than it is to be sullen and sour or even just to go one's own way.

It cannot be said too often that nothing worth accomplishing with children in their homes is accomplished without an all-pervasive atmosphere of affection. Children always learn best from persons whose good will they trust and whom they are therefore willing to work *with,* instead of against. This is not as simple as it sounds, for although most parents love their children, they sometimes have difficulty in *liking* all of them all of the time. Children are quick to sense meaning in a tone of voice, in a facial expression, or in our overeagerness to get them out of the way or hustle them off to bed, "for their own good." In the last analysis they will disregard our words —"Of *course* I love you. Mothers always love their children." "Certainly I love you as much as Danny"—and will respond instead to the pleasure or lack of pleasure which we get from being with them. This is the only kind of loving that children understand, and it is this knowledge alone that makes it possible for them to perform the dozens of dull, daily tasks we require of them.

The crying need of most fumbling young parents is to stop worrying about "habit training" and to turn their attention instead to what the child is feeling about his parents, about the other people in his world, and about himself. Is he comfortable about his ultimate ability to measure up to the standards exacted of him? Is he happy with his contemporaries? Does his relation to his parents make him feel warmed and wanted and loved despite the disappointments in him they must sometimes feel and express? These are the questions parents should ask. Here is where their efforts should be turned. In the deepest sense it is true that childhood is the golden period of personality formation. Whatever the direction given by our inherited constitution, our earliest nursery experiences play an overwhelming part in determining whether in later life we will be happy or sad, generous or mean, friendly or hostile, suspicious or trusting, reasonable or stubborn, and how well we will be able to express or control our aggressive and our sexual impulses—in short, all that is most important in life. And these are the consequences not of direct and mechanized training, but of the feelings released in the family drama of the early years.

CHAPTER THREE

DISCIPLINE

M<small>OST</small> <small>PARENTS</small> would agree that their purpose in training their children is not blind obedience, but rather gradual progress toward self-discipline. Perhaps obedience has its place, but it is as a means to an end, not as a goal. Those of us who believe in the American way would like, if we knew how, to bring up our children to make intelligent choices for themselves, not to depend on the man higher up to make choices for them. But we also want children who can accept the inevitable disciplines that life imposes, who are able to see the necessity for self-denial when it is called for, and who are willing to make themselves do the difficult task, the dull chore, and the distasteful job, at least as a step to something else which is not dull or distasteful. But self-discipline is more than a negative virtue. In the human mechanism it is important to have not only the brakes, but also the accelerator in good working order. Self-discipline means the ability to initiate as well as to inhibit, to "go" as well as to "stop," and it is disconcerting to observe the extent to which, as people reach maturity, the mechanism for *going* seems to be out of order more frequently than the mechanism for *stopping*. The world, in fact, is full of people in whom growth, initiative, and progress seem to have given way to a merely passive participation in life. Disciplined living degenerates too quickly into docile living.

In the child this is rarely noticeable. His "go" mechanism seems enormously effective; it is the brakes which are feeble. We marvel at his energies. He wants to go everywhere and to explore everything. Watch the year-old infant crawling about the floor, tirelessly working hour after hour to learn new co-ordinations—pulling himself up by chair legs and table tops, seizing lamps, ash trays, matches, vases, turning them about with solemn interest, pulling them apart if he can, and crashing them to the floor with glee at his power. When he is a little older he will never want to come in from play, or sit quietly, or go to bed, though the signs of fatigue are there. He will stand noises which drive adults mad, he will ask questions by the hour, will climb, run, punch, and kick. It will be hard to make him sit at a desk with books, or keep himself neat, or pay attention to the demands of time, or submit to the social amenities.

How can we preserve for him all this fine energy, this inquiring spirit, this insatiable will to explore and to pursue his own ends, and yet at the same time tame and civilize him so that he can meet the demands of living? The problem is critical and it is fundamental. It cannot be solved by embracing either horn of the dilemma. Are we "modern" parents who believe in self-expression and freedom for children, or

[71]

"old-fashioned" ones who admire discipline? Obviously, let us hope that we are neither one nor the other, but both. There is no real freedom without discipline for either child, adult, or nation. The very preservation of our democratic institutions and of the liberties we value most depends ultimately on the ability of individual citizens to achieve self-discipline. Yet we discover at the same time that for both children and grown-up citizens life cannot and should not be wholly orderly and rational. Children, though they need authority, also need to break out now and then, to defy their parents, to feel their oats, to kick up their heels, to long for and to taste the independence which someday should rightfully be theirs. Desiring obedience, parents should never aim for "implicit obedience." Routines should be flexible, rules should have exceptions, the doctrine of parental infallibility should be discarded early. Children like to mind; they also like not to mind. Routines are necessary; so are breaks in routine. Laws are made to be broken.

ROUTINE—THE BASIS OF DISCIPLINE

The quiet execution of the ordinary routines of existence is the earliest form of discipline. Grownups have become so habituated to the rhythm of daily life that they take it far too much for granted. For most of us it is no longer a great effort to brush our teeth, to come to meals on time, to dress and undress, or to go to bed. For children these things and others like them are the first real experiences in discipline, and in their early years they need much help in getting through the day in an orderly fashion. Furthermore, the attitudes acquired in the process are of the utmost importance in determining whether children are to grow up anxious and tense or easy and good-humored.

As we have already seen, much wear and tear is saved if the grownups, instead of constantly exerting pressure, allow the child to assume responsibility for these things at his own rate of development and can refrain from prematurely shifting too many responsibilities to the child. Most young parents are too ambitious and too eager to hurry a child on to the next step. They are also far too inclined to worry about how to teach an infant *not* to follow his natural impulses. They would be better off if the question they asked themselves would be: "How can I let him be as active and adventurous and explorative as possible and still keep him and the furniture safe?" This means an almost constant job of supervision, and the young mother's day, especially if she is tense and fussy by temperament, is often exhausting.

"My Day"

For example: She puts her fifteen-month-old youngster, who has just learned to walk, in his play pen with some toys —a woolly dog, a string of beads, and a box with miscellaneous objects in it. He starts to play with these, while she goes to the telephone to make arrangements for the day, or into the kitchen to make the dessert. She hears a violent shaking at the bars of the pen, and a voice shouting, persistently but not angrily, "Out, out." She lifts him out, realizing that after all he has just learned to walk and it is only right that he should want to try his new skill. She sits at her desk to go over some bills, and he at once follows her, chatting amiably and trying to seize envelopes, pens, the ink bottle. "No, no," she says, and perhaps administers a little slap on the hand now stained with the ink. She takes the toys from inside the play pen, demonstrates their charms, and tries to get him to sit on the floor beside the desk and play with them. He, however, has another plan—to climb on the couch, scale the back of it, and reach for the picture on the wall. The picture groans a bit on its wires, threatening to come loose. She leaps up, pretty annoyed by this time, and struggles to unfasten the small hand from the edge of the frame. "No, no," she insists, "you are a very naughty boy. You may not touch the picture. It will fall and hurt you." A final twist extricates him, but he bursts into cries of protests, and stamps his feet as she puts him down. Does he deserve a good spanking, as his father suggests? She tried it once and it didn't seem to settle anything. She feels helpless, and in her mind the fear rises that she is no good at this business of being a mother. Better get him outdoors as fast as possible. She carries him, still sobbing, to his room. He fights her every inch of the way as she tries to get his outdoor things on.

Is this a discipline problem? Is this a spoiled child? It seems to be more a problem in management which requires, first of all, some knowledge and acceptance of what a healthy fifteen-month-old child is likely to be and do. Second, it requires planning ahead to provide safely and practically for his interests and impulses; and third, it requires a mother who is prepared to change her plans at a moment's notice in order to meet the unexpected. A runabout child should not be required to spend hours in a play pen or even to sit quietly on the floor. His very nature will make him run about and he should have a chance to do so, but he will also lack the co-ordination and the judgment to move about among attractive and breakable articles in safety. Something can be done, of course, to teach even young children not to touch or do certain things, but this is a process which takes time; it is also far easier to accomplish with some children than with others of a more headstrong and aggressive make-up.

No small child can be completely relied on to resist temptation when temptation is really strong. This does not mean that parents should not try to teach and to train. By suggestions and example they should keep right on with quiet attempts to have the child accept certain rules of living. But they must realize that this process takes time and that long-range education is preferable to short-range training. Meanwhile, when the child cannot or will not comply with reasonable demands, parents must be ready to step in themselves and take the responsibility for seeing that certain things are done. With very young children they must also be able to reconcile themselves to giving a great deal of purely custodial care. This is why we put bars at the nursery windows, or gates at the head of the stairs, instead of relying wholly on instructions and prohibitions. Let us hope also that we put expensive bric-a-brac on a top closet shelf and postpone getting the new satin bedspreads for a good many years. A home with children in it must be furnished in a way that takes into consideration their needs and natures as well as the adults'. We are heading for trouble if we bank much on "training" to rid them of childish desires or to turn them into controlled adults overnight.

What could have been done to prevent a headache for the mother just described and anger for the baby? There are no guarantees, of course, and no formulas. The best of mothers get headaches and have moments when they feel they are failing, and even the children with the wisest parents must sometimes be confronted with some definite "noes" which may provoke anger. But neither the headaches nor the "noes" should ever become chronic.

Here is the way one mother met this actual situation: when her child climbed to the back of the living-room couch and reached for the picture she did not snatch him away. Instead, she steadied it in his grasp, holding him up and naming some of the objects in it. This, however, was not what he wanted. So, still holding it, she allowed him to twist it slightly and look under it. He ran his finger underneath and along the picture's back and began to sneeze and look very surprised at his black finger, since his mother's housekeeping was not exactly perfect. She said, "Oh, look, dirty!" and carried him off to wash it. He protested, of course, but his mother knew when enough was enough and continued on her way, and once in the bathroom they soon found other interesting things to do. Back in the living room she introduced him to a cubbyhole in her desk always full of things which her child *might* have. Here she kept an empty ink bottle with a cork to take out and put in, papers and envelopes, a dull pencil with a cap, a box of clips, a paperweight—and she varied these things occasionally, so that any day there might be some surprises.

Good Management Equals Good Discipline

This kind of management is the foundation of good discipline. By this means the child learns daily and hourly that the world is full of interesting chances for exploration, but he discovers too that there are some rules to the game and that even the people who love us impose those rules. Such discipline is far more effective than the slap which brings compliance through fear. It teaches more reality, more experience of the ways in which civilized people live together. It has two virtues —it demands some conformity and at the same time encourages activity. When quits are called they are called firmly and definitely, but help is given in discovering delightful possibilities elsewhere.

It is the besetting sin of conscientious parents, particularly with their first babies, to begin to worry much too soon about discipline in its merely negative forms. They are afraid of having a spoiled child or a child who "gets into bad habits." They therefore center their efforts on making their child conform to civilized standards as quickly as possible. Usually they are not concerned enough with giving him a contented infancy and with helping him make the difficult adjustment to life and its routines with the minimum of friction. They make the mistake of regarding the impulse toward independence and self-will, which emerges at the age of two or three, as an indication that their discipline has been faulty or that the child is exceptionally unruly. Actually neither need be the case. The normal, energetic child who is endowed with enough spirit of adventure and aggression to get him through a tough world begins to feel his oats when he is about three, and he loves to experiment with his new-found sense of power. He behaves selfishly, egotistically, often violently and aggressively. He indulges in outbursts of defiance against his parents. He slaps and sometimes bites, he gives vent to rages, he seizes his toys for himself alone instead of sharing them with guests, he refuses to eat, to go to bed, to get washed. Of course, he does not do these things all day long. Between times he may behave quite angelically. Most children between two and five or older, however, show several of the items on this list in greater or less degree.

During this period, a child is discovering both his power and the great limits of his power. It is exciting to be able to walk about instead of crawl, to use words which get definite reactions from adults—"No, no," and "I won't"—or to gloat over the distress caused by refusing to do what adults demand. But adults are also bigger, stronger, and more determined to have things their way. They make children get washed, go to bed, say please and thank you, and they won't let children do many of the things they wish to do. No matter how reasonable or necessary these demands or these denials are, the child is likely to consider them arbitrary and to regard adults as enemies as well as friends. From time to time the desire for opposition and revenge grows very strong.

GOOD AND BAD BEHAVIOR

Some of this is inevitable and proper, and the first great lesson parents must learn is that some actual hostility and aggression must be understood and accepted as a necessary phase of a child's development. The second point for parents to understand, once they have grasped this first and fundamental one, is that in spite of appearances to the contrary a child also wants his hostilities and aggressions to be controlled by his parents. Discipline is something far more important than a mere device for making children bearable to adults. It is a profound emotional need of children themselves; without it they are uncomfortable and in constant inner conflict. The undercontrolled child is not a happy one, any more than the overcontrolled one. Nor is he free. He is constantly the victim of unbridled egotism, aggression, and unco-ordinated impulses of all kinds which prompt him to bite, to destroy, and to be "bad" even to those he loves. Such impulses are terrifying to the child himself and if permitted to run riot produce only a deep sense of guilt and inferiority. He can be relieved only when he discovers that there is someone in control who will not let certain things happen, who can oppose the "bad" things and keep him "good." If we knew how to listen we could tell that children ask all the time to be saved from the consequences of their own unbridled and dangerous impulses—consequences which, after the momentary pleasure of gratification has passed, are far from pleasant. For even when the adult does not punish a child for being "bad,"

[79]

there is no doubt that his own conscience does and he suffers accordingly.

Conscience

Conscience in children develops earlier than is usually realized. Long before he can really conform to its demands or is able to discipline himself, a child is busy in his own small world with this problem of "good" and "bad"—words that recur again and again in his vocabulary. Even the very naughty child has an active conscience, and part of his reason for being bad is that he is caught in a vicious circle. He feels inferior because his conscience reproaches him for being naughty, and this sense of inferiority makes him crave even more the momentary gratifications that come from indulging his naughtiness. This situation, in which nearly every child is enmeshed from time to time, calls loudly for two things from the parent. It calls for a firm, sure, quiet control that *prevents* unbridled, disorderly behavior. It calls even more for a parent whose affection and understanding, though quiet, are real, all-pervasive, and unconditional. Only in exchange for love can a child accept disappointment and denial. If he doubts this love or if he feels that it depends on good behavior ("Mother doesn't love you when you are a naughty boy"— this attitude, when it becomes extreme and whether expressed in words or actions, is a very destructive one), anxieties arise that express themselves in more and more misbehavior. The difficult child and the naughty child need more love and reassurance, not less, for they can accept discipline only on this basis.

Counterfeit Love

There is a whole class of gushy, emotional parents who are always protesting their love by words and embraces and by excessive fussiness about health and safety. They are over-protective and they cramp the child's independence at every point. Their egotism, their fears and anxieties, and their own lack of self-control are also apparent in a thousand ways, so that the child soon learns that both the affection and the discipline are wholly undependable. This is not love; it is counterfeit. But even quite sensible parents make the discovery that although little babies need cuddling and handling, children of two or three and older begin to get enough of it, and affection must find new forms. Most children respond to interest and companionship, not words and embraces or even gifts. "His presents and things are nice," said one child commenting on the attentions of a certain adult he never liked much, "but he doesn't really love my dog." Where his misdemeanors are concerned, what a child needs to feel in the attitude of both parents is something like this: "Of course, I love you and always will, but the naughtiness makes us both unhappy, and so I am sorry and am going to help you to get over some of it." This should not come as a sermon, but as a way of life which the child senses from the moment he begins to discover that he is living in a society which has certain rules.

Parents, in the stress of living with children, often lose the art of expressing what they really feel. They become merely strict, nagging, or quick to punish, and when this is the only sign they give of their interest in their children they run the risk of arousing the maximum of antagonism and resistance. It is a good rule for all parents who decide (as which of us do not periodically?) that we have been altogether too lax and easygoing with our Johns and Sues to plan, not only a new and firmer regime, but new interests and new things to do together, more time, more trouble taken, more experiences shared and genuinely enjoyed together. Often enough, when we do this we find that the actual discipline required is far less than at first appeared. This very process of increasing friendliness makes the subborn, resistant child far more amenable and friendly.

Managing Children

Here, then, are some suggestions which may be helpful at those times when parents feel that their children are really out of hand and are headed straight for calamity unless the proverbial foot is put down:

1. Be sure that your affection and interest are expressed in actions which the child understands. Do not let your contact with him degenerate into a series of "don'ts," "you musts," "hurry ups," and all those other innumerable reminders of his faults and errors. Keep these at a minimum and spend as much time as possible doing things together which you can both enjoy.

2. Give careful consideration to the places where you intend to tighten your grip. Are your demands suitable to the child's development?

3. Be firm, but be good-humored and companionable. Substitute a funny remark (if you have it in you) for that tense, patient, martyred look which is becoming such a habit.

4. Give a reason for a demand once, or twice at the most. Never argue. When pressed, all children will try to seduce you into talking to keep you from acting. Often you can treat a child's "no" as if it had been a "yes" and so get the thing done. When a child asks "Why?" make up your mind quickly whether it is a genuine request for information. If it is, treat it with respect and explain carefully. Remember, however, that the "why" which follows a request to do something that is no fun is usually a mere noise which the child has invented to set you talking again. Don't be caught in this trap more than a hundred times.

5. With young children, "getting a thing done" is usually not at all a question of repeating your orders—it may mean that you have to get up yourself and start to do whatever is to be done. If it is bedtime, for example, start putting toys away and turning down the bed. Keep the conversation away from the topic of going to bed and what a healthy, sensible thing it is.

6. Do not challenge the child by offering him radical choices, such as: "If you don't go outdoors and play like a nice boy, Mother won't take you to the beach tomorrow." By doing this you not only risk spoiling a happy afternoon, you also dare the child to defy you. In these early years, a more suita-

ble approach would be: "Now it is time to go out. Will you take your skates or your scooter?"

7. Remember always that *chronic* irritability and negativism, *chronic* bad temper, unhappiness, and defiance that do not yield to suggestions like the above may have deeper origins than mere mismanagement. It is always wise to consider the child's life from time to time, with a view to discovering the causes of dissatisfaction. What these causes may be cannot be summarized briefly in a chapter, though it is the purpose of this book as a whole to introduce parents to the commonest of them. It must be remembered, however, that they are individual with every child.

8. An intelligent and experienced mother who has the ability to identify herself with her child and to feel as he is feeling often becomes expert at ferreting these things out. Yet she should beware of the too-prevalent notion that common sense and affection can solve all the problems of childhood. Even the wisest and most "normal" of parents sometimes need professional help. They should have no more sense of guilt or failure in seeking psychiatric help than in consulting a doctor about their child's physical problems.

REWARDS AND PUNISHMENTS

What place in child training should be assigned to the use of rewards and punishments, spankings and penalties? Are they a necessary part of the process of discipline, as they were certainly thought to be in the old days? Or are they wholly obsolete? Of course, every child is "punished" when he encounters his parents' displeasure. But is this enough? Do we need to add external punishments besides? Is virtue its own reward, and can children learn the rules of life through nothing but sweet reasonableness, the power of example, and moral instruction?

In answering these questions we must first understand that reasonableness is not always what it seems and that too often it merely cloaks the confusion of an indecisive adult. Also, certain brands of moralizing are not so gentle as they appear and may be essentially more cruel than a simple spanking. Yet, however we feel about the use of force on children, most parents quite rightly are eager to make their homes places where a sense of moral obligation exists independently of external coercion. Our goal is not a well-policed and docile family of children, but a family where children are gradually learning the meaning of decent behavior and are acquiring the power to discipline themselves.

Once we have adopted this point of view we are likely to find that penalties, bribes, rewards, threats, and all the paraphernalia of discipline turn out to be either ineffective or unnecessary. Perhaps they are sometimes justified as short cuts on occasions when a child needs just a little prod to make him stop stalling and shilly-shallying. For example:

"If you hurry up and get dressed in time, you may ride with Daddy and me to the station."

"No story tonight. Sorry, but you wasted so much time undressing that it's much too late now."

Show That You Know How He Feels

Children need to know, too, that we sympathize and feel like showing it when something really unpleasant is required of them.

"When we're all through at the dentist, we'll stop at the drugstore and have some ice cream," we may say, without making this happy ending in any way conditional on good behavior. Or if a child has shown unusual fortitude under trying circumstances, or has kept at something which required patience and effort, he certainly deserves recognition:

"When that boat is all done and makes its first trip in the lake, I believe this whole family is going to celebrate. What shall it be? A picnic? A boat ride?"

On the other hand, there are certain inevitable consequences of failures:

"You didn't come home when you said you would when I let you go to the Smiths' alone. That shows you aren't old enough yet to play away from your own yard. So you'll have to stay here to play until I am sure you can remember about coming back."

If these things are rewards and punishments, they are fair enough and necessary for the conduct of any reasonable household. There is, however, a real difference in the spirit of such procedures from that which prompts parents to send a child to bed because he came home late, or to make promises of dimes for good behavior at the doctor's. Moreover, parents who have depended consistently on rewards as the only means of winning good behavior are likely to be startled when they find that their children, as they get older, have learned only to demand their pound of flesh.

"I won't wash dishes unless you pay me a quarter," says a twelve-year-old.

"What's the use of doing all that schoolwork just for A's? I say, Dad, how about a new bicycle?" says a rising young businessman.

In these cases, one child has failed to learn that a home is a co-operative enterprise where each member does his share because that is the decent way to live together. The other child misses the point that education is something for himself and that his obligation to work has no relation to immediate and tangible rewards.

These Things Count Most

In making for successful discipline, whether or not we use rewards and punishments as teaching devices, the most important factor will always be the understanding which exists between parent and child and the soundness of the parents' characters as adults. If these things are right, rewards and punishments may or may not be used, but they will not be the real source of success. It is unfortunate that so much discussion of child management should revolve around this question of spanking and punishment versus nonspanking and nonpunishment. There are certainly parents who punish and who are eminently successful with their children. There are other families where, in spite of three or four high-spirited young ones, arbitrary disciplinary devices are rarely, if ever, resorted to—yet things run smoothly and on the whole amiably. It would be a mistake, therefore, to conclude that success is attributable either to the punishments or the lack of them. By and large, we find that those parents who do not depend on external punishment alone get along the best. Their choice requires them to bring more thought and intelligence to the task at hand. Having decided not to depend on force or fear, they find that they must work harder at the task of understanding the forces which underlie misbehavior. The danger of continuous recourse to punishment is that this essential issue is thereby likely to be obscured. Punishments are an attempt to suppress misbehavior after it has happened instead of trying to bring about a situation where the very impulse to misbehavior is reduced. This latter approach is far more difficult than any other, but, because it considers fundamentals, it is the only course really worth taking.

This does not mean that the parent who resorts to punishment in an emergency or in a fit of temper or exasperation has committed a crime. Most parents have at some time lost their temper with a child and smacked him in anger. They are likely to feel guilty about it afterwards, and perhaps they should. A child has a right to expect a pretty high standard of behavior in his parents. Yet if it is unfair to demand perfection of a child, perhaps we should not demand it of ourselves either. We too are human, and the child might as well find it out. He should also learn that adults have feelings and that there are limits to their patience. Righteous indignation is something worth discovering, as well as the wholesome truth that there are some kinds of behavior which will surely evoke hearty and heated resentments even in people who are ordinarily quite calm.

But if parents find themselves continuously angry, or in a chronic state of administering punishments, they can be perfectly certain that they are on the wrong track. The only thing they can do to remedy matters is to prepare for an entirely new angle of attack on their child's problems. This attack must be one which sets in motion an inquiry into the child's whole life and perhaps their own life as well. What caused the failure of those fundamental, emotional satisfactions which children need as truly as they need food and water? What forces within the entire system of family relationship are driving this particular child into misconduct?

Again and again we find that the most important point about discipline is not a question of correct procedures and proper techniques; ninety-nine per cent of it is made up of two things—the way in which the person who is in control understands the child's inner problems at various stages of his growth and the relationship which exists between that person and the child. The mother who is aware of the stresses and anxieties in her child, and is yet forbearing, can make dozens of mistakes in "method" without doing any real harm. The mother, on the other hand, whose feeling for her child is dominated by a fussy anxiety, whose genuine enjoyment has been supplanted by a tense concern about doing her duty, is in a bad way. She can read all the books, attend all the lectures, take a Ph.D. in psychology, but her correctness will get her nowhere unless these attitudes undergo a fundamental change. It is true that she may be a good disciplinarian and her children may toe the mark, or, if she is a different type, she may grant them unlimited freedom. In either case, unless her unhampered acceptance of them shows in their daily contacts, neither the discipline nor the freedom can make her children really disciplined or genuinely free. Both will be colored by the child's resentment of his mother's disappointment in him, of her nagging, her ceaseless criticism, by a sharply condemnatory attitude, or perhaps most of all because there has been an underlying indifference to him and his needs.

A young child never wholly recovers from such antagonism in his mother throughout the early years. He may struggle through to a maturity that seems adequate enough, but inwardly he is to some extent crippled. His freedom, if he has it, tastes sour. Discipline is something to be resented and overthrown wherever possible, if that is all his home has offered. Coming without the assurance of love, it will seem to him an inescapable, crushing burden, since it has never brought him anything really worth having. It is therefore unacceptable and he will be unable to make it a real part of his mature personality.

A CASE HISTORY: THE STORY OF TWO BROTHERS

This principle is illustrated in the case of two brothers. Their reactions to a family setting which failed to offer them the essentials for sound development were quite different, but equally destructive. Their mother was an ailing neurasthenic who alternately "adored" her children and withdrew from them because their childish actions upset her and brought on an attack of nerves. She worried about them constantly, feared for their health, pestered them with a multitude of petty orders, and completely failed to produce an atmosphere in which a normal child could be himself.

The father of the family was seldom at home. He was a successful businessman, a molder of events, and in some ways was also a dictator at home, but he could not cope with his wife; fundamentally he was afraid of her and yielded to her particular form of tyranny. With the children he took a strong hand, and to them he was chiefly a figure to be feared. His demands seemed arbitrary, his rules rigid. When he was at home they had to behave in a manner which took only his wishes into account, and infringements were met with punishment or angry outbursts which terrified both children. When he did show interest in them it was largely through taking them to visit places or people that *he* enjoyed. On these occasions they were on exhibition, to be admired by his friends for his personal gratification. Further, he always checked up on how they behaved when he was not at home, and if the reports were bad he exacted penalties. While he claimed again and again that he did this for their own good, it was perfectly clear to the children that his own pride was at stake and that he cared nothing for their personal problems. Obviously he made no attempt to discover what they were thinking, feeling, or wishing. It is interesting that in the eyes of the world he seemed a good father, one who tried earnestly to give his boys the attention which they lacked because of their mother's illness. People did regard him as strict, but since the boys had good manners and seemed intelligent this was all to the good. Nobody questioned much whether the father's interest was real or selfish, or whether the strict discipline could ever become self-discipline.

Of course it did not. As the older boy grew up, he cut loose. At adolescence he abandoned sullen submission at school and became insolent and defiant to his teachers. In high school, trouble was always being made and always being patched up. Just before graduation he used the occasion of examinations to write an "open letter" to his teachers, telling them what was wrong with the courses they gave and with themselves and offering suggestions for improvement. This nearly cost him his diploma, but his good academic record and his father's influence saved the day.

At college, more serious trouble began. In the middle of his sophomore year he ran away, announcing that he was going to work. His father immediately sent him a long, indignant letter full of righteous moral advice, ending with the conclusion that the boy could now sink or swim, entirely on his own. Maybe this would make a man of him. The boy then embarked on a series of business ventures which ranged all the way from the merely phony to the positively shady. On occasions, in order to save the family honor, the father had to step into the breach with some cold cash that would gloss things over. Two adventures in matrimony ended each time in divorce and additional unpleasantness. Today, at thirty, this boy shows no signs of having learned anything from experience. Or, to state it far more accurately, he has never succeeded in unlearning the deepest lesson of his childhood: that discipline is something which people who don't love you believe is good for you.

The younger of the two brothers was at first thought to be a great success. He was big and strong, a fine athlete, was socially popular, did excellent work through school and college, and "greatly admired" his father. Since he got his pleasure in life out of successful striving to please, it was almost inevitable that he should go into his father's business. Actually he had wanted to study medicine and had taken premedical work in college, but he gave up these plans because it meant so much to his father to have him in business with him. This plan worked fairly well until the depression curtailed many of the firm's activities and left the son with almost nothing to do. Father and son spent their time being as cagey as possible, guarding the family investments, and cursing the government. There was also squash and handball to fill in the leisure hours and to provide an escape from a sense of futility. At no time did this young man dare to think of branching out for himself; he lacked the nerve to ask his father's help, he lacked the initiative to discover what else he might do with his life—in fact, he now lacked even the will for anything else. He too had married, and his marriage was considered both "suitable" and a success, but a close observer could quickly see that through it ran a strain of irritation and disharmony. His wife was at constant odds with her mother-in-law, a condition which was caused partly by the fact that he himself had developed a close and deeply attentive relation to his mother, leaving his wife with the feeling of being excluded from her husband's life or at best secondary.

This second son is typical of a certain kind of "successful" adult, who has never been able to unlearn the lessons born of his early experiences. What this man feels, though he is unaware of it, is something like this: "It is wicked for a boy to hate his parents even when they are selfish and indifferent. If you do everything they want you to and are a good boy and act as though you love them, you won't feel quite so wicked."

Despite the external differences in these young men, the similarities caused by the common experiences of their early training are fundamental. Both lacked self-discipline, though one showed it by an impaired "stop," or control, mechanism, and the other by an impaired "go" mechanism. Both had an unconscious hatred for the parents, though one showed it by overrebellion toward authority, the other by oversubmission. Both failed to find satisfaction in marriage and their relation to women because the generally unsound emotional relationships in the family had deprived them of satisfying love experiences while they were growing up. Both were therefore seriously crippled, though in the case of the older boy the failure was far more apparent to the world. The younger son is more likely to be regarded as a success since he is amiable and popular, a good provider, and a dutiful husband and son. Such an estimate, however, overlooks the sense of inner frustration and depression and the defeat of real potentialities, which is as true in the one case as in the other.

It cannot be said too often, then, that if discipline is ever to become acceptable and genuinely incorporated into the personality as self-discipline it must come through an adult who possesses both warmth and strength and to whom the child feels himself genuinely acceptable. Children must suffer definite denials in the course of growing up; there are bound to be many "noes" and "don'ts," and parents are constantly called upon to put pressure on children to live up to certain standards which have come within their capacity. Yet everything will depend on whether or not the child discovers that the person who makes demands and imposes discipline is the same person who offers him love. Beside this basic condition, the methods used and the disciplines imposed are trivial. Questions of whether to spank or not to spank, or of what formula can be used when a three-year-old refuses to take his bath or wets his bed or slaps the baby, are all useless unless they serve to focus parents' attention not only on what it is fair to expect of the child at a particular stage of development, but also on what is even more fundamental —the quality of the whole relationship between child and parent and the nature of the family drama as it unfolds during these early years.

CHAPTER FOUR

BROTHERS AND SISTERS

QUARRELING AMONG BROTHERS and sisters is one of the most common of family annoyances, but that does not make it any easier for the whole household. One thing that makes this condition especially hard for parents is that it represents a disappointment and a defeat of their plans, for among the things they hoped for most in their home life were harmonious, affectionate, and companionable relationships among the children. Since they may even have decided to have their second baby because they thought he would prove a delightful companion for their first child, it is no wonder that they feel defeated when their two-year-old wantonly destroys the elaborate block construction of their five-year-old, who responds by hitting the baby on the head with a fire engine. This is only one of the many proofs that it is better to have children simply because we want them and not for any ulterior purpose or because they will fit into a preconceived scheme or correspond to some charming picture painted by our imaginations.

To be sure, not all children quarrel. Sometimes they seem to form deep attachments which are apparent from the first. More frequently, however, this attachment grows only with the years, and jealousy, envy, a sense of inferiority, and bursts of anger may in the meantime produce antagonisms which are not always outgrown. Sometimes children in the same family seem wholly indifferent to each other, displaying a lack of congeniality which persists for a lifetime. Usually, though, a kind of blind loyalty does grow up among them, an affection which outlasts irritations, the stuff that binds family members to one another despite countercurrents. This kind of loyalty does seem worth cultivating if we know how; it is one of the genuine sources of inner strength still left us in a world of desperate insecurity and bewilderment.

Most informed parents today know that a real and fundamental crisis occurs in the life of a small child when a new baby arrives as a member in good standing of the family group. If the child has so far been the only child it is doubly hard, for he has reigned supreme in his small world. He was cock-of-the-walk, the kingpin. He possessed his mother in a peculiar and exclusive sense. But whatever the situation, the older child is likely to regard the new baby as an interloper and may even receive a shock that will take years to undo. Most books on child management are full of advice on how to prevent jealousy. This advice is usually good as far as it goes and is worth attention. But few students of young children—especially those who have worked with them only in nursery schools or psychology laboratories rather than in homes—seem to understand that these measures never fully meet the situation and cannot be expected to resolve all the difficulties. Jealousy, it is true, can be helped to run a normal course instead of settling into a continuously corrosive force in the child's development, but it cannot be wholly prevented. Parents who have been led to believe that they can eliminate jealousy entirely, if only they follow the rules, usually emerge discouraged and insecure, beginning to doubt their own fitness as parents.

HOW TO PREPARE YOUR FIRST BABY FOR YOUR SECOND

Here, however, are some suggestions that may help: prepare the older child for the new baby's birth. The extent of this preparation will depend on his age. A child of three or four in most cases needs to know only a short time before the date that a brother or sister is coming to be a new member of the family and that it is now growing inside the mother's body, but older children require more information. This will create one of the natural moments for some of the sex instruction which will be discussed more fully in a later chapter, and like all sex education it should convey feelings as well as facts. If the child discovers that his parents are happy about the coming of a baby and that he himself is included in the preparations, he is more likely to feel that this is to be *his* baby too, something for him to look forward to as much as his parents do. He can help his mother buy, wash, sort, and put away the baby's clothes. Their purpose can be discussed with him. He should be invited—but not urged—to become an active partner in his mother's enjoyment and in the things to be done, and this should continue in his relation to the baby after it is born as well as before. He should have a chance to hold the baby (on his lap, sitting on a bed), to hand his mother the clothing as it is needed, to help pat the baby dry after his bath, and to share in the details of baby tending whenever he gets pleasure from doing so.

It seems wise also to let a child know that his mother will go to the hospital so that the doctor can help the baby get born and that she will come home again as soon as she can. If she has to leave hurriedly or in the middle of the night without saying good-by, it would be a good idea to leave a little note to be read to the child the next day. One mother who was clever with her pencil drew some funny pictures for her small son to laugh over after she had left. Something intimate and reassuring is what is needed, for a child often feels without saying so that his mother has been spirited away, perhaps never to return, and that the new baby is at the bottom of all the trouble and worry which he feels. An air of mystery about the whole matter should also be avoided, for it tends to increase whatever anxiety exists. Since children aren't permitted to visit their mothers during the lying-in period, telephone calls, notes, or messages help. Of course the father, the grandmother, or someone who is naturally close to the child is especially needed at this time and should keep eyes and ears open to the child's questions and comments, unspoken as well as spoken. At this time it is not entirely a question of telling a child what we think he ought to know;

[99]

it is also necessary to try to decipher and help him with what is really on his mind.

Jealousy

While some children show clearly and at once that they feel the baby threatens the security of their world, many do not betray their jealousy directly, or until later. The helplessness, smallness, and apparent insignificance of the newborn baby may make the older child feel at first that he is unimportant, little more than a nice new toy to be played with. But time passes quickly and babies grow rapidly, so that soon it becomes apparent to a child that here is a real and positive personality who is a definite rival and who is just as important to his mother as he is.

At this point the older child often becomes frankly hostile, openly expressing hatred: "I want him to go back where he came from." "I hope he dies." "He's ugly, he's horrid, I hate him." When angry he may strike out at the baby, slapping, pinching, tripping. His hostility and anger surge up, his aggression overflows, and though they make him miserable, he has not yet learned either to mask his feelings or to control them. Usually, of course, these things take his mother wholly by surprise. She is unprepared for this display of primitive ill-will; she had hoped for love and chivalry toward a weaker creature. She is morally shocked, and while struggling with her own bewilderment she has no idea how to help the child. Blindly she exhorts him, moralizes, threatens, and punishes, pointing out his greater age and greater obligations. And, in so doing, her whole behavior makes him more sure than ever that he has lost her affection, that he is "bad," that he is outcast, and that the baby has taken his place. And whenever a child—or an adult either, for that matter—feels thus rejected and judged "bad," he usually responds by behaving worse, not better.

There arises, then, a real dilemma, for obviously the mother cannot altogether ignore the older child's behavior. She cannot pet him and tell him what a good boy he is, for he knows perfectly well that he is not. Not only does she have to see that the baby is physically safe and leads a tolerably comfortable existence, but she has a sense of obligation to her older child's emotional conflicts as well. She feels, and should feel, that she must help him, for he is struggling with a problem as real for him as for her. But she must realize also that there is no formula for curing this condition overnight; she needs to know that children have had this same trouble from time immemorial, whether or not they remember it as adults, or whether their parents remember it. This problem of jealousy in some form is part and parcel of growing up in a family.

Handling Jealousy

Instead, then, of exclamations like, "It is naughty to hate the baby; you are a bad boy. Good boys love their little brothers. If you don't love him God may come and take him away again, *then* how bad you will feel," the mother may say or, better still, *act* something like this:

"I know you don't always like the baby. Many children feel

just the same way about brothers and sisters at first. But it will all get better someday and meanwhile I love you anyhow." Here then are some points to remember:

1. The mother should be ready to listen patiently and without too much concern to verbal expressions of hate and should avoid making the child believe that he is very bad because he *feels* that way. This does not mean, however, that he may *do* anything he wants. When irritations between the children begin to mount, she may quietly remove one of them.

2. In their efforts to prevent jealousy, parents should beware of actually favoring the older child and neglecting the baby. This is bound to seem unfair even to a jealous child; his confidence in his parents' sense of justice is sure to suffer.

3. As her children pass beyond infancy, a mother should be ingenious at finding occupations which will keep them somewhat separated instead of constantly provoked by contacts in which the one is the easy superior of the other. Sometimes their outdoor play as well as indoor routines should be arranged so that they are separated at least part of the time.

4. Instead of punishing a child for an attack on another it is wiser to try, if possible, to catch the hand about to strike or to hurl the toy and, with quick resourcefulness, to find other things for the child to do. Such prevention of continual acts of aggression or surreptitious teasing is of great importance, for it keeps the child from accumulating a heavy burden of guilt and a hopeless sense of his mother's disapproval. This is one of those numerous occasions when a child really

craves someone who can control him. He wants to be saved from the results of his own angry impulse. He does not want to be allowed to slap people constantly or to break his favorite toy in a rage or even to have underhanded meanness tolerated indefinitely. He wants to be good. A mother, he feels, should be someone who can physically *prevent* him from being too bad. This is an extremely important principle and runs through parent-child relationships at all ages and even into adolescence. It is when they are behaving worst that children, in their hearts, want parents who continue to stand firm for certain standards.

5. Prevention should not depend on punishment; punishments always come too late. The damage is done; and when a child is already under a cloud, punishments usually make the cloud heavier. Of course, the mother cannot always successfully circumvent clashes between children; there are bound to be some quarrels, fights, and scenes—and perhaps it is just as well that there should be *occasional* outbreaks. Unbridled discharges of feeling are to some extent healthy if they are not too numerous. Most of us have learned quite correctly to be suspicious of the child who is always good, as well as of the child who is always bad. While we work toward control we must realize that there are dangers in overcontrol and in premature self-control.

6. It goes without saying that parents must be scrupulously fair in dealing with their children and must try to bring about a situation where other adults—grandparents, friends, and servants—are fair also. However, here, as always, the

[103]

parents' attitude counts most. Children can tolerate a great deal of mismanagement from others if the quality of this parental relationship remains sounds.

7. Parents must guard against causing injustice by arriving on the scene just as violence between children begins and, seeing only the final act of aggression, administering blame or punishment without considering what has gone before. Often the child who finally strikes has been constantly provoked by the other in the hope, no doubt, of getting him into trouble while the real offender stands by innocently during the storm which follows. It is important to recognize these nursery *agents provocateurs* for what they are.

HOW TO HELP YOUR MOST TROUBLE-SOME CHILD

The oldest child is not always the one who has the hardest struggle with jealousy or who suffers most through these early rivalries. Sometimes younger ones live in a continuous state of envy of the privileges of greater age—or whatever else they fancy they lack—and are inwardly irreconcilable. Such children need special attentions from their mothers to a far greater extent than the better behaved ones who may "deserve" it more, and it is strongly urged that a mother arrange to give some *exclusive* time each day to her more difficult offspring. This simple plan sometimes works wonders in a month or two. With the other children safely disposed of elsewhere the mother should use the time to try to re-establish

satisfactory relations and to share a good time with her difficult child—not on a bribery basis or as a reward for good
behavior, but as something due him, like meals and vitamin
drops. The worse a child's behavior, the more he needs this experience.

A child who is giving trouble also needs ample opportunity
for growth in physical and mental skills according to his age.
As never before it is essential for him to have a world of his
own where he is busy and adequate and free from problems
demanding adjustments to people   parents or brothers and
sisters—with whom he has deep emotional involvements.
Now is the time for the new tricycle or roller skates, the
white mice or the dog. He can learn to play ball or to swim,
or to become a trapeze artist, or to paint or model. He should
have a chance to discover the larger neighborhood of children
outside his own home, playgrounds, and playground life. He
can "sleep out" at the home of a friend or relative, or pay a
longer visit, or go to camp. Anything that either widens his
world, increases his satisfaction, or adds to his sense of worth
and adequacy is fundamental for a child at this difficult time.
Nursery school is often of immense value, providing as it does
a chance to acquire new interests and to enter into new relationships, as well as several hours away from the family group
and its problems. Such a child is also fortunate if he discovers
or rediscovers in his father a friend and companion with the
special things that a man has to offer which a woman does
not. Experiences such as these are strengthening. But this
does not mean that he should merely exchange attachment
to his mother for attachment to his father, at least not per-

manently. Whether boy or girl, the child will also need to re-establish a happy relation to the mother and the ability to get along in the family. Ultimately he must learn to meet the emotional as well as the other requirements of home. There is no escape from these. But the more resources he has, the more privileges and compensations he discovers there are in being *himself* and *his* age, the more capable he will become of appreciating the needs of others and of responding with increasing generosity.

Look Beneath the Surface

It would be a mistake to assume that all children respond with open hostility to the coming of a new baby. Even little children are complicated and indirect in their behavior and at an early age learn to mask or actually to deceive themselves about their real feelings. Others are so secure in their relation to their parents and to living that they handle this crisis quickly and relatively easily. Like a light case of whooping cough, it may be over before it is fully recognized, so that from an immediately practical point of view it seems scarcely to matter.

There are, however, many indirect expressions of the child's hostility to the new baby which should be recognized for what they are. One of the most common ways in which the older child betrays his real protest against the coming of a rival is in apparently unrelated outbreaks of misbehavior, which may take almost any form. Frequently he begins to wet his bed again, to demand milk from a bottle, to suck his thumb, to talk baby talk. One six-year-old, who had begun to read quite nicely, baffled his teachers by completely refusing to do so after his baby brother was born and by becoming apparently unable to recognize the simplest of printed words. It is as though these children said to themselves, "Babies have it soft. They get all the good things. I will be a baby, too," and accordingly they *act* baby wherever they can. When this happens it is far from easy to know how far to indulge the children and to what extent to hold them to standards suitable for their age. The first thing is to understand what the behavior means. If they understand, parents will at least not begin to punish blindly what appears to be sheer perverse naughtiness. Attempts to discourage these flights back into infancy should be largely directed to encouraging all of the activities and skills already suggested and also working for a parent-child relationship which is leisurely, warm, and mutually enjoyable. It will take time.

A Physical Illness From Emotional Causes

The following case, where a child actually became neurotically ill following the birth of a baby brother, is exceptional but it illustrates what may happen in less extreme form even to normal children. Here the difficulties, though wholly masked, were wreaking havoc none the less.

A girl of about eight was subject to continual night terrors, bad dreams, fears, and anxieties of every description. Someone had to sit with her almost every night before she would go to sleep. She saw "great bad black faces coming nearer and nearer" out of the darkened room. She was almost hysterically anxious about her baby brother's well-being, "loved him passionately," her mother said, was desperately afraid something would happen to him when he played in the yard, and insisted on watching over him whenever she could. Once when he had been slightly ill, she had "gone wild" with anxiety, wandering disconsolately about the house, unwilling to go to school lest something happen while she was away. Finally she had developed what appeared to be a heart disorder—she was seized with palpitations, became dizzy, and once or twice had fainted. Thorough medical examinations by several specialists revealed that there was no organic disease; the attacks were said to be nerves and the mother was advised to ignore them. Of course she was much relieved, but as time went on it became clear that the child was becoming increasingly ill despite the absence of a real physical ailment. She was re-examined by several specialists who continued to pronounce her organically sound. Finally the parents consulted a psychiatrist who drew from them the following items in the child's history.

When four years old, healthy and apparently well adjusted, the child was brought to her mother's room to see the new baby brother the morning after his home-coming from the hospital. She found her mother in bed with the baby snuggled beside her and was asked to come and take her first look. She did so in silence, the mother continuing to talk about the baby and to display his charms, whereupon the older one burst into tears of rage, tried to snatch the baby away from the mother, screaming, "I want him to go away, away, away!" She was quieted; it was pointed out to her that everyone loved the baby, that he was her own little brother and she must love him, too. No harshness was used, but the moral obligation to love and accept him was emphasized. In a few weeks the child appeared to have settled the problem so completely that the mother, in telling the story four years later, had practically forgotten that the child's initial feeling about the baby had been anything but loving. She recalled this as something of little importance since it had disappeared so quickly.

Although all the facts and subsequent developments in this child's struggle back to health cannot be given here, it is worth pointing out that one of the things which had to be accomplished was to find a way by which this child could face her real feelings toward her small brother. The truth was that the excessive love and anxiety for his welfare were a sham. They masked an underlying resentment, jealousy, and actual hopes for the baby's removal or death which she had never dared express. With the help of the psychiatrist she had to learn that many children hate the new baby in the family and that for her to do so did not mean that she was "wicked," that she would lose her parents' love, or that punishment was bound to descend upon her. This realization was accomplished only after several months, after which the excessive "love" for the baby vanished along with the fainting spells, heart attacks, and punishing faces in the night. Her fear of punishment as expressed in these things disappeared because she had finally faced the full extent of her "badness" without any of the awful consequences she had somehow assumed were sure to follow.

This case, though extreme, is not essentially different from many milder nervous disturbances that children show and that are traceable to inner conflicts regarding a new baby. Usually they work out of them in their own time, especially if parents keep in mind that various idiosyncrasies of behavior in children are often related to this event. It is always important for a child to feel that his parents continue to be reassuring in spite of "bad" thoughts or even "bad" acts, whether these consist in hating the baby or any other kind of "bad" behavior. This does not mean that we condone or permit him to indulge his impulses indefinitely; it does mean that by our attitude toward him we manage, in spite of restraints, to make him aware that we know how he feels and that we stand ready to help him.

FAMILY FRICTION—VALUES AND ABUSES

Friction between brothers and sisters sometimes works out quickly, and real companionship, or at least a working relationship, begins to emerge early in life. On the other hand, years may pass before this comes about, and sometimes children have to grow up entirely before they discover the possibilities for companionship in each other. This need not necessarily be an unwholesome situation. A home where all is sweetness and light, or seems to be, from the very start may not be as good a preparation for living as one where there is an opportunity for various personalities to encounter one another and to clash, to work out compromises, and to appreciate each other despite differences. Friction is often a constructive force, and parents need to understand that there are values to be gained from learning to fight one's own battles and to work through some of the jealousies and rivalries of the nursery years without constant interference. If the children can hold their own most of the time and if give-and-take is on a fairly equal basis, a great many quarrels can be ignored. Above all, children should not feel *obliged* to love one another, or anybody for that matter, at a time when they obviously cannot.

It is essential for a healthy development in this respect, however, for parents to have achieved a working relationship with each other and, whatever their differences and clashes, not only to tolerate but also to appreciate each other. Living with people who have learned to get along together is of far more value to children than a hundred moral lectures on the value of harmony. For here again it is not the mere absence of friction that is desirable. Like children, parents are human; husbands and wives do annoy one another. Far better, therefore, than a continuous false front and the masking of smoldering antagonisms between parents are occasional honest clashes with genuine feeling openly expressed. This is something children can understand, provided they can also take for granted their parents' fundamental affection for each other. Moreover, they usually learn from the process a good deal about human feelings and their management. Such clashes are likely to prove destructive only when children doubt not only the quality but the very existence of their parents' affection for one another.

In contrast to the healthy give-and-take of nursery bickerings there may also exist between brothers and sisters a situation in which one child is constantly top dog and another constantly underdog. Here it becomes more important for the parents to take a hand. No child should be dominated all the time; no child should always be dominating. Parents who are alert to the dangers of the former role often ignore those inherent in the latter. One child may occupy continuously a position where he feels outstripped and inferior—perhaps because he is younger, or not as articulate or as outgoing, or as good-looking, or as quick at skills and sports. This makes not only for unhappiness; continuous defeat may lay the groundwork for lasting difficulties of development. When this happens a certain amount of physical separation may be very useful. As has already been suggested, several hours of the day spent apart, with different pursuits, different schedules, different companions, may serve to tide children over such difficult periods. Instead of experiencing nothing but conflict and anger, with the sense of guilt and defeat that is bound to result, each child learns to find himself in his own way and to establish a sense of adequacy in a world of his own. Thereby he becomes strengthened to meet home relationships more effectively.

One word of warning—avoid superficial judgments. The more aggressive child, the one who boasts or bullies or more energetically strives for first place, is often the very one whose trouble is deepest and whose feeling of jealousy and insecurity is the more acute.

NO TWO ALIKE

Observation of many two-children families leads to the suspicion that in a large number of cases the older of the two is temperamentally the more "difficult" and the harder to get along with. Although there are, of course, very definite exceptions, innumerable mothers describe their children thus:

"My older boy is intelligent and sensitive. He is high-strung, introverted, negativistic. He is also shy and likely to seem rude with strangers; he is also inclined to be timid and delicate—susceptible to colds and infections. The younger? Just a happy-go-lucky baby! Everybody loves him, he's so friendly and good-natured. You never have to worry about him!"

The reasons for the frequency of this picture are doubtless complex, but a few things stand out. The mother, in all probability, made most of her mistakes on this first child. These mistakes, at least among the educated and intelligent classes, commonly consist of overanxiety, fussing, too-great strictness in training and discipline and not enough easygoing pleasure in the whole relationship. In addition, the first baby is more likely than subsequent ones to be born at a moment when the parents are most disturbed personally. Often their marriage problems are in the foreground; they are in an un-settled state of mind, and the tensions in their own lives be-come transferred to the baby. But possibly more important than either of these situations is the fact that this first child suffers a shock that befalls none of the others. He alone has had a brief span as the *only* child and is therefore subjected to a period of violent readjustment when this safe world is shaken. The marks remain, perhaps permanently, in the character structure of the child. While this need not necessarily mean that he is damaged by the experience, his personality is likely to be colored and to some extent shaped by it.

Middle and Youngest Children

It should be clear, then, that no two children, even those in the same family, have ever really had the same environment or the very same bringing up. These things will be subject to modification not only by the child's numerical position in the family and the difference in experience which this implies, but also by the various shadings of the parents' attiude toward each child. Middle children often learn to regard themselves as nonentities, sandwiched between the oldest and youngest, and of no particular interest to anyone. The youngest child stands in a still-different relation to the rest of the family group and is likely to face the extremes of one sort of treatment or another. For example, he may be underdog in the family, suffering from the full weight of the elder ones' piling down on him, so to speak. If these elder children are permitted to act as bosses and everyone tries to squelch the youngest whenever he raises a voice, this child may become timid, passive, and browbeaten, or, if he possesses a more aggressive temperament, markedly ambitious and self-willed in a desperate effort to defend himself or outstrip his elders.

In many families, however, parents tend to regard the youngest as the privileged baby. Discipline is reserved for the others, and he becomes a favored character, overindulged and overprotected at every point, so that he cannot escape a highly exaggerated notion of his importance. Unless something shakes up this child thoroughly he is likely to become either a dependent nobody or else the victim of a "crown prince" psychology, believing that everything good will surely come his way by divine right and without effort. Both reactions make for an essentially infantile character; neither accords with reality, and, despite a kind of precociousness or superficial brilliance, any real progress in the direction of genuine self-mastery is seriously retarded. To ensure the best development of a youngest child, it seems wisest for parents to remain firmly in control and to circumscribe this child's determination to act older than he is and to emulate everything his other brothers and sisters do. A yearning to grow up and be independent is fundamental and necessary, but when exaggerated this tendency can keep a child constantly striving to be something beyond his powers and, in consequence, feeling perpetually frustrated.

At the same time parents should see to it that a younger child is not continuously bossed by older ones or arbitrarily subjected to their immature notions of what is good discipline. Control should remain in the hands of the parents unless the age differences in a family are so great that the eldest is unusually mature in judgment and understanding as well as in years.

The Only Boy and the Only Girl

Both the only boy and the only girl in a family of several children have difficult problems, despite the fact that in the case of the girl it is supposed to be fun to have a lot of brothers, who can presumably secure for her the attention of their friends. It is never considered quite as much fun, however, for a boy to have nothing but sisters, and the feeling that boys are somehow better than girls dies hard, if at all. Nevertheless, girls as well as boys are better off if brought up in surroundings where there are plenty of both sexes as part of their intimate world. Girls need girls *and* boys. Boys need boys *and* girls, if they are to form sound notions of the differences, psychological as well as physical, between the sexes and if they are to learn to make the necessary adjustments to each other.

The lone girl with several brothers is likely, whether she knows it or not, to feel at a disadvantage because of her sex and may react either by becoming hopeless about it and subsiding as a weakling or by striving to become masculine like her brothers. Such weakness is only a handicap and, at the other extreme, a deep-seated envy of maleness threatens the happiness of her later adjustment to men and marriage. The dangers for the boy in a family dominated by women are a matter of common knowledge. Most sensible people are aware of them; they fear he will become a sissy and take steps to see that he finds a boy's world in addition to the woman's world at home. With the only girl the dangers are less obvious; she may continue to appear very feminine even though she is deeply envious of males. She too needs intimate associations with other girls her own age. More especially, she needs a mother who is truly and happily a woman if she is ever to become truly and happily a woman herself. Lacking this, every effort should be made to bring another such "mother person" into her world.

THE PROBLEM OF THE "ONLY" CHILD

The fact that certain problems and conflicts seem to be inherent in family life fortunately does not keep most normal men and women from having children. It might appear, on the face of it, that the "only" child avoids all the nursery conflicts that children in larger families have, but, unfortunately, he runs into others that are worse. The "only" child, even more than the youngest, is, at least proverbially, spoiled and overindulged. It is feared he may become too adult in his tastes and interests and may be unpopular with other children because he has been forced to get all his satisfaction through pleasing adults. He is supposed to be selfish and a bad sport, to lack adaptability and determination, because his path has always been smoothed by a pair of adoring parents. He has never had to make his own way in a family where a certain amount of devil-take-the-hindmost attitude has prevailed and he is therefore likely to run to cover when he first encounters difficulties outside his home.

Probably some of these accusations against the "only" child are well founded and may assume serious proportions. But such characteristics can be mitigated if the parents are sufficiently aware of the dangers. "Only" children need other children as vital parts of their lives from the age of three on. The nursery school, kindergarten, or play group offers at least a substitute for life in the larger family. There are other ways, too, if parents are willing to take the trouble, of finding company for an "only" child. In this way he learns that, although the sun may rise and set in him at home, there is another and equally important world where he counts for one and no more and where he must learn some of the rules of give-and-take. In addition, sensible parents *can* take common-sense steps to avoid spoiling. They *can* see to it that he is not constantly overstimulated to be precocious or used to satisfy their own selfish need for a bright child.

Only Means Lonely

Yet even the wisest parents, using the most sensible management, cannot eliminate additional difficulties which are far harder for the "only" child to meet than those involving his social contacts with other children. These difficulties are inherent in any triangular situation, and in his home the "only" child cannot help feeling that in the father-mother-child setup, he is the extra spoke in the wheel, that he is bound to be left out, that his parents' relationship is complete without him. These feelings persist whether or not they are true. No matter how deeply his parents may be wrapped up in him, the "only" child continues to see his existence as a two-against-one situation. Both his parents are bigger and more powerful than he. They can speak to each other in words or by glances or jokes that he does not understand. They go out together in the evening, leaving him alone in a dark room or with a "sitter" who is not "really family." In matters of discipline he finds that his parents always stand together.

Unlike the child with many brothers and sisters, he has no allies to gang up with and to be his companions in misery. Because of these things he cannot escape a sense of his inferiority, and this feeling stimulates him to unwise and unsuccessful attempts at power. Further, he suspects that his parents love each other more than they love him, and this, without contemporaries in the family, leaves him especially isolated and jealous. Sleeping arrangements, though apparently accepted, are an additional reminder of loneliness.

"Why do you always have to sleep with Daddy?" said an only daughter, aged seven. "It isn't fair. We should all take turns sleeping with each other. Why should I always have to be alone?"

The mother explains in vain. "That's just the way things are. Fathers and mothers share a room; children sleep somewhere else. When you grow up and have a husband, you can have a room with him, too."

For a child that is small consolation. Here is medicine which just has to be taken.

For the "only" child, therefore, the essential problem consists of the heightened intensity of emotions in a small, closely knit family group. These emotions fall full force on him alone, and the resulting inner conflicts and struggles with jealousy and guilt in relation to his parents and others are immensely heightened. One has only to watch children in a large family to observe how quickly they ally themselves against adults. They may quarrel among themselves, but they quickly learn to back each other up and display very early a code of behavior which demands loyalty to each other and constitutes a mutual-aid and protective association. This is as it should be. It makes their lot in life far happier and enables them to accept with better grace their position as children. One of the important steps in a child's psychological development is just this type of alliance. Ganging up with other children of the same age is essential—even though it results in the child's feeling that adults are, to some extent at least, his natural enemies.

How to Help

What to do about it? First of all, understand it. After that, it will be easier to do everything possible to help the "only" child find compensations and wider interests. Many of the suggestions offered for helping any difficult child in his adjustment will be useful for the "only" child, too. He stands in particular need, for example, of experiences outside his own home. Encourage him to make friends in families where there are lots of children and plenty of rough-and-tumble family life. As he gets older, it is sometimes possible to borrow another child for several weeks—in the summer vacation, for example. Even under ordinary circumstances it is possible to keep the home pleasantly filled with younger guests, whether for the afternoon, the night, or the week end, thus giving the "only" child some experience, no matter how incomplete, of living with other children.

All children should have a chance to develop skills and hobbies and many kinds of activities, but the "only" child stands in special need of things to make and do and so to get away from the intense involvements of personal relationships.

He needs, also, parents who understand that he can be lonely even when every care is lavished on him and who, even while they can do nothing to change the situation fundamentally, do what they can to offer substitutes. Perhaps this means such slight things as being allowed to ride between his parents on the front seat of the car instead of alone in the rear; or having a real, live dog for a pet, who is a genuine companion and sleeps near or even *on* the bed with him, even if the dog, from the parents' standpoint, is a nuisance. Or his parents may take him with them occasionally for an early supper "out" instead of packing him off to bed before they go; or include him in at least a part of a wedding-anniversary celebration, so that their special closeness to each other is not continuously rubbed in. One "only" child was granted her wish of sleeping with her door open, even though noises and reminders of the rest of the household drifting to her room may have kept her awake longer than if the door had been closed. At least she went to sleep less lonely.

The best advice of all is to have more children. But if you have only one beware of his special stresses.

PARENTS—MEET YOUR CHILDREN!

Whatever our family turns out to be and whether we have an "only" child or many children, nowhere do parents need more flexibility of character than in serving the individual needs of each. First and foremost, parents must be ready to give up the image of a dream child they may have been nourishing for years. They must be ready to relinquish old ambitions, to revise their standards, and to change their tactics. Otherwise their relations to their children will be spoiled by continuous pressure to conform to a pattern that suits the parent rather than the child. Having children is, in many respects, a grab-bag proposition. We have to take what comes and we often spend the first five years or more of a child's life getting acquainted with what is actually a stranger and putting aside much of our wishful thinking. Only then can we clearly see this particular child and his needs.

A father, for example, may have visions of a son who is manly, courageous, practical, and a regular fellow with the other boys. He looks forward to receiving him someday into his business, or to making a doctor or an engineer out of him. He gets instead a shy, introverted, dreamy child who dislikes baseball and spends hours reading. Years are spent trying to effect a change, to the great detriment of the child and to the anguish of the parents.

A mother has visions of a charming little daughter, companionable and affectionate, with whom she will share her own intellectual and creative interests and enjoy a close personal relation. She gets a rather hoydenish, overgrown girl, devoted to sports and the inconsequential doings of others of her own age, indifferent and even resentful toward her mother's efforts to interest her in music, literature, and other cultural matters.

Any chance for a happy outcome for either of these children is seriously jeopardized as long as they are forced to live in daily contact with parents who are unable to accept and enjoy them as they are. Constant determination to make them different merely increases stubbornness and closes the door to whatever potentialities for wider growth may exist.

"To Each According to His Needs"

As a family grows, it becomes increasingly clear that getting along with several children means the ability to become wise to the individual needs of each, for no two ever feel, think, or act alike. They come into the world with different physical and mental endowments, and, in spite of being born to the same parents, they all have different life histories and experiences. What works with one child fails signally with another, so that everything depends on the parents' willingness to make fresh starts and learn again with each child. Older parents discover the extent to which the principle "to each according to his needs" must govern. Young parents, on the other hand, are apt to make the mistake of believing that fairness to children consists in treating them equally, and by equally they are likely to mean similarly. If the eldest was allowed to eat at the family table when he was six, then the younger must be allowed the same privilege at the same age, regardless of the important difference that their first child was ready for this new step and that the younger, at six, gets tired and irritable during a long meal with grownups. Or, if we bring one child a present, we feel compelled to bring the other a similar, or at least equally expensive, one, though the reason which prompted the gift for the first child may have been that he had lost an adored kitten and we felt like singling him out for a token of sympathy. As our children grow older we are constantly finding that the needs of one may require us to adopt a wholly different course than we take with the others. Camp for the summer may be a constructive experience for the child who needs athletic skills, while, if the budget is limited, a brother who is good at sports anyway can stay home. Piano lessons may be indicated for another. Or perhaps more expensive clothes for the growing daughter with the hard-to-fit figure turn out to be among those trifles that matter.

Against a background of confidence in their parents' good will, it is not too hard for children to understand and accept the reasons behind what may at first seem like a favor to one at the expense of another. Older children, and sometimes quite young ones—if we take time to explain—are quicker in their comprehensions than we give them credit for being and often respond generously when one member of the family needs something that another can well do without. On the other hand, if this confidence is lacking, the slightest attention to one child may be interpreted by another as favoritism and start a storm of anger.

Our children differ from each other in native endowments as a result of hereditary factors beyond our control. We need to recognize these differences and, instead of demanding what is not there, strive to help develop the best of what there is. But children differ also because each was born into a different constellation of forces in the family group. Not only numerical position, sex, health, and bodily structure, but also the special interactions of each personality with another, conspire to make each child unique and to shape the course of his development.

In addition to these things, and perhaps most important of all, is the fact that the parents' own problems as adults are constantly playing into the situation as well; they actually present different selves to each of their children. In the same family there are not just one father and one mother, but as many fathers and mothers as there are children. Therefore, if parents are ever to understand the forces which have gone into the making of their sons and daughters, self-knowledge is the first and most imperative step.

CHAPTER FIVE

THE CHILD AND
HIS FRIENDS

IT TAKES TIME to become sociable. The newborn baby is concerned wholly with a world limited by his own person. He is absorbed in bodily sensations of hunger, thirst, and the desire to sleep and to eliminate. Pleasures come with food, warmth, stroking, rocking. Light and sound penetrate his world, too. Gradually he becomes interested in things to touch and, finally, to grasp—though it is a long time before he realizes that his toes are part of himself and a toy is not. Quite early, though the time is variable, babies also show the beginnings of social responses. They begin to recognize the face of either mother or nurse and smile in evident pleasure at her smile—and in anticipation, no doubt, of good things to come, which may be either food, or handling, or play. Babies make discriminations and show preferences very early. Some babies resent everyone except mother or nurse. Others reserve a particularly warm smile for the father, or an eager waving of arms and arching of back, accompanied by gleeful sounds, according to age and development.

Babies show aversions, too. These are often hard to account for—men with mustaches, for example, or all women with handbags. It is not uncommon for any stranger to be regarded with suspicion, and for the baby to register anything from a slight questioning of the stranger's rights to violent screams of rage and fear, accompanied by hiding of the face and even tantrums. Sometimes early associations play a determining part. If the baby has learned to connect an unpleasant experience with a certain person, or even with someone who is *like* that person, this whole response of displeasure may be carried over and may persist until the child has a chance to build up new, pleasurable associations.

SOCIABILITY STARTS EARLY

Yet whatever part such conditioning plays, it is hard to escape the conclusion that some babies are by temperament more sociable than others and that all their lives some people find new experiences challenging and delightful and others turn away from them. Even at birth, or shortly after, infants differ markedly from one another. Some lie placidly in their cribs, waving their fists contentedly or sleeping. They take their food easily or with gusto; at first they don't mind being bathed and dressed and then they actually like it. Other babies are restless and fretful, cry a great deal, and get little pleasure from food; the gift of life seems to be a very doubtful blessing to them.

What makes these differences and what do we mean by

temperament? Do we refer to traits and tendencies determined by heredity and contained wholly within the material of the germ plasm itself? Or are these characteristics influenced by prenatal conditions, or built into the child in the first weeks of life by his very early experiences? We are just beginning to ask such questions. Without a doubt heredity plays a part, though geneticists themselves would be the last to claim full knowledge of its contributions. Increasing evidence also shows that the child's first satisfactions, or lack of them, through the taking of food, through eliminating, through experiences of warmth and handling, color his attitudes toward life and have much to do with how he goes out to meet the world—whether he faces it with a secure sense that he will find it good and pleasurable or whether he anticipates frustration and pain. No positive predictions can be made. However, we may guess that *on the whole,* despite definite exceptions, people who find life hard at nearly every point—including their social relations—found it so in early life as well; and that, conversely, our optimists were optimists in the nursery.

How Optimism Begins

To help a child develop a welcoming attitude toward life and toward other human beings, everything should be done to further his physical and emotional satisfactions *during infancy.* Illness and the discomforts that go with it are often unavoidable, but sometimes with the best of intentions misguided parents impose unnecessary deprivations on a potentially healthy baby. Everything that, in the name of "instilling good habits," frustrates and denies a child the normal pleasures of infancy tends to produce a human being who anticipates painful experiences at every turn, who cannot believe that a fair share of love and comfort is likely to come his way, and who consequently becomes withdrawn and distrustful. (These matters have already been treated at more length in Chapter I.) A satisfied infancy, of course, is no guarantee of later social adaptability, but it does constitute the best foundation we know. Here are some further suggestions:

1. The child should not live in a hygienic vacuum with an "expert" standing guard over him like a dragon. First and foremost he needs a mother or motherly person to whom he can form a lasting attachment. Two or three people may do things for him, so long as they are not carriers of infection or too inconsiderate of the baby and his schedule.

2. A child's friendship must be won, not demanded. Sudden pounces, loud talk, and forced embraces are likely to startle him and cause resentment. Often the better course lies in quietly offering a toy or glittering object, or simply sitting and letting the child take his time about accepting approaches.

3. If a child seems genuinely frightened or discomfited by strangers, despite sensible efforts to win him, do not force the issue. Keep strangers at a distance and, after several weeks have elapsed, try again—but gingerly. Remember that increasing maturity often solves problems.

4. A shy child is better approached in his own room, among familiar objects, than when carried out for display.

5. With slightly older children especially, encourage visitors to dispense with nine tenths of those useless amenities— "How do you do? My, how big you are"—and start quietly *doing something* which interests the child and makes him forget himself.

Playing Together

When children are about a year old they usually begin to show an interest in each other. Sometimes this interest takes an apparently unfriendly form. One baby will hit or push another, or grab his hair in a sort of experimental approach just to see what sort of response will follow. Actually this is merely clumsy, not unfriendly at all. Sometimes children will eye each other with evident curiosity, but without approaching, seemingly aware of something about them that is different from adults. Sometimes they will offer a toy, attempt to open a conversation, or make other overtures to get a response. By the age of two these responses are more marked, though usually children do not begin to play together until they are about three. "Playing together" means engaging in some joint enterprises requiring a division of labor. For example, one child may load pebbles into a cart while another hauls it to some dumping ground. Or one may hold a chair steady while another climbs on it to reach for some desired object. Even at this age, however, there will be wide differences in their sociability, depending greatly on the child's individuality.

Some of them prefer to play alone much longer than others. They differ, too, in the characteristics they bring to their play and their social relations. Even at an early age some are so absorbed in people that they tend to neglect the world of things and activities. Others play so hard with whatever they find around them that people might as well not exist.

Parents should be aware of these inevitable differences and should guard against feeling that all children must be equally sociable or must be trained to become sociable according to a preconceived schedule. Here, as elsewhere, individual characteristics deserve great consideration, and constant pressure to change them simply results in strain, discontent, and irritability. What children do need, from the time they are about three, is adequate opportunity for associating with others of approximately their own age, preferably with some supervision from an adult who understands what is going on among the children and who has some skill in helping each to find an avenue of expression in the group. This does not mean constant interference or a prescribed program of play. But, on the other hand, it involves much more than merely putting in an appearance when civil war is well in progress and attempting to enforce order without understanding what has happened and without knowing anything about the personal problems and characteristics of the individual child.

The same kind of understanding that can control the nursery battles among children in the same family helps their outside relations as well, and many of the same principles apply. Whether within the family or in a wider group, no child should be permitted to dominate all the others constantly, or to be dominated by them. Whenever such situations arise, as they frequently will, children need some adult help in arriving at a happier arrangement in their relationships. No set prescription for accomplishing such a change can be given; it will be necessary to know the individual children involved. It is fair to say, however, that it will call for someone possessing understanding, tact, skill, and willingness to take time and trouble.

HOW ONE PARENT CURED ONE BULLY

In one neighborhood where children between the ages of three and six or seven played on the block and in each other's yards, one powerful six-year-old, Christopher, emerged as the political boss and bully. He appropriated the belongings of the other children with false promises of favors to be rendered. He laid down the law as to what games should be played and how and he punished infringements with tripping or punching, so that the younger children were frightened and tearful when he was there. He also invented a superman, known as the Giant, to whom all had to promise allegiance. "The Giant says you must take that mud and wash it all over your face," he would tell a timid little girl who was known for her dislike of dirt. And everyone knew that she had to obey. Many children refused to go out to play at all so long as the tyrant went unchallenged. Eventually, of course, the parents began to hear of these things. Occasionally they left their houses long enough to rescue their own offspring and to tell Christopher what they thought of him and to forbid him their yard.

One day Mrs. Brown, the mother of a five-year-old, called on Christopher's mother, who stiffened visibly when she saw the visitor, since she had been expecting trouble. But Mrs. Brown merely smiled and said that she had come to ask if Christopher would go with her and her husband and the children to the beach on Sunday. This was not what the other mother had expected, but she continued to look glum and suspicious and replied that Christopher was being made to stay home on Sunday instead of going to the movies because he had been disobedient and deceitful. That started her talking and she went on with a long tale of woe, to which Mrs. Brown listened sympathetically, agreeing that children were like that. Later a grandmother joined the conversation and added some complaints of her own about Christopher. It ended, however, by Mrs. Brown being told that Christopher might go to the beach with her—although his mother assured her that he would probably ruin her day.

The day was certainly not an easy one. Christopher wanted an indefinite number of hot dogs, although the Browns considered three the limit. He scattered paper napkins and bread crusts around the beach and refused to pick them up and put them in a receptacle. He was jubilant, however, when he developed unexpected talents at the near-by rifle range. Mr. Brown was good at it too, and the two played amid cheers from the rest of the family and a gallery of onlookers.

"Oh boy, oh boy, oh boy, maybe I'm not good!" said Christopher. And he was.

All the way home he was in high spirits and extremely amiable, and Mr. Brown promised to set up a range in the Browns' back yard. He said that Christopher would, of course, always have to ask Mrs. Brown for the rifle first and find out if she had time to act as umpire. Christopher couldn't see why an umpire should be needed, but the Browns changed the subject and the matter rested there.

After that Christopher came often to the Browns'. Sometimes he stayed to lunch. He spent the night, too. At first the Brown children disliked him; then they agreed that he was "O.K. when he was nice." Christopher grew fond of them, and they gradually became pleased by the attentions of an older and bigger child. Mrs. Brown sometimes visited Christopher's mother, and they became friendly. Mrs. Brown said that she thought the boy seemed happier and that they got along very well when he came over. Christopher's mother said she couldn't see why he should be happy, there was nothing to be happy about—everybody in their house was worried all the time and the grandmother nagged and complained and held the purse strings. Mrs. Brown, as her husband said later, "got an earful," but she was careful to keep it to herself and just went on being friendly. In time, Christopher improved. His mother took more notice of him, feeling that if Mrs. Brown could see anything in him to like he might not be a total loss after all. Matters somehow settled down for the neighborhood children. Christopher had more fun; his mother liked him because the Browns liked him, and because his mother liked him he felt better about himself and didn't have to show how important he was by bossing everybody and beating them up.

Christopher, in other words, was not such a problem child

after all. He was mostly a neglected child; though, as it turned out, his mother's indifference was not so deep-seated. It was comparatively simple to turn it into genuine warmth and interest—things that make a world of difference in a child's outlook. Difficult children in trouble are not always as easy to help as this one, yet Christopher's case does point to the fact that, when a child becomes a bully, something is needed besides moral censure, punishment, and a firm hand. Firmness has its place, but it will be useless without an inquiry into the causes of bad behavior and an effort to remedy the trouble at the source. In this case, the mother's neglect and discouragement about her child were of paramount importance, but for each child the trouble will be something different.

PRIMITIVE EGO IN THE NURSERY

Aggressiveness is one of the commonest problems among children of nursery age. It is as normal as cutting teeth, but much more disturbing. Christopher's behavior, it is true, had lasted too long to be laughed off on the assumption that he would outgrow it. But between the ages of two and four most normal children are still struggling to make an adjustment between, on the one hand, a strong and primitive ego and, on the other, the dawn of a social conscience. Sometimes one side, sometimes the other side of this conflict is uppermost. If we observe closely we can see how a child wavers as to whether or not he prefers social approval and the friendship of another child to selfish possession of some toy or unfair advantages

[135]

which will give him the lead at play. The parents' job is to help a child find a satisfactory compromise between the demands of his ego and this gradually emerging need for love. This will be a slow process, and high standards should never be demanded all at once or at too early an age. In other words, we must expect some selfishness and violence in the nursery years. The average child's own growth process, plus an emerging consciousness of the standards by which the adults in his home regulate their lives, will probably guide him to more civilized living. But with a child like Christopher, who is harassed by feelings of inferiority, by doubts of his parents' affection, and therefore by general insecurity in all his relations, the process will be harder. Unless this kind of situation is remedied the child will be driven to seek quick and easy pleasures by playing the "big strong man" and by grabbing material satisfactions wherever he can find them.

We Learned Slowly, Too

Because they often tend to be perfectionists where their children are concerned and are far too intent on "training" certain habits, parents frequently demand too much of little children in their social relations and especially in their duties as hosts. As adults, we have learned to exercise self-restraint. We offer the guest the most comfortable chair quite automatically and we have learned to choose whatever entertainment the guest would prefer. Most of us have forgotten the many years over which this battle was fought before it was won. But because we are now able to live by such a standard, we expect it from our children at too early an age. In the nursery years, fair play

[136]

THE CHILD AND HIS FRIENDS

and equality are quite enough. Giving preference to a guest is asking too much, and a child is better off taking one step at a time. Two-year-olds are usually too young to observe even the standards of give-and-take which three- and four-year-olds are learning. The parents' role in the supervision of these very young children lies largely in maneuvering to see that each has a chance to go his way unmolested.

Judith, for example, at the age of twenty-two months delights in knocking down the block building of a five-year-old companion. Although we can try saying, "No, no, Judith," and shaking our heads, probably the best plan is to remove Judith to the other end of the nursery and see that she is sufficiently occupied with her own activities to forget the thrill of toppling over a pile of blocks. Punishment here teaches very little because Judith is not yet old enough to control the impulse, even when she realizes vaguely that it is "bad." But at the age of three or so, though there will still be plenty of infringements of rules of fair play, children are old enough to discover that certain behavior will be demanded more and more and that uncontrolled aggression and selfishness will not be accepted. In other words, at these ages they can begin to take some responsibility for their own behavior. While it is certainly not the same amount of responsibility we expect of ten-year-olds, the time has definitely come for them to find that giving up what they want on certain occasions is a necessary experience. With young children, antisocial behavior can usually be handled quite simply by removing them from the group, with full assurance that they will be welcomed back with no hard feelings as soon as they are ready to play fair.

Chronic and continual aggressions or other forms of trouble-making that continue until a child is six or seven, without any signs of improvement, however, call for an inquiry, often under professional direction, into the child's whole adjustment to living.

They Shouldn't Be Too Good

It is not always recognized that a more difficult problem arises with the child who is not aggressive enough and so is unable to hold his own and defend his dignity and his person against others. Grownups, especially teachers, make the mistake of regarding these children as "sweet," "amiable," and "unselfish." They therefore fight their battles for them instead of helping them to stand up for themselves. Such children are regarded with great favor, since they give adults no trouble. Actually they probably have the same share of self-interest and hostility in their characters that the more aggressive ones have, but somewhere in the course of their development these things have become so repressed that they do not seem to be there at all. But the feelings *are* there, and a sense of defeat along with them. Unless something happens, while they are still in the nursery, to help such children express themselves more freely, they are likely to carry resentments all their lives, carefully concealed under skin-deep amiability. Furthermore, since they feel at a disadvantage with their contemporaries, they are inclined to seek so much satisfaction in the approval of adults that they are hampered in the free flow of normal social relations. These children need to be allowed, or even urged, to assert themselves. Self-depreciation is not a virtue.

Unselfishness is not always what it appears. Love for one's fellow man, if it is really to become free from admixtures of its opposite, depends to a very large extent on a fundamental esteem for oneself and faith in one's own dignity and power. Everyone instinctively dislikes and distrusts the goody-goody, and for sound reasons: the child, or the adult, who never gives vent to strong, definite feelings or is unable ever to assert himself will probably release his feelings in indirect meanness or tyranny—or, as we now know, in neurosis and illness.

A visitor to a nursery school was astonished one day to see a small child turn suddenly on another for some very slight offense and hit him in a towering rage, not once but three or four times. The teacher stood by and did nothing. She did not even rebuke the child. The visitor, quite naturally, asked the teacher later if she would explain.

"This," said the teacher, "has been a great day for Jean. For six months she has been browbeaten by the class unless I protected her. Everybody pushed her around or laughed at her, hit her, or tried to grab whatever she was playing with. I tried to stop them and did stop them—up to a point—but that didn't really help Jean. She had to learn to stand up for herself instead of just looking helplessly at me. Today, for the first time, she took matters in her own hands. Of course she *would* choose the wrong boy and the wrong moment, when nothing much was happening! Never mind. Carl can stand it, and for Jean it was a great moral victory. She has taken the first step in the right direction.

"Last year there was Mark," she went on. "Mark was five, and so amiable and good-natured that everybody imposed on him. When they were waiting in line for the swings he'd give up his place to anyone who asked him. Mark had to learn, too. He never hit anyone, though, and I don't believe he ever will; that's not his style. For some children hitting is the only way, and you have to let them—at least for a while. Mark just gradually learned—partly, perhaps, because we have encouraged him—that holding his place in line was one of the things he *ought* to do, like putting away his toys or anything else that's expected of him. I suppose that method is better than hitting, but we can't be too particular, and if I explained all that to Jean I might just scare her back into her old ways."

Children Are All Different

To a large extent each child has to develop his own style in getting along with others. Some will fight at the first provocation. Though they have to learn eventually to give this up, they must be given time. Others, especially when they are boys, distress their parents because they never fight and are thereupon instructed in the technique of boxing, usually by their anxious fathers. But, like Mark, each child must find his method of holding his own and winning an accepted and respected place among his fellows. Some children are miserable if called on to assert themselves in purely physical ways, and parents and teachers should beware of demanding that they all act alike. This attitude has been caused, in part, by mistaken notions about qualities that make for leadership. Parents fail to understand that in a group of children the dominating boss rarely holds first place long. Eventually the child with intelligence, resources, and adaptability comes to the front. It is an advantage to have physical strength and size and athletic skills, but in the end the better qualifications seem to belong to the stamp collector, the skilled airplane builder, and the child with ideas and plans.

While every child sooner or later must find some way of getting along with others, we are too likely to forget that he has an urgent need for some solitude as well. We begin very early to drive and press our children just as we often drive ourselves, feeling that we neglect our duty unless a child is always "out playing ball with the boys." Often children who have been with other children all morning prefer to spend their afternoons at home alone, doing nothing in particular. To be sure, there are dangers in wanting to be alone all the time. Regular experiences with other children are necessary, and parents must see that they are provided. Ability to work and play with others, in some degree, is a prime necessity and if, over a period of years, a child makes no progress, it should not be neglected. But this does not mean that children should never play by themselves.

Parents forget that there is also a more introverted type of child who will always proceed more tentatively in his social relations than his outgoing, easygoing brothers and who should not be expected to do otherwise. A sensitive, quiet child is not necessarily suffering from a character defect. Here is a special kind of person, but not a handicapped one. Solitude and even idleness, with plenty of time to invite one's soul, are an essential part of living, and most adults today suffer from the lack of just these things. Where our children are concerned we would do well if we should occasionally temper our enthusiasm for "worth-while activities." And, if we happen occasionally to find our young one lying on his back on the floor, quietly waving his legs in the air, let us depart in peace and leave him alone.

HELPING THE SHY CHILD

Shy children usually need the same kind of consideration. There is no hurry; they have many years ahead in which to find themselves. It is important that they should develop skills, whether athletic, artistic, manual, or intellectual, because these skills help to offset their inability to be at ease socially. Encourage a child to develop what he has; do not continuously press him to acquire what he lacks. Usually he will work out relationships with other children in his own time. Children also need encouragement from parents as they meet socially difficult moments.

"You see, Mary, when I was your age I was shy, too. I was afraid of other children. But I learned to get over it, and so can you."

Something like this can be said to our five- and six-year-olds who cannot greet a guest or who are overcome with fear at the thought of going to a party. But whether spoken or not, a note of encouragement should always be implicit in our attitude toward a shy child at any age. Words, no matter how wise and true, can never be so effective as concrete help when strangers appear. All of us have too much faith in word magic. We rack our brains for a verbal formula, but it is our actions that are most eloquent. No words can ever help the shy child as much as the kind of person who can produce, at a difficult moment, something that wins the child's attention—a set of toy automobiles, for example, or a game of parcheesi—and who can stimulate so much interest in these things that the child eventually forgets his self-consciousness.

Those children who tie themselves to their mother's apron strings and refuse to be untied often need a firm but gentle push.

"Here come Bill and Jack," we may say, making no especial attempt to extricate our own David, who cowers close to our side. "Come on, boys, do you want to see a stunt I can do with a string? See, I'm going to knot it. Now you can hold the two ends over your hands like that. All right, Jack's turn next, then David's."

When the time comes, David is quite absorbed and holds out his hands eagerly, but he is still silent and has not yet said a word to Bill and Jack or seemed to notice them. However, all begin to play, and by slow degrees David is drawn in, too. Bill and Jack take him for granted and let him alone, but eventually the contact between the children becomes more natural, and David actually forgets himself and has a good time.

This is not the moment for David's mother to retire with a book and feel that the matter is settled. The children need watching or there may be an explosion that would wreck all the progress. While she may retreat for strategic purposes, from a distance she should give a good deal of attention to what goes on. In this way she can rescue the situation from a catastrophe before it happens. As a rule, shy and timid children need to play under some supervision, or the difficulties of coping with their rougher and more aggressive playfellows become so great that they may withdraw from the scene entirely, with a sense of defeat and humiliation increased rather than diminished.

Help Them Find Skills

In trying to help shy or timid children to build skills by which they may win the respect of others, efforts should in part be directed to the field in which the child is deficient. But this should never be all. We must be quick to help him capitalize his assets. One little boy of six, for example, was no good at all at throwing a ball and at climbing; it was perfectly apparent that when it came to physical daring he was just a sissy, and he suffered accordingly. Then it was discovered that he could draw and paint boats better than anyone else in his grade at school. All the other children tried, but none had such intricate rigging or such billowy sails or such realistic water as his. When they had all tried their best, they gathered around this timid child's easel to admire and to envy. His prestige soared. Even more important, as soon as the others began to think these things quite wonderful he began to think so, too. He painted boats passionately, but besides that—and without any special cajoling or pressure from the teacher—he began to hold his own much better in physical contacts and to lose some of his shyness. His feeling of competence in one field spread to other fields as well.

PLAY GROUP OR NURSERY SCHOOL

In most communities today many practical obstacles prevent children from fully enjoying those give-and-take relations that are the beginnings of friendship. Families, particularly in large cities, tend to be smaller than they were a hundred years ago. Companionships no longer happen as spontaneously as they did when village life was more cohesive and more homogeneous and when it was safer to play on streets or back lots than it is today. Automobiles have tended to break up neighborhoods. A great many families live far from their friends and would have no social life at all if it were not for transportation facilities. In the apartment houses of large cities we often do not know a single one of our fellow tenants. Even in smaller towns our home may be located in a place where there are few children of the same age as ours.

Schools offer a partial solution and, for children old enough to attend, create a genuine community. But the enormous and highly organized public school of today cannot altogether replace the intimate neighborhood life of past generations. For most children under five or six, moreover, school life is not available. They must wait until the law opens the doors to them. Meanwhile they are often lonely and disconsolate, needing companionship of their own age and also a world in which the stimulus of new interests offers freedom during several hours of the day from their emotional involvements with home and parents.

For these children the nursery school, or a more informally organized play group, has definite values. The primary goal is not intellectual learning. No good nursery school sees its function as "teaching," in the usual sense of the word, or as preparing children for reading, writing, or other techniques of the school curriculum. What these groups do offer is a variety of activities—things to make and do, chances for bodily development, for music and rhythms and dramatic expression, and a chance to create as the imagination prompts. But even more important are the opportunities for social contacts and the dawning capacity for friendships inherent in these early years. This is the "learning" which the preschool child needs most; his school is a laboratory in which he experiments with his selfishness and his affections. Here his need to possess and dominate conflicts with his need to win the love and esteem of others, and in working out methods of compromise and control he makes discoveries that should last him a lifetime. These experiences are among the greatest values of the modern nursery school; they are the same things the old-fashioned neighborhood offered to children abundantly and in so many cases offers no more.

Choose a Good One

But some warnings are necessary. There are many groups calling themselves nursery schools that are hastily thrown together and have little to offer. Their "teachers" may not be suited, either by training or personality, to educate small children; and the children may be housed in places inadequate to their needs. In most places there is no system of state supervision for preschool groups, and parents alone must assume the full responsibility for making sure that the place where they send their children is something more than a mere parking place where they receive custodial care for a few hours a day. The good nursery school should be under the direction of someone whose experience and training qualify her to know the problems of young children and to handle them with skill. If planned and improvised by the parents themselves, they should understand their responsibilities.

Health should be a primary consideration. There should be regular medical advice from a physician on how to keep children *in groups* from exposure to infection. There should be skill in detecting the beginnings of an illness, and provisions should be made for immediate isolation, no matter how slight the danger. If this problem is properly provided for, nursery school is not undesirable from a medical standpoint. There is some evidence to show that children are likely to contract more colds and other passing infections *whenever* they begin to associate with groups of others, whether they begin at the age of three or six. Perhaps there are some, therefore, for whom it is wiser to postpone this exposure until they are older. But, in most cases, there is reason to believe that the increased mental stimulation and general happiness resulting from regular associations with other children actually improve a child's general physical tone and more than offset any disadvantages.

However, there is no general answer to the question of whether or not a child should go to nursery school. It must be settled individually. The answer will depend not only on health factors, but also on what the child's home and neighborhood have to offer and on whether the school in question is prepared to meet the emotional and physical needs of a child of that particular age and temperament. With shy, dependent children of two or three years, one should proceed cautiously. Usually nursery school helps them grow beyond these traits, but there are times when the experience is too hard for them and they are better off at home for a while longer.

Besides safeguards of health, a nursery school should offer children every opportunity for physical growth and social development. Swings, slides, climbing apparatus, blocks, wagons, crates—whatever seems calculated to stimulate physical and mental activity should be available. Equally important are materials with which a child can express his feelings and enjoy sensations, such as clay, paints and crayons, or hammer and nails with which he may pound and bang as hard as he can. He needs, also, a chance to get wet and dirty without being scolded and to play freely with water and sand. Dolls have eternal values for both boys and girls, for while playing with them they are able to act out and find relief for many of the problems they struggle with at home. Outdoor space with plenty of sunlight and freedom from wind is also essential, as well as provisions for rest and for eating. These should be arranged according to the length of the child's day. If he stays into the afternoon there must be facilities offering a chance for an unbroken sleep of an hour or more, after a lunch that is well served and of proper quality. Even the child who goes home at noon requires a mid-morning snack—milk or orange juice and crackers—and a period set aside for quiet when everyone rests for ten or fifteen minutes.

Parents and Teachers

Most important of all are the experience and temperament of those in charge. If they know their job they understand the importance of health, equipment, and competent assistants who can get along with young children. With wise teachers in charge, there will be full recognition of the importance of parents. Mothers will be made welcome, and the development of parents as well as children is often a genuine result of a school experience. Both mothers and fathers should be given a chance to understand the purposes and philosophy of the school as a whole and to know what a teacher is trying to do for their particular child. During their many informal visits parents may learn to see their child in relation to other children and thus to consider his development more clearly and objectively.

Though some conceal it better than others, most young parents have many misgivings about their children. They welcome an opportunity for wise and sympathetic counsel from a teacher who, having known and worked with many children, has watched them through a variety of trying phases and helped them to mature. Warm relationships with such teachers give the mother self-confidence and a sense of sharing responsibility with someone she can trust and someone who cares—not, of course, as intensely as she cares, but whose concern is none the less real. Meeting other parents and observing the behavior of their children contribute to the mother's own maturity.

A good nursery school, then, to some degree must always be an extension of the home. Though it offers experiences which the home, by its very nature, cannot offer, it should not break sharply with all that has gone before in the child's experience. There should be a continuous interchange of experience and counsel between parents and teachers. Teachers must recognize the parent-child relationship as the cornerstone on which the child's life is constructed and must understand the part they can play in strengthening it.

To further these ends, some nursery schools have been organized on a co-operative basis, with parents included as a necessary part of the plan. For example, each mother may pledge, as she enrolls her child, that she will give a specified amount of time each week to the school, acting as assistant to the teachers, assuming certain responsibilities—and, in the process, sharpening her own powers of observation and her skill in management. It would be hard to overestimate the value of learning in this way, through this kind of close association with many children and with teachers whose experience is likely to be wider than the parent's own—though not always as deep. Perhaps not every school can adopt this scheme, for it is not a simple one and requires careful planning as well as expert supervision, but when it has a chance to succeed the educational values are doubled.

FRIENDSHIPS

Whether in nursery groups, the large family group, on the city block, or in the small-town neighborhood, children at this period of their lives are making their first experiments with friendships. Their development in this field is likely to be irregular, as it is with so many other things. Not all of them will feel friendly toward all children and devoted to a few, as their parents might wish. Children are often fussy or capricious or unreasonable in their tastes. Some of them for years may never "really seem to care for anybody" and, though not definitely unfriendly, may remain casual and indifferent. Others will take to a bosom friend early in life, concentrate upon him exclusively, and resist every attempt to make them appreciate the charms of others.

Children do not always choose friends who are desirable from the parents' point of view. Sometimes they choose much younger children, or unpopular ones, or rough and bad-mannered ones, or even the troublemaking, so-called problem child of the group. Parents are afraid that such connections will leave indelible marks and should therefore be carefully controlled. But this is likely to be too superficial a view. Sometimes such attachments fulfill a temporary need and pass of their own accord as a child's development proceeds. Sometimes, when we know the friend better and take into consideration the things he gives our child that we cannot, he may seem less undesirable than he did at first. Children from well protected homes, for example, may learn much that is valuable from the neighborhood "roughneck." Occasionally, two children do actually stimulate the worst in each other— the infantile and regressive forces instead of those which make for wholesome growth. In this case, and if we are sure of what we are doing, partial separation at least may be necessary. But whatever the situation, parents should always regard their children's choice of friends as valuable clues to their inner problems and unspoken needs. With this in mind, they will be cautious about trying to influence or regulate their friendships and will hesitate a long time before they definitely prohibit any of them. Children who are unsure of themselves, lacking in self-confidence and self-esteem, as a rule will choose friends who are younger or duller or "not as good" as they are. These children are selected because they constitute no threat, impose no challenge. In their company, a timid child's own supremacy is easily assured and he finds release from his habitual sense of inferiority.

When this is the case, criticism, exhortations, and complaints from parents are useless. These methods attack the symptom, but not the cause of the trouble. Even if our children are quite tactfully and imperceptibly prevented from association with "undesirables," we have accomplished little or nothing unless we can take steps at the same time to build our child's self-esteem and rid him of the need for such companionship. "Why does my child choose this child for his friend?" is a question which must be asked and answered if parents are to be genuinely helpful. What children need is not enforced companionship with the "right" children, but the capacity to hold their own among children who have something to give. If this capacity is real, they will spontaneously find friendships that are constructive instead of those that offer nothing but an escape from the problems presented by their own personalities.

As the years progress, there is nothing that parents can do to promote happy friendships for their children that will help more, in the long run, than setting up the kind of home where their children's friends love to come. No home should be so clean that a child is made miserable when he tracks mud in, or so sanitary that it cannot admit dogs, cats, and pets of all kinds, or so routinized that there is never a bit of cake between meals; or a mother so busy that she gets cross if children dare set foot in the kitchen. A play yard with equipment for all occasions is a fine thing—so is an attic or indoor room to accommodate the gang on rainy days—but to these things must always be added the kind of mother who "smiles so nicely" or a father who is "swell." One of the big thrills of childhood is to have a home that is the envy of the other children because they have such a good time whenever they come there. If the other children think your father and mother are good sports, then you have to believe that they probably are, and their advice and opinions about things become easier to take. Against such a background and in such an atmosphere children invite their friends in freely and learn to see them realistically. They measure them by the standards of their own homes. It becomes unnecessary to regulate friendships. The wheat and the chaff eventually become apparent for what they are, and the foundations are laid for developing powers of discrimination that will last a lifetime.

CHAPTER SIX

SEXUALITY IN CHILDHOOD

LIKE EVERYTHING ELSE, sexuality has a history. Far from spring-
ing into full-fledged existence at the onset of puberty, sexuality must be viewed as a set of forces which, like the organs
of sex themselves, is present at birth and undergoes certain
changes as the individual matures. It is true, of course, that at
puberty the speeding up of growth in the glands of reproduction is accompanied by rapid psychological changes as well.
Overnight the child seems to become a youth, almost an
adult. Yet, strictly speaking, all this sudden flowering is not
new at all. These events, physical and emotional, have had
their roots in early childhood; their particular form and
color, their vigor or its reverse, are intricately related to the
experiences of the nursery years.

Infantile Bodily Pleasures

No discerning observer of the intimate behavior of little
children can fail to perceive how interested they are in their
own and other people's bodies and bodily processes. The in-

fant delights in the discovery and handling of fingers and toes and any other parts of himself and likes tickling, stroking, and muscle sensations of all kinds without discrimination. Soon, however, he learns that there are special pleasures connected with mouth and lips, and he accordingly carries everything to his mouth, to bite, to suck, or to chew. It is at this time that many children become thumb or finger suckers or develop addictions to the corner of a blanket, to the ear of a woolly dog, or to the railing of their cribs. As we have already seen, during the first year or so of life the mouth is one of the chief pleasure zones of the body, not only because food is taken through it, but because it yields pleasurable sensations that have nothing to do with the physiology of nourishment. Though it is related to the child's developing sexuality, there is no evidence that sucking tends to make a child "sensual," as some parents used to fear. On the contrary, sucking is a legitimate need of infancy that is more likely to run its normal course and yield to a new and more mature phase of growth if it is interfered with as little as possible.

Although some children apparently get all the sucking they require while eating, the majority supplement it with toys, fingers, or other objects. Mouth pleasure is highly important, and whether or not we choose to call it sexual, we can scarcely fail to recognize its close relation to the sex instinct. Common sense and ordinary observations tell us constantly of the closeness of this tie-up. While mouth stimulation and sucking usually cease to be the primary source of pleasure after the first year, so that most children of three or four are nearly through with it, the mouth nevertheless continues to occupy a highly important place in the expression of love and in human sexual behavior all through life. Even in behavior not ordinarily called sexual, mouth stimulation as a source of pleasure or as a relief from nervous tension continues into adult life. One has only to watch a group of average people at unguarded moments to see how often fingers are carried to the lips and how pencils and anything else at hand are sucked. What are the pleasures of smoking? A complex of many things, perhaps, but certainly the pleasurable nature of the mouth sensations involved plays an important part.

BOWEL TRAINING AND SEX

There are other bodily interests typical of early childhood, and the attitude that parents take toward these interests may strongly influence the course of sexuality. At the age of about two, more or less, children's concern in their bowel function and everything that goes with it is likely to be intense. This matter is a problem of great concern to the mother also, but unfortunately her interest and the child's are likely to run counter to each other and to conflict. Most mothers, with the problem of training uppermost in their minds, with a strong desire not only for fewer soiled diapers but also for a child of whose cleanliness they can boast, create an issue long before the child is ready for it. To the mother, as we have already seen in an earlier chapter, the child's stool is "duty"; but to the child it is pleasure. The mother usually wants the matter speeded up and disposed of as fast as possible. The child, on the contrary, prefers to linger over his performance, delighting in the size of his stool, pleased by its smell, and with an inclination to touch and even to smear which is often irresistible. The more the mother urges conformity to set routines, the more likely the child is to resist. He may tease his mother by holding back his stool altogether or by reserving it until he has left the toilet seat and can soil himself just as he wishes.

It is of the utmost importance for parents or anyone else in charge of young children to understand that their pleasure in the whole process of bowel functioning is normal and necessary. Grownups, because of their training, have forgotten or nearly forgotten these pleasures, though traces do linger in a variety of ways (for example, our pleasure in the whole class of toilet jokes—not sexual in the usual sense, but certainly regarded as "dirty"). But, for the most part, childish pleasures in toilet matters are forgotten, and the sense of disgust that comes later usually hides whatever other feelings still exist beneath the surface. Consequently, we are all inclined to be hard on the naïve pursuit of these pleasures during the nursery years. Although without question children must learn to give them up, experience has taught that we can be of most help if we are careful not to demand compliance too early and if we understand the relation of this matter to the child's whole life.

Is Pleasure Bad?

Viewed psychologically, toilet training is far more than toilet training. It is part of the child's training in his whole feeling about his body and its functions. Therefore, in a highly important sense, it also serves to train him in his later attitudes toward pleasure itself. If such training is severe, all pleasure in life tends to become something which one's mother forbids and which is therefore "bad"; only giving up what we enjoy is "good" and can win us our mother's love. Moreover, since the organs of excretion and the organs of sex lie so close together, it is impossible for a growing individual to escape the conclusion that if the body's excrements are somehow bad, then everything else connected with this region of the body must also be bad. Long before the so-called facts of sex have been told, or sex questions asked, sex attitudes are in the process of building. They are built by the mother's "dirties" and "disgustings" and "naughties," with her tense and disapproving looks, the way in which she forbids the things that a two-year-old finds interesting and pleasurable. Or they are built by a tolerant acceptance of the child as a child and by a gradual, kindly, and good-humored manner of introducing him to adult customs as soon as his behavior indicates that he is ready to go forward.

In the child's sex development, more than anywhere else, the parents' attitude speaks louder than words. Children continually forget our words; they misconstrue them or ignore them. But the parents' unspoken and often unconscious attitude toward the body always makes an impression, and the parents' feelings about what is good or bad in this connection are inevitably communicated. For this reason, it is difficult to answer parents when they ask what they should tell their children in reply to sex questions. Giving information the "right way" is futile unless the parents' unspoken feelings are sound or unless they at least recognize at what point their feelings are likely to be colored by the mistakes in their own early training and will do what they can to guard their children from similar impressions. Sometimes parents themselves are so confused about sex matters that they should seek professional help in straightening out their own attitudes before attempting to help their children.

THE CHILD AND HIS BODY

Usually the child's first questions center around the body. He notices differences between children and adults and, if he has the opportunity, between boys and girls. Somewhat later he discovers that new babies come into the world and he wants to know how. If he has a chance to ask these questions openly and receives straightforward, accurate, unabashed answers, he learns that a grownup is someone he can talk to about anything he wants to know. If, on the other hand, he is put off with evasive half-truths or the promise "when you are older" or with a flushed and halting attempt to spiritualize the facts out of existence ("God makes little boys different from little girls so they can grow up into men and women," or, "Because Daddy and Mother loved one another, you grew under my heart out of that love"), he realizes that adults are likely to be unsatisfactory in this matter and he turns elsewhere for information. Worse still, he is afraid even to wonder about his own and other people's bodies. When this moment comes, a door is quietly closed between him and his parents. Perhaps it can never again be opened, and the child is thus left to struggle alone with a phase of life in which, somewhere in the course of his development, he is likely to need help. Not only is he left alone outside; he may be left with the feeling that the whole subject is dangerous and that he himself is bad for having been curious.

In answering children's questions, parents are often afraid of stirring to activity forces that they feel are best left quiet. They know how long it is between the time when sex interest begins and the time when our civilization will permit sexual expression and marriage. Wouldn't it be better, they ask, to keep it all in the background as long as possible, until the young person becomes mentally mature enough to cope with this difficult matter wisely? This plan of postponement would be a very good one if experience had not shown again and again that it does not work. Whether we give direct misinformation as our grandmothers did or whether we are merely evasive and silent, the result is the same. We leave the child alone with his unanswered problems, running the risk that he will begin to feel that the body and all of its functions are something vaguely bad, in which it is shameful to be interested.

Some children, it is true, survive such a course and perhaps work their way through unaided to a healthy enough solution, but, for a far greater number, parental evasions merely lay the foundations for increased difficulties. Our problem therefore remains. How can we help a child to be willing to forgo premature sex experiences without letting our fears and prohibitions implant a sense of guilt regarding sexuality that may persist for a lifetime? How can we best give sanction to a child's inevitable concern with the body, and to all the questions and experiments that are likely to arise, and at the same time impose some control on unrestricted gratification? It is no wonder that with the best will in the world mistakes are often made.

Facts and Feelings

To some extent, such sanctions are given by the way parents respond to children's questions and their willingness to answer clearly whatever is asked, regardless of the child's age. Some parents, however, make the mistake of trying to tell too much at once. The young child needs simple explanations.

"What's that?" says a three-year-old, pointing at the genital of her new baby brother.

"That's his penis," the mother may answer. "Little boys and men, too, have a penis to urinate with."

Often this is enough for the moment, though from time to time a child will chatter about it, forget what he has been told, or misinterpret what the mother has said. The job has to be done over again, but, as any teacher knows, there is no such thing as imparting facts "once and for all"; they are only vaguely understood at first and the same questions keep recurring. Sometimes, however, they take a new form and express more than mere curiosity and a desire for information. In their sex questions, children's feelings and fears are betrayed, too.

"I want one. Why can't I have a penis, too?" asks a three-and-a-half-year-old girl.

The mother begins all over again with the unchangeable facts of sex differences.

"No, that's not true," the little girl said, quite gravely and positively, when her mother had finished. "All babies have a penis when they are born; girls lose them when they get older. Why do they lose them?"

Since this child had never heard anything but the truth from her mother, this query illustrates how even very young children develop firm ideas of their own to explain bodily differences. These fantasies are likely to be related to whatever anxieties children may be entertaining at a given time about the whole mysterious and momentous question of the body. The mother, if she is to understand, must be alert to the state of mind behind the spoken question or comment. She must try to help the child with what really troubles him as well as with what he asks. It is worth noticing that, at just this time, this same little girl had a boy doll which she liked very much. When she first got him she undressed him eagerly and, noting important omissions in his structure, appended a string of small safety pins in the proper place, with evident satisfaction. Somewhat later she had an even better idea. She pinned a string of larger safety pins to the front of her own underpants and wore them happily for many months. The mother removed the pins whenever she put the pants in the laundry, but left them where the child could get them if she wished, with the result that the child always promptly put them back on her clean pants.

This child's question, especially when supported by her actions, clearly said, "I wish I had a penis. Why did I lose mine?

Did I do something bad and get punished? How can I get it back?" This state of mind is more general than most people realize. It is not unusual for little girls to want to have a penis and to be inwardly irreconcilable. They feel deprived and somehow cheated and will either become discouraged or later on look for ways to make it up to themselves through an attitude of deep-lying competitiveness with men—a poor foundation for marriage.

They Are More Worried than You Think

Neither boys nor girls take sex differences quite so for granted as their elders suppose. The boy's attempt to solve the problem is fraught with anxiety, too. If there are human beings who have no penis, how did they happen to lose them? Is it possible that even a boy might lose his? Sometimes a grownup adds to his fears by threatening him, when he misbehaves, with actual loss of his genital. It used to be common for parents or others to try to break a child of masturbation by telling him that if he does not stop someone will come and cut off his penis. Such threats or suggestions of bodily mutilation are dangerous and can readily give rise to nervousness and fears.

But even when every effort is made to avoid such mistakes, it is nearly impossible to keep the situation entirely clear of anxiety. In one home where simple and direct explanations were to be had for the asking, a boy of three watched in silence as his baby sister was being bathed. It was evident from his expression that he was troubled by what he saw, now that he was face to face with the fact that here was a human creature who lacked what he had and prized. He did not comment on what he saw, but he became more and more restless and finally, looking up with a troubled face, said merely, "Mommie, I'm afraid."

These anatomical differences are facts that both boys and girls must learn to accept. Though the mother cannot wholly prevent anxieties from developing, much that she does will either help or hinder the process of ultimate understanding and acceptance. She can prevent threats and give reassurance. She can let her small daughter know that girls have something unique that boys cannot have. A girl has a place in her body called a uterus, where someday a baby can begin to grow and get big enough to come out into the world—and how much fun it is to have a baby! You can give it milk and change its diapers and bathe and dress it and soon it learns to know you and smile at you. It is a great advantage to a little girl's normal development to have a mother who has been glad to be a woman, one who has wanted babies. All children delight in stories of their own birth, and children who know that their coming meant so much to their parents that they love to tell about it are likely to acquire a healthy sense of importance and also will begin to look forward to having families themselves.

GIVING INFORMATION AND LIMITING
EXPERIENCE

Besides questions about the body and its meaning, children will ask about babies. Where does a baby grow? How does it get out? Where does it come out? Even to the youngest child the mother can explain that the baby grows in the mother's uterus from a tiny thing so small that you can't see it. It grows and grows until it is a baby and is strong enough to live in the world. The right age to tell him this and anything else is *when he asks.* A little later he may want to know how the baby gets out and can learn that it comes out through an open-ing in the mother's body, called the vagina, which leads from the uterus, where the baby is, into the outside world. A child should learn, in the course of time, where the vagina is. This is usually enough for the time being, though sometimes chil-dren want to go right on and ask their mothers to show them the place in her body where they came out. This is a natural demand but it brings us into range of actual sex experience and the necessity for limiting it. Sex curiosity, whenever pos-sible, should stop short of actual physical contacts, especially such contacts with parents. Certainly parents must say no to such a request, making it clear that people always want to keep this part of themselves private. One of the major prob-lems of growing up is learning to shift the emotional center of life from parents and home to others whom one learns to love more and with whom one is destined to found a home of one's own, and this transition is made harder if too many sexual associations with parents are mixed into all the other memories of early childhood.

Sleeping with Parents

For the same reason, it is definitely undesirable for children to sleep in the same bed with their parents or even in the same room, after they are six months old. This does not mean that children should never romp on their parents' bed now and then. But prolonged physical contacts past babyhood may disturb sound development. So may sharing the parents' bedroom even if the child's bed is at a distance from the parents'. Children observe or overhear far more than we may care to believe and, even when they cannot fully understand what goes on between their parents or what they imagine goes on, they are impressionable and may retain memories that trouble them deeply. Whether or not they know the facts of sex relations, children increasingly realize that parents are men and women, that they are different, and that there are special and private things between them. Curiosity and guilt and disappointment at being excluded are stimulated if children are allowed to draw too close to the center of the mystery. This is hard advice to offer to the millions of families living on small budgets and in cramped quarters. Having the baby sleep in his parents' room seems the easiest thing to do and this often drags on into childhood. But resourceful parents make adjustments. The most practical plan is to turn the bedroom over to the children while the parents occupy a daybed in the living room.

The Right Word Is the Best Word

Children who have lived closely with parents whose attitude to physical processes is natural and easy will have learned, among other things, to call the various parts of the body by name by the time they are four or five—or even earlier. There should never be one word, such as "private parts," for example, to designate the genitals of both sexes. It is far better for a child to know that a boy's genital is a penis, the girl's a vulva. Moreover, a girl should know that she has a vagina and where it is, as well as its ultimate purpose. Too many girls grow up with only the vaguest notions of their own anatomical structure, a fact which tends to retard the normal development of sexuality and to confirm their feeling that they have no genital organ at all and no part to play in life that is comparable to the boy's. They should learn also that there is a difference between child and adult, that grown women have breasts from which they feed their babies, that hair grows in certain places, and that sizes and shapes of various parts change in both sexes with the years.

Nudity

In most cases, this knowledge is acquired like any other set of facts. Young and old in families today are far more casual about going nude before one another than they were a generation ago. Many parents today have no hesitation about taking showers or performing other toilet functions while their children wander in and out of the bathroom. But it is questionable whether this break with usual conventions solves any problems. Confusion about anatomical differences continues even in children brought up this way; seeing is not necessarily believing. Whatever the family customs, as the child grows older, parents and children alike usually find they want more privacy and spontaneously prefer closed doors at certain times. This usually comes about naturally and is perhaps better than setting an arbitrary date for a change or forcing an abrupt, self-conscious reversal of household habits.

Most young children make comments (often far from flattering) on their parents' bodies and ask questions about what they see. Some seem to take their knowledge easily and appear to digest it without emotional disturbance. Others are clearly over-stimulated. Even those who have seen nude adults since birth, may suddenly begin to stare long and perhaps guiltily, or they may want to talk continuously, demanding explanations for what they already know. Sometimes they try to touch and handle other people's bodies, or when in bed with parents or each other show obvious signs of sexual stimulation and excitement in close physical contact. While this is by no means abnormal, it shows that these children are going through a phase in their development that is loaded with tension and inner conflict. Parents, therefore, should see that these occasions for stimulation are reduced or eliminated. When excitement is clearly evident they should manage to keep themselves covered when the child is in their bedroom, to make it known that they prefer not to be bothered while dressing or bathing, and see to it also that physical contacts are less prolonged, and less intense. These should be replaced by play that is focused on the outside world—new knowledge, new skills. It is hardly necessary to add what we *do* for children is always more important than what we *do not* do and that new interests and absorbing activities in the world about him naturally enable a child to solve by himself the problems raised in the course of his emotional growth.

Father's Role

A great many parents find no hesitation in answering children's questions about the body and its workings or about the baby's growth in the mother's uterus, but feel reluctant to tell them the father's part in reproduction and constantly beg to be told authoritatively "at what age" children should be told, and how. Here, too, the answer is the same: "As soon as the child asks." But such information should be given simply, a little at a time, and the scientific details of fertilization and embryology can wait. A child should not be rushed beyond his capacity to understand in the hope of settling the matter speedily, "once and for all."

There are some legitimate reasons for the parents' hesitation. When a child has asked this question he has asked one with enormous implications, and we are overwhelmed by our inability to make him really understand. As in the case of questions about death or God, we feel we can give him so little he can understand that we hesitate to give him anything at all. But no matter what the question and no matter how impossible a complete answer may be, a child still has the right to expect some help in at least beginning to understand. When a youngster says: "But how did I *get into* you, Mother?" or, "Why can't Aunt Kate have a baby? Why do babies only

[169]

grow in married people?" we need not evade the question. Every mother will want to choose her own words and should be guided by what she feels her own child can understand, but nevertheless she should be ready to tell the elementary facts. This is far easier if both parents and children are already accustomed to calling parts of the body by their right names. Children who have learned that the baby grows inside the mother's uterus from a tiny seed can also be told that there must be a father to help it start growing. There are seeds in the father's body, too, inside his testes, which have to meet the seed in the mother's body or there can be no baby. Somewhat older children ask how the seeds get in. It can be explained that a man's penis, besides being the organ for urinating, is also the organ by which the seeds enter the mother's body through her vagina.

Sometimes children ask whether they cannot make a baby right away with a boy or girl they know. They may be told that the seeds are not ripe in children and that babies only grow from the seeds of men and women. And that, besides, it is very important for babies to have a home and a grownup father and mother to take care of them. That is why people must wait until they are married before bringing a baby into the world.

Your Child and Your Neighbor's Child

This may seem like a great deal of information with which to burden a small child, but if it is asked for and given bit by bit, as is usually the case, it will gradually be understood. In addition, children will always get sex education from one another and from the raw material of their own experiences. This is not necessarily undesirable. In their sex development children need the crude approach of contemporaries as well as the refinements of adults. Parents are not mere purveyors of facts according to a fixed schedule. Their role is not that of keeping a child protected from all outside influences. It is, instead, to help a child to sort and arrange and comprehend his experience, the feelings as well as the facts. Parents represent the point of view of mature people, a view which supplements but never takes the place of what children will inevitably learn from each other and for themselves. In the long run, the *facts* of sex are a very small part of a real comprehension of sex in life. Far more momentous are the feelings and emotions which arise as the whole individual develops and, although children are unlikely to talk much about them, it is these that play the dominant role.

As children's freedom to express themselves develops, it seems fair to warn them that not all parents care to talk to their children in just this way and that their friends' parents may not like it if they talk to other children about how babies come and about the differences in male and female. They might be told that most parents prefer to tell their children what they want to in their own way and that because of this it might be a good idea not to say too much to their friends. This is instruction in social usage and should have no more weight than any other such instruction. It seems unwise to forbid such conversation; children inevitably will talk to each other as time goes on. This is a necessary phase of their development, and not dangerous, provided they also feel free to go back to their parents for clarification of the unsavory and garbled accounts that they are more than likely to get from their contemporaries.

SEX PLAY AMONG CHILDREN

Although all our present knowledge shows strongly that reassuring guidance from parents will in the long run help the young child to a sound sex adjustment in later life, it is certainly no guarantee that he will willingly put all such things out of his mind until he grows up. Sex curiosity is not so easily stilled, and normal children, even when sexually enlightened, often seek to satisfy curiosity or get even more exciting stimulation from challenging one another to exposure or exploring each other's bodies. Games of "doctor" furnish such occasions in more or less disguised form; franker bodily comparisons carried on in the bathroom or behind the proverbial barn may result in children exposing and sometimes manipulating each other's genitals. Some of this sort of thing is likely to go on among groups of young children and if it stays within bounds much of it can be treated casually. But continued preoccupation with it calls for some redirection from adults. This does not mean punishment, threats, shaming, and moral lectures on the wickedness of such conduct, or even the ostracizing of a child who may be the leader. It does mean that parents should have some idea what children are doing when they are alone for hours or locked in the bathroom together; and it does mean that parents should see to it that children should have plenty of genuinely interesting things to do and that there is some unobtrusive supervision of their play. Sometimes when the parent is sure that such experimentation is definitely going on there is nothing he can do but meet the situation openly. Father or mother, as the case may be, can explain in whatever words seem suitable that this sort of play is a mistake for children. Sexual contacts are for grownups, and children must learn to wait. As long as the child is able to talk about sexual matters freely, such simple, dogmatic statements are usually more effective and less terrifying than those veiled threats of mysterious illness which come so readily to the tongue of the frightened parent.

Certainly there is no denying that these occurrences are difficult to handle. A child is incapable of understanding all that is involved. The adult is again faced with the task of postponing, if possible, premature sexual experience and the anxieties it is almost sure to arouse, without fastening so much moral censure to what has taken place that the child is forced into a course of secrecy and shame. Evidently there is no perfect way of avoiding the sense of guilt in connection with sex matters. All that parents can hope to do is mitigate it. A chance to talk it all over with a grownup who is trusted and liked often helps a great deal. Whatever else is done, however, such children should be helped to find plenty of other active interests to absorb their energies. But when these things have been tried and, as sometimes happens, failed, professional advice is indicated.

There is no reason to suppose that children who have been told the facts frankly and fully are more likely to engage in sex experimentation than those who have not. On the contrary, the weight of evidence, in so far as we have it, seems to be the other way around. The most extreme "sex problems" are found among neglected children and are not infrequent in those whose parents flatter themselves that "they have no interest in such things." A child who has always felt that he has free access to his parents' mature knowledge in all matters including this is certainly better off than the child who is forced to be secretive and who lives in the knowledge that only punishment and shame will follow discoveries of sex activity. It is not true, though, as the more ardent of the early advocates of sex education once fondly supposed, that giving children "the facts of life" satisfies their curiosity once and for all and safeguards them against further impulses to experiment.

THE CHILD WHO "NEVER ASKS"

Children's sex interests and the behavior of individual children may be enormously different, at least on the surface. Children, who are essentially normal, show gradations all the way from marked preoccupation with sexual matters to apparent indifference. Between these extremes are the majority who, although they are occupied most of the time with a variety of other matters, have definite sex interests, who exchange occasional "dirty" jokes with friends, and who are in the process of discovering that sex is something of special consequence, as indeed it is. This majority group represents the children who are perhaps coping most successfully with the whole matter. They are doing it in their own way, without priggishness, without rejecting the mores of their group, and without closing the door to some adult guidance. It is the children in the two extremes who give us most concern. Like the sexually overactive child, the one who is wholly unaware and who never seems to notice or ask a question raises special problems as to what has happened to check his natural curiosity.

What shall we do about the child "who never asks"?

All Children Are Interested in Sex

In the first place, the indifference of many of these children is either pure bluff or only skin-deep. They have learned plenty, but feel it wiser to keep quiet. Others, however, definitely reject opportunities for knowledge. Some children cannot bear any reference to sexual matters and strongly disapprove of other children whose behavior is freer. Clearly, they are afraid of their own sexuality, not devoid of it. Frequently they have learned their fears from mother or nurse, or through chance experiences which often operate subtly. Most puzzling of all are those children who have put their early questionings so completely out of their minds that there is scarcely a trace left. The usual opportunities for questioning fail to arouse curiosity. Whatever the precise situation may be, parents of such children can be of most help if they can find ways to open up the whole subject. By giving their sanction to sex curiosity they can perhaps free it from the fears which have held it in check. No child really lacks sex interest; this has been demonstrated over and over again from closer study of those who apparently lack it. What has happened is that curiosity and everything connected with it has become bottled up so strictly that the child himself is unaware of it. This bottling-up process has definite dangers, and there is an increasing burden of evidence to show that the roots of much neurosis and later maladjustment originate here.

Natural opportunities to help a child out of this dilemma are likely to present themselves and should be utilized. The best of these is likely to be the arrival of a new baby in the family, but if one does not arrive somebody else's new baby will do. Even the occasion on which the family cat or other pet produces a litter may be a good time to open a conversation.

"Fluffy is so fat, I do believe she has some baby kittens growing inside of her," we may say. Or, "Isn't it nice that Aunt Jean and Uncle John are going to have a baby? Where do you suppose babies come from? They have to be *somewhere* before they come into the world."

Often we find that our child knows more than we thought he did, but we must remember that our purpose is not to see merely that he has the facts, but that he understands that here is something easy and right to think and talk about. Our task is not to fill the child full of correct information, but to set him free to say whatever concerns him. In sex education, as in all other kinds, we need to be good listeners, prepared to shift our course and change our tactics as we discover exactly what is on a child's mind. We may be all primed to tell him where babies come from or what the father's part is, for

example, only to find that we are on the wrong track altogether and that what he wants to know, at this particular
moment, is the meaning of some phrases or bad words
which he has heard other children use. Or perhaps he is confused because he has always believed that babies are born
through the mother's navel. As soon as a child begins to express himself at all, we are on comparatively easy ground. We
have our cue. Silence is harder to cope with and, if it persists,
perhaps the best thing the parent can do is supply answers to
questions that are *probably* on the child's mind, hoping that
this will bring the child a step nearer to asking them himself.
Often, too, a child can be led to talk about what other children
think about these matters, and in this way the parent learns
much about his own child's speculations. Or the child may
say what he used to think "when he was young," especially if
we take the initiative and tell him first what *we* used to think.

Don't Start with Bees

It should be added that children rarely want to know anything at all about the sex life of birds, bees, and wild flowers.
They are concerned with events within their immediate experience—humans or animal pets—with their own bodies, and
with practices and suggestions encountered in other children.
These, then, are the places to begin. Comparative biology can
wait.

MASTURBATION

Of all phases of sexual development, probably none is more subject to misunderstanding through masses of superstitious lore than masturbation. Even today, when the clouds of unmentionableness have begun to lift, for most people it still remains loaded with vague and unanalyzed anxieties. We may have succeeded in scrapping most of those wholly false horror stories that hold masturbation responsible for insanity, epilepsy, eye trouble, impotence, sterility, and the like, and we know that it is so common a practice in both sexes at some stage of development that it is nearly universal, and yet we keep right on regarding it as "a very bad habit"—one that we should help children get over as fast as possible if we do not want it to interfere with their social or sexual adjustment as time goes on.

This view, though an improvement on the old one, continues to beg the question, for it represents a final and dogmatic attitude toward a phase of sex life that is not yet completely understood. What is the meaning of masturbation at various stages of growth? In the infant as compared to the older child; in the adolescent? In girls as compared to boys? What are the variety of thoughts and feelings that accompany it and alter its significance? Is masturbation in children wholly useless or harmful, or does it serve a necessary purpose in sexual development as one of the means by which sexual feelings become localized, as is normal, in the genital area?

Should parents attempt to prevent or regulate it or, on the contrary, completely ignore it?

The causes of masturbation lie, for the most part, within the nature of the developing individual. Children find that handling their genitals gives pleasure in varying degrees. In some children it seems to be little more than the kind of pleasure they derive from idly fiddling with any other part of themselves. Other children, even very young ones, masturbate with every evidence of a real sexual climax. Alleged causes such as local irritations, tight clothing, and uncleanliness should, of course, be eliminated for the child's general health and comfort, but their part as a cause of masturbation is likely to be exaggerated. There are cases where children have been introduced to the practice by deliberate instruction from another child or by a perverted adult, but such accidental factors are not likely to fix the habit with any intensity unless they fall on fertile soil and serve a need already existent within the child himself. Parents should do all they can to keep such experiences at a minimum. They are terrifying because they stimulate thoughts and impulses of many kinds which the child is not equipped to cope with. But masturbation as a habit never arises from these things alone. Like thumb sucking and other practices that are characteristic of certain ages, masturbation comes and goes more because of changes in inner needs than because a purely repetitive pattern has been established or broken. Observation shows that it is very common in one form or another from the age of one year to five. From then on until puberty there may be quantitative or qualitative changes for in these years the child's interests seem focused on the outside world. At adolescence, however, masturbation again reappears with a good deal of inner conflict about it until the struggle to fulfill maturer psychological needs is successful.

As for the parents' role, the most important thing for them to know is that if a child is healthy, happy, interested in life, and busy with friends and other activities, he should be let alone and the masturbation entirely ignored.

What Not to Do

Mechanical restraints, such as bandaging the hands, should *never* be employed for any child, nor should parents ever threaten, humiliate, moralize, punish, bribe, or tell children that they will make themselves sick. In the case of the little child it is undesirable to remove the hand from the genitals, because this soon teaches him that his mother (and therefore his own emerging conscience) must regard this area as strictly taboo—an attitude inhibiting to normal sex development. Encouraging him to substitute other activities is probably harmless, unless in doing so the parent betrays anxiety. Nothing need be said to the little child, though sometimes he may need reassurance that it is permissible and necessary to handle his genitals for certain purposes, such as cleanliness. Somewhat older children may be told that they will find as they get older that they may learn to prefer all sorts of other activities and will find them more interesting.

The Parents' Role

By these means the parent exerts a mild but consistent pressure toward relinquishing the practice, not on the grounds that there is something disgraceful and harmful in it, but because, in most cases and no matter how carefully parents refrain from condemnation, children grow to condemn it in themselves. This is a crucial point, for it embodies two fundamental principles that should govern all parent-child relations. The first is the recognition of the child's need for a mother who is tolerant and "understands." The second is the recognition of his need for parents who are also "good"—and by good the child means that they support all his forward-moving, growth-making impulses, those which lead toward a satisfying and disciplined maturity rather than backward into infancy and dependence. With all their tolerance and understanding of childhood, therefore, parents must also be prepared to line up consistently on the side of all those tendencies in a child which lead to a conscious mastery of impulses but not to great guilt which leads to their repression. To achieve a balance between, on the one hand, some tolerance for childhood and, on the other, pressure to go ahead and grow up—this is the parents' most fundamental problem.

Occasionally there are children who masturbate with increasing frequency over a long period of time. They seem driven to the practice even while getting little satisfaction from it. Evidently they are attempting to make up by quantity for the qualitative absence of pleasure, much as the gluttonous eater takes food far beyond the point of satisfaction and with decreasing pleasure. This type of masturbation cannot be ignored. Like all extremes of behavior, it indicates a need which is out of the ordinary. Such children are never happy or well adjusted. They are likely to be unsociable, inactive, irritable, or hard to manage. It cannot be said too explicitly or too often that the physical act of masturbation is not the fundamental cause of these traits; on the contrary, it is probably a result of them and arises as a mode of escape from the task of coping realistically with other problems. But at the same time it is also true that a vicious circle can be established whereby the practice, through a sense of isolation, and shame of the thoughts and fantasies that so often accompany it, helps to produce other maladjustments. A child continually and obsessively involved in masturbation feels more and more withdrawn and inferior, no matter what his parents may do to avoid implanting a sense of guilt.

Ask Yourself Questions

Therefore, attention must be directed toward the child's total problem, not merely toward "breaking a habit." Why is this child troubled and unhappy? Why does he feel unloved and unwanted, inferior to other members of the family or to his friends, picked on, teased, depreciated? What are the tormenting sexual thoughts he cannot banish? His need for this quick-and-easy type of pleasure can only be diminished if he is helped to find relief from inner struggles and can improve his self-esteem and general satisfaction. If parents can find the answers to these questions they can do much to help such children. Ultimately, perhaps, they are the only ones who can really bring about an improvement. But the problem is not always a matter of simple, common-sense measures; it may call also for the advice of a child-guidance expert. This is also true of children whose obsessive concern with the whole matter of sex does not yield to sympathetic and sensible efforts at redirection. Such children are confused and ill-adjusted, at least temporarily, both to their inner problems and to the outside world, whether excessive masturbation or some other extremes of sex behavior are prominent. When such professional help is available, parents have been increasingly grateful for the added insight and practical counseling that result.

REVALUATION OF GOALS

If we are freer than our grandmothers about sex, it is because the older ways proved inadequate. At first, some parents went all out for giving every detail; now they have found a better balance. "Imparting facts" to children is less momentous than conveying attitudes. We now realize that we face a problem of educating the emotions and of all types of education, this is the most difficult. Moreover, it is a dual problem that confronts us, because the soundness of the child's sex development will depend in large measure on the soundness of his parents' development. Let us hope that we have given up the false goal of raising children who "aren't interested" in sex and are trying instead to use every scrap of knowledge available to develop a positive and vigorous sexuality which will form part of a character healthy enough both to express and control this instinct. Sex, after all, is not a separate department of living, and sex education is necessarily a part of the larger task of character education. It has to do ultimately with relationships between people and especially with the ability of two people to live together in a responsible and adult fashion. In this sense it is moral education, but we have begun to realize that moral education will be more and more successful as it is based on a widening understanding of the conditions for healthy emotional growth.

What we would like most to give our children, if we knew how, is the capacity to love; this then is our goal. But stating a problem does not, unfortunately, solve it. Perhaps we know the fundamental fact that being deeply loved by parents in early childhood lays the foundation for this capacity, and that children who have felt rejected in these early relationships are seriously handicapped. But we need further knowledge to recognize and encourage those infantile manifestations which may eventually flower into this capacity. We need the wisdom not to confuse the capacity to love with its dangerous imitations. We must distinguish it from those pretenses of love which are merely a concealment of unconscious hate; from sentimentality and self-love; from a destructive trend toward self-depreciation and self-punishment; and from an empty or childish kind of doing or being good in which no real self-discovery has ever been attained.

In the end, parents will teach children with their lives, not with their words; with what they are, not with procedures and methods. Growing up in a home where two adults have lived together lovingly, loyally, and responsibly teaches more than any other experiences or any special methods can possibly teach about the circumstances in which sex relations are most satisfying. Parents, then, must put their own house in order as best they can and must be willing, if they feel in danger of failing, to seek help for themselves as well as for their children. Their way of working out their problems as adults, the manner and direction of their own loving and hating, will, when all is said and done, be the paramount facts in their children's emotional development and happiness.

CHAPTER SEVEN

THINGS TO MAKE AND DO

EDUCATION DOES not wait for school. It begins with the infant's first experiences of the world and with all that he senses and does. Toys and play are far more than childish pastimes to be replaced as soon as possible by serious work and lessons; on the contrary, they have positive and intrinsic values, since they furnish the materials by which a child experiments and learns much about the fundamental nature of the world in which he finds himself.

A child will discover playthings whether or not we provide them; he will find them in places where we would be least likely to look—in parts of his own body, in the brass knob of his crib, in the contents of a wastebasket, in the mud puddle by the side of the road. From the time he is a few months old the child's activity is ceaseless and his interest in exploring and testing anything and everything is nothing short of prodigious. Through his activity he is training his senses and his powers of co-ordination and with amazing rapidity is gaining knowledge of a constantly expanding world. He should be encouraged in this yearning for adventure which carries him farther and farther on the road toward mastery of his environment.

The first thing parents must do is see that a child, even a young baby, has the opportunity to play with and make use of everything his natural surroundings offer. Store-bought playthings alone may be meaningless. They should be preceded and supplemented at every point by contact with ordinary objects and direct experiences. For the baby, this means crawling on the floor, pulling himself up by chairs and tables, prying into nooks, grasping and examining objects of all kinds to learn their uses and how best to move about without hurting either himself or the household belongings. A child needs to be allowed to explore as far as he can safely do so and he must learn, too, a few things that are forbidden. Parents should realize, however, that compliance to their rules and obedience concerning certain restrictions will not be learned overnight. Instructions and regulations must be made clear again and again, and even when a child "understands perfectly" what is expected of him, as we often say, he may still be too young to be able to check some of his own strong impulses. Until a child is three or four or older, it is usually more practical to provide actual physical supervision than to try to train for implicit obedience. There should be as few forbidden things as possible; and instead of trying to think up ways of preventing a child from doing what he wants we can try teaching him skills that protect him and encouraging him to go ahead for all his worth. "Don't go near the stairs," for example, can be replaced by instruction in how to use them safely by crawling down backward on all fours. A child as young as three can learn to strike matches correctly and in the presence of a grownup instead of struggling constantly with the temptation to experiment behind someone's back. The old gag, "Go see what the baby's doing and stop him," expresses the habitual attitude of the lazy or unresourceful mother.

WHAT TOYS SHALL I BUY MY CHILDREN?

Before anything else, a child needs direct experience with his immediate world. He needs toys, too; this means materials which enable him to live and relive his daily experiences, things that are his very own to play with in his crib, or bath, or play pen and later on to find on his own shelf or in a corner of the yard.

As long as shops offer playthings in such profusion and since children grow and change so quickly, a few criteria may help in choosing toys which will stand the test of time.

First, we must ask: Does it afford *opportunity for making and doing?* Does it lend itself to many different uses according to the child's own imagination and choice? Does it help to develop manual or bodily skill or—and this is equally important—does it stimulate emotional, artistic, and imitative expressions?

Second: Is it *suitable for the child's age?* Does the activity involved present a problem too easy to be stimulating or, on the other hand, a problem so far beyond a child's present powers that he becomes discouraged?

Third: Is it *sturdy* enough to last as long as the child's interest, and is it *practical and suitable* for our particular home or yard?

The toys suggested in the following list by no means include every possible object of interest to a child; they do, however, represent many that have been found especially desirable, tried and true. Most of them are equally valuable for boys and girls, though usually when children are around six or thereabouts the differences between the interests of boys and girls become more pronounced. It is well to let these choices take a natural course. A boy will not turn out to be a sissy because he plays with dolls, and a girl will not be a tomboy because she prefers carpentry to sewing. Some of the toys listed, notably dolls, books, and blocks, are likely to be of interest over the entire age range because they are adaptable to wide levels of development and to every taste and temperament. Children vary greatly in the ages at which they use certain play materials. This classification makes no claim to comprehensiveness, but offers a guide to approximately when a new activity may be introduced.

One to Two Years

Indoors
Soft, cuddly animals or simple dolls

Rubber balls
Boats or wagons—to pull on floor
Large pegboard
Trains of blocks
Picture books, magazines, catalogs
Large wooden spoons for beating on tins
Boxes with lids to put small objects in and out of
Bath toys

Outdoors
Kiddy-car
Express wagon, wooden
Wading pool
Push and pull toys
Sand toys to play with in earth

Two to Three Years
Indoors
Dolls with clothes to put on and take off
Doll carriage or bed with covers
Unbreakable tea set
Story books, crayons and paper
Small cars, simple trains (not electric)
Boats that float
Bean bags, large beads to string
Low table or work table

Outdoors
Pail and shovel, sandpile with awning
Wading pool

Swing with wide seat
Slide
Large packing case
Hollow blocks
Kegs
Wheelbarrow
Garden hose or sprinkler—water play of all kinds

Three to Four Years

Indoors

Box of large, unpainted wooden blocks in a variety of shapes
and sizes, well sandpapered or shellacked
Barnyard animals
Many small dolls or figurines to use in connection with
dollhouses, cars, barnyards, etc.
Storybooks with pictures—to be read aloud
Simple musical instruments of good tone—piano; record
player; nursery rhymes and other records (see catalogue)
Rhythm instruments—drums, cymbals, etc.
Small stoves, sweepers, dustpan, dishes, washtubs
Plasticine
Blunt scissors, paste, old magazines (to make scrapbooks)
Hammer and nails (to use on soft wood or soap)

Outdoors

Roller skates (wooden wheels for beginners)
Planks
Seesaws
Sled
Tricycle

Four to Six Years or Over

Indoors

Jars of a few good water colors
Muffin tins to mix colors in
Large paint brushes
Easel and paper
Metal trains on tracks (wind-up type, not electric)
Jigsaw puzzles—very simple
Doorway gym—swing, rings, trapeze
Dollhouse and furniture
"Dress up" box containing old scarfs, jewelry, costumes, dresses, etc.
Games—simple card games (slapjack), jackstraw, tiddly-winks, darts, ring-toss, etc.
Craft equipment of many kinds

Outdoors

(For children of six years or slightly over)
Jumping rope
"Softball"
Bicycle
Larger and sturdier wagons than those for younger children

PLAY—MANY MEANINGS AND MANY USES

We must remember that play is far more than intellectual or muscular learning; it is work, thought, art, relaxation, and feeling. Through it, emotions of many kinds are evoked. It enables children to experiment not only with the tangible universe, but with their relationships to other people and also with the inner world of their own feelings. Through play, they can give freer scope to emotions and desires which in the course of daily living they dare not express or feel they are forbidden. But in a world of make-believe they can say and do anything they feel and wish. Watch a small girl when she feels quite alone with a family of dolls—father, mother, sister, and baby brother. She is absorbed in trying to find out how it feels to be a mother, to tend and care for two small children, to love them and to guide and discipline them. We will find that children begin early to struggle with warring elements within themselves, and that the loving and tender impulses may alternate rapidly with cruel or wantonly destructive ones. Even a child who has never been roughly dealt with or spanked may take our breath away by beating her doll children unmercifully, as though such treatment were a commonplace and a matter of daily necessity in all families. Children's thirst for simple aggressive acts and their belief in the inevitability of anger and punishment are usually on display for almost anyone who will take the trouble to observe.

Children are best left to play freely at these times. Rather than a continuous attempt to influence a child's play or to mold it into forms which grownups consider desirable, parents should ask themselves, "From what need does this kind of play spring? What can I learn about this child by watching what he does when undirected?" Correction, if any, must take place within the child's whole relationship to life. Angry

[193]

feelings, destructive tendencies, and other manifestations which parents object to cannot be altered by curbing their external expression alone. They must be treated at the source if there is to be a fundamental change. If a child's life is full of opportunities for getting about and exploring his home and neighborhood, and if he has materials in his nursery for re-creating these experiences, he can, to a large extent, be left free to express himself as he will. Make-believe and dramatic activities of all kinds have real value, even when these activities express "bad" feelings. We cannot let children actually destroy their belongings, but we can permit them to *pretend* to be destructive. The child who beats her doll babies without conscience may be sparing herself the necessity for committing aggressions against real people or against herself.

Another word of warning about toys. Don't feel that all toys have to be taken with deadly seriousness as "educational material." It is true that the best ones are, and it is also true that most normal children, if free to choose, really enjoy this sort of education. But there is always the unpredictable in children's preferences, which should not be rejected because it does not fit our theory or standards. For example, a child may greatly prefer the objects on our dressing table, designed entirely for adult use, to those on his own toy shelf, or the contents of the kitchen cupboard to anything else we may try to substitute. Parents may discover again and again that a child will reject a charming Teddy bear as a going-to-bed companion, preferring instead some apparently meaningless object like an old and faded blanket. Somewhat older children are likely to be attracted by toys which enable them to express their native impulses to fight and punish. Guns, knives, battle-ships, and soldiers hold a perennial fascination, and there is little evidence for believing that these things play any part in predisposing children toward militarism. Nevertheless, many parents may prefer to play them down, feeling that our press, radio and T.V. are already offering too much in the way of violence.

It is interesting that the Soviet Union forbids the sale of war toys. Fragile tin toys with ragged edges, like some horns, are dangerous. There are also cheap mechanical gadgets so flimsy that they break down almost at once or come apart in a day or so.

Certain toys may offend an adult's sense of good taste or esthetics (I admit to an aversion to some grotesque dolls and T.V. characters popular today), but it would be rash to say that a child's taste suffers permanent corruption by such con-tacts. Taste is built slowly, over a period of years, and fortu-nately is not conditioned by a few bad experiences. I also have an aversion to large, clumsy, elaborate, and expensive toys, perhaps from motives of thrift but also because as a housewife I resent having to find storage space for things which give a child only momentary pleasure. An enormous stuffed elephant, for example, always stands around gath-ering dust because it is too big to put away. There are also large toy automobiles, very tempting at first, in which the child is supposed to pedal himself about. Unfortunately, he finds great difficulty in doing so because it is badly contrived me-chanically. Such automobiles offer nothing that a tricycle does not offer more satisfactorily. An expensive costume

THE PARENTS' MANUAL

doll with one elaborate peasant dress, from which an adult gets great pleasure, usually offers less long-run pleasure to a five-year-old than the simpler doll with a trunkful of machine-made dresses that correspond to a little girl's own experience of what clothing should be. Though children need a variety of toys, easily accessible on low shelves, too great a profusion of them is useless and distracting. Some should be put away for a rainy day, so to speak, for convalescence, or for any period when the familiar objects of the child's daily life need a little revamping.

PLAYING HARD AND WORKING HARD

Parents often want to be told for how long a time children should be expected to play alone and how to train them to be willing to do so. The answer can only be settled by watching to see what each child can tolerate. Merely forcing a child to remain alone, no matter how he protests, does not necessarily get results, even if it is started in earliest infancy. Most normal children crave human companionship. Nothing that they might do alone seems to interest them nearly so much as just being with people. When they are young, this means Mother. Parents should realize that they will rarely be left undisturbed for long though their resourcefulness in directing a child to a fascinating pursuit may win them some time. Yet parents must take care not to yield altogether, but should try instead to direct the child's attention to the pleasures of making and doing things alone or to the possibilities for pleasure in active play with other children. Those who bask in adult attention and surrender to just being entertained are not developing either mastery over their physical world or social experience in the everyday give-and-take that exists only between equals. Independence in play comes through interest in the task itself, and while in some children it seems to come as an altogether natural outcropping, in others it is built only over a period of time and requires a good deal of help from someone who can keep the goal constantly in mind.

Learning to Play Alone

It must be remembered, too, that the attention of small children is necessarily limited. Very few year-old babies will play alone for an hour or so in any constructive way. Sometimes they fall asleep on the floor of their play pens, gnaw the rail, or sit moodily sucking their thumbs. Still more likely, after twenty minutes or half an hour they start to fuss and then to howl. Parents had best abandon their more rigid notions in this matter and find out what is the most practical plan for their own individual baby. Usually if they make a judicious selection of several playthings for him to keep in his pen, or arrange his room when he reaches the runabout age so that he cannot do constant damage when left on his own, he will learn to play by himself for ten or twenty minutes or perhaps even for an hour or so. To avoid arousing stubbornness through enforced periods too long for the child to tolerate, it may be best for the mother to reappear from time to time with a suggestion for some new way of play, thus reassuring him, by the mere fact of her appearance, that he is not condemned forever to solitary confinement.

Somewhat older children often become deeply interested for long periods in what they are doing. "I have to work now," says the small boy who wants his mother's visitor to stop annoying him with frivolous questions about his age, or with comments on how fast he grows, and let him get back to his block building. Watching him, we find that he brings to it all of the intense concentration and seriousness of a trained engineer. We would give a lot to know the formula for preserving this joy in work and this ability to bring every ounce of energy to whatever problem is at hand. Occasionally this concentration manages to survive growing up; there are a few fortunate people for whom work continues to be a compelling adventure compared to which "play," as adults mean it, has little to offer. But whether the fault lies within ourselves because of a slowing down of our vital forces, or in our educational system, or in the defects of modern civilization, we must still face the fact that such concentration of energy is likely to be short-lived. It is a tragically brief time until "play" is what you like doing and "work" what you have to do.

"My Child Won't Stick to Anything"

While for many untroubled youngsters this evil day is long postponed, there are others who even when young show a lessening of interest in play. They become easily distracted and refuse to overcome minor obstacles. This may be because they need to get away from toys and nurseries and re-turn again and again to direct, personal experiences. This is rule number one for stimulating activity in seemingly bored children. Play materials, at best, merely offer them a chance to re-create. If they see someone washing in the kitchen, their own toy washtub takes new meaning. A visit to an air-port makes toy airplanes new again. How can a child con-tinue to enjoy a toy barnyard when he has never known what a real one is?

Sometimes, however, in spite of everything we may do, a child seems unable to play hard. "He gets discouraged too easily," parents say. "He won't play long at any one thing." They hope for some way of "teaching concentration." Later, when the same tendencies appear in schoolwork, they are increasingly disturbed and accuse the school of failing to in-still "good study habits" early. But teaching concentration is nothing so simple as training and practice. Concentration itself is a combination of many things; it is not a simple fac-ulty that can be instilled by repeated practice, like piano scales. It depends upon interest and the ability to integrate interest. We cannot teach a child to be an absorbed block builder by merely setting him down with his materials when he doesn't want to use them, any more than we can get re-sults by setting a child down before a paper with arithmetic sums when his mind is woolgathering.

The answer to the question of how you *do* get results is likely to be different for each child. A child who is habitually inattentive and whose interest fluctuates far more than is usual for his years is probably daydreaming, and almost anything may go on in the mind of the daydreaming child. He may be absorbed in dreams of himself performing heroic or difficult feats, with the result that this vision gives him so much satisfaction that he is unable to attend to anything else. He may be busy, on the other hand, with thoughts of revenge against a playmate or a younger brother or sister, or with anger toward a parent or teacher. He may be puzzling about sexual matters, or he may be preoccupied with other obsessive thoughts which refuse to be banished. Children rarely confess their thoughts to their parents, so it is hard to get at what is going on. Nevertheless, ability to concentrate comes only when the child stops living in a world of fantasy and is able to attend to the matter at hand. Usually he does this in his own way and time, especially if the circumstances of his life offer the opportunity for happy relations to family and friends of many kinds and also encouragement to wider experiences and the development of whatever skills his interests may lead him to. But if distractibility is extreme and persists long into the school years so that school failure threatens to be added to already existing problems, it may be wise to call for professional psychiatric advice.

Keeping Interest Alive

In the average case, however, the following suggestions are likely to prove helpful in stimulating initiative and activity.

1. Try playing with a child long enough to get him well under way. Start a block building of your own, for ex-

ample. Since interest is contagious, get very excited about it. Then help him get started on his own.

2. When he meets an obstacle and his interest threatens to disappear, step in without delay and help him find a way out so that he can go on again immediately, or offer something entirely new. What he needs, however, may be not· new materials but new experiences in the real world.

3. Be sure also that your plans for him are not too ambitious. Take an interest even in humble products. Gear your standards to his *actual* level of achievement, not to what you think children his age should do. Raise these standards gradually.

4. Watch for any signs of spontaneous interest in some unexpected phase of living. Then try to help him find related activities. An interest in pets, for example, starting as nothing more than pleasure in the looks and feel or amusing quality which they have, can, with skill, be extended into a wider study of animal life and animal habits, and later on into the making of collections of insects or butterflies, which in turn will involve the construction of cages and other equipment, and so on into many other ramifications. One child who was interested only in his pets and who neglected everything at school developed his first impulse toward books when a skillful teacher showed him how much more he could add to his knowledge of animals if he could read.

[201]

5. The presence of other children who are not too much his superior in achievement may stimulate a child's interest in doing things and rouse his previously dormant ambitions.

6. Be sure that in your desire to make your child happy you don't use playtime for merely amusing him while he looks on passively. Get him to do as much as possible himself, stimulating your child to be active and creative as you play with him.

7. Don't press him beyond the fatigue point or get irritable if he doesn't live up to what you want. Be ready to call it a day when he wants to.

8. Remember always that parents are teachers and that teachers differ in their skill with children and their ability to inspire enthusiasm. Don't conclude that you just haven't got it. You can learn. Visiting a nursery school and watching the teachers for a week or so may give you lots of useful ideas that can be adapted to home conditions.

9. Be patient. Many normal children go through periods of daydreaming and inability to sustain attention for long. This does not mean that you should not try to help. As has already been suggested, you may need to give the most effort to trying to improve your child's satisfaction with his life *as a whole;* otherwise he may become so preoccupied with his discontents that he cannot turn his energies outward.

Children need plenty of chance to play with other children, but they are lucky if they have parents who do things with them, too. Fathers and mothers who enjoy hobbies or handicrafts are in a better position to hand these things on to their children, and the sharing of these pleasures goes a long way in building basically happy relations and often eliminates family friction at many points.

Hobbies

If a child's father has always been a nature lover, if he is the kind who is always making discoveries in fields and woods, if he works in a garden, or knows something about stars, it will be natural for him to include his growing children in these pleasures, though usually an interest in "nature" is not very characteristic of childhood. Parents who love music or books stimulate the love of music and literature in their children more easily than others. Those who love hiking are most successful at developing similar enthusiasms in their children. Usually this is true, not always. Sometimes a child refuses to see the fun in our own pet hobbies, and in this case, though it is harder, we must help him find others of his own which may not be ours at all.

But it is not necessary for parents to have a fully developed or unusual hobby in order to draw children into their activities. A mother who can sing even a little should do so and should encourage her child to listen and imitate. For the youngest child, nothing in music education takes the place of singing songs himself. A mother does not have to possess a "voice," as long as her memory is well stocked with nursery rhymes or popular songs—and she is able to sing in tune. She should sing often and freely while the child is dressing and undressing, going to bed, or riding in the automobile. If she does this, the child will soon follow both tune and words and will learn to think of music as an inevitable part of life.

Even small children can acquire rudimentary skill in the ordinary cooking or sewing that goes on in a household. Children of five or six can roll out dough and pat it into biscuits for baking in a small pan while their mothers are busy with the larger supply. While their elders do more complicated dressmaking, they can sew patterns with bright wools on colored materials. They can help make beds, set the table, dust, and clean—and their pride and pleasure in their home is all the greater. Besides these things, parents should investigate the possibilities for themselves among a child's possessions. Most grownups have forgotten what fun it is to lay out a barnyard, with house, garage, an auto, fenced-in fields, and animals, and to take the farm produce on the "truck" to be loaded on the "train" for city markets. They may be surprised, too, to find that with their child's paintbox and easel, or with ordinary crayons, they can make pictures in which they become genuinely absorbed. Clay or plasticine are fun for grownups. Try making a flat "man" in the gingerbread manner, while the children are rolling "worms" or "balls" of these materials. Always let a child work out his ideas while you work at yours. Don't try to make him copy you. Working together is stimulating and lots of fun, but it should not mean just imitating each other.

Getting Out

No matter how fine a child's home may be or how perfectly it is equipped with the most "educational" toys, he will still need to expand his horizon to include some of the outside world as well. Parents who have a tendency to "surround children only with what is beautiful and lovely," under strictly hygienic conditions, seriously cramp their lives. An ivory-tower existence limits growth. Children are soon able to take good stiff doses of reality in a world full of noise and dirt. Even out of apparent confusion they can select certain things that have meaning for them, without damaging either health or nerves. Resistance to infection is not built up by living in cotton wool, but by gradual exposure to the ordinary germs around us.

From the age of two on, unless there are special circumstances, a child should have a chance to ride in trains, busses, streetcars, or subways; to explore the neighborhood of his own home; to stop to look in shopwindows or to stroke a kitten; to join other dirtier children at play; to hang around while workmen mix cement; to watch a steam shovel digging the foundations of a new building. Parks and playgrounds offer opportunities for certain kinds of development, but wharves offer another—wharves where boats leave for unknown parts, with cargo for distant cities. There are also other industrial processes which, as time goes on, can enrich a child's experience—his father's office or factory has special charms, and so does a visit to a bottling plant for milk or ginger ale, or something else with which he is familiar. It is fun to take a familiar object—like milk, for example—and trace it to its source. Before it came to the table it was in a big bottle in the ice chest, and before that it was brought to the front door by a milkman who drove a truck. If you're awake in the early morning you can look out and see the milk truck stop and see the man lift the bottles out and put them by the door. And before the bottles got into the truck, the milk came in huge cars from the dairy farm in the country.

Country children should, whenever possible, have a chance to see cities and to know where the food they see growing in the fields goes to be distributed and to be bought by women in markets. City children need to reverse the process, and most children are hungry for these everyday facts about the daily processes of their lives. Such knowledge stimulates everything they do. A New York child who has made a round-Manhattan trip on an excursion boat, seen the wharves of the transatlantic liners in the Hudson, visited the Statue of Liberty in the harbor, rounded the end of the island, and passed under the bridges of the East River has a new incentive for play at home. With blocks, boats, toy autos, and anything else at hand, he may lay out his own Manhattan and carry on commerce for days. He has seen the world widen far beyond the walls of his room and he has also brought the world back into it, to digest and enjoy. Toys grow meaningless if they are not constantly supplemented by experience.

BOOKS AND LEARNING TO READ

Nowadays, parents are in a hurry to teach children their letters and often want them to learn to read at a time of life when firsthand experience has far more to offer than book learning. They become overanxious for fear their children will never learn to read or are sensitive if they do not learn as fast as a neighbor's child. They seem to feel that achievement in this respect is the very sign and symbol of mental alertness—which it is not. Yet, when the world of books opens, it is certainly a further stimulus. Homes which naturally have books around, parents who read themselves and read to their children, are the best foundation for learning to love books. But the child must also have matured inwardly to the point of readiness. Until this readiness exists, children need no formal instruction. Some, of course, are ready earlier than others, and we can then help them go ahead. Many of the alleged dangers of premature bookishness have been exaggerated, but it cannot be denied that certain children who are confronted with the necessity of facing difficult personal problems—notably their relation to other children— may make use of reading as a ready avenue of escape. Even under these circumstances, however, by no means curtail your child's reading. You might, at times, try to find other outlets for him if he spends every spare moment with his books, but, in general, reading should be encouraged.

Picture and story books fill a very real need for children over two, especially picture books about the familiar here and now. Young children particularly seem to prefer trains, policemen, automobiles, and grocery stores to the fanciful and the far away. Animal pictures are always in demand, but for city children should be supplemented by visits to the farm or zoo. Similarly, books about fire engines and trains will mean more to a country child after he has seen them. The need for a thorough grounding in the facts of his immediate life seems to guide the youngest child's literary choices, and it is surprising how often the advertising section of a magazine or a well-illustrated but prosaic department-store or mail-order catalogue is preferred to anything else. Picture books, of course, carry captions and simple texts, and reading aloud to a child can begin early, provided it is done slowly, with plenty of time allowed for conversation and comments.

Tell Them a Story

Children love storytelling, some more than reading. The youngest child especially enjoys a retelling of the simplest events of the day. "The doorbell rang, ting-a-ling-a-ling. Joan opened it. The postman had left a letter. I said to Joan, 'Hurry, hurry, Joan, I want my letter. It must be from grandmother.' And then you brought it in and I knew right away that it was, because grandmother writes in a special way that nobody else writes. I opened it and grandmother wrote, 'Give Joan a great big hug and kiss from me and tell her—' " and so on.

For most children, however, the time comes when the fantastic and imaginative hold a unique position and meet a need that reality cannot fill. "Here-and-now stories" orient the growing personality to the realities of living, but the make-believe world of fairy tales, where anything can happen, is a welcome release from reality and offers equally fundamental experiences. It is wise, however, to postpone them until a child can recognize the stories as "pretend." Folk tales, whether they are beautiful, or stark and cruel, have contributed to the culture of nations and are part of our literary heritage. If some children show that they are afraid of these stories, they should not hear them until they are older and no longer distressed by them, and can accept the cruel step-mother, the wicked witch in the oven, and Red Riding Hood's Wolf, even displaying a lusty relish for the gory details. Rhymes and jingles and nonsense of all kinds offer their own delights. Rhythm is pleasure in and for itself. Mother Goose, while almost completely obsolete in content and often incomprehensible to a twentieth-century child, is enjoyable anyway and needs no apologies or explanations.

I have a few pet hopes for children and also some *hope-nots,* at least for the very young ones.

SOME HOPES

I would hope that children under six should *not* go to the movies. If they must go it should be very seldom, perhaps to an animated cartoon, remaining in the theater no more than twenty minutes or half an hour. Even if their older brothers and sisters go, the younger children can be taught that the time has not yet come for them. I would hope that their T.V. diet be limited to what is truly good and suitable to their ages. These media are strong stuff, a highly exciting stimulant, and in general it is true that the more we depend on having thrills shot into us while we sit passive, the less effort we are likely to exert to create our own pleasures. Effort is an important element of growth, and it can be preserved or crippled. Movies and television must be accepted as part of our civilization, but we must exert control and selection in their use, instead of merely wringing our hands when our children first discover them. There are now some excellent programs. These will have a legitimate place in the life of the child.

There has been much alarm about whether continuous exposure to crime and violence incites children to delinquency, even where it is shown that "crime does not pay." Though these are not claimed as the sole or even the main cause of juvenile crime, we are right to question such a constant diet of violence. For the ill-balanced child, they are especially dangerous. Even for the "normal" child, too much viewing of gun-play, slugging, and killing is questionable. Though some children sleep soundly even after a hair-raising thriller, some do not, and we. shall have to act accordingly, helping a child see the common sense of our refusal to let him listen to or view a program that always arouses anxiety or terror. Parents are often afraid to take a strong stand when they really should. Let us hope that absorption in ready made thrills can be postponed for several years and that they do *not* assume too-large proportions in these early years when, with a little help, a child can find de-light and satisfaction through his own activities.

And some hopes:

Just for Fun

First, of course, let us hope that we make use of play to preserve joy in life as long as possible. This presupposes that parents can draw upon their own humor and flexibility and can find a place for the perfectly ridiculous as well as for the genuinely educational. I took my own five-year-old to the zoo. She had a wonderful time, but the high spot that made the day positively glorious was not the seals, nor the elephant, nor even the giant panda. It was a baby's pacifier, dirty and old, dropped from a perambulator. She pounced on this and treasured it above all else as a memory of that day. We took it home, I boiled it for ten minutes, and then figuratively shut my eyes and let nature take its course, which it did in a quite violent addiction to the object for several days.

Another hope is that all children may have pets. Dogs are perhaps not especially suitable for children much younger than seven or eight. They are not yet mature enough to take the responsibility for a dog's care and are too egotistical to appreciate and satisfy a dog's need for love. These things come later, and for many children there is a time when a dog makes an important contribution to their whole emotional expansion. But kittens are cuddly and comforting and can soon take care of themselves; they will not tolerate cruelty as a dog will, and cruelty is common in many young children. Anything living which needs some care and appeals to a child because it is strange or beautiful or soft or adorable does some thing for him that mere knowledge "about" these same things cannot do. Not only kittens and rabbits, but birds or alligators, turtles, fish, and even ants can be housed success-fully. Some families have been successful with snakes, lizards, toads, and other creatures that are not usually domesticated. White mice, though they smell, have a charm of their own and are much nicer than rats. They are gentle and pretty and their habits of reproduction are adequate but not excessive. When children are still young they should not be expected to assume full responsibility for their pets' care. They will need help, and parents might as well reconcile themselves to taking an active interest and doing a good deal them-selves. Children will follow the parents' lead and can eventu-ally take over.

HOLIDAYS

And still another hope is that parents should remain simple enough to preserve and perpetuate the holiday spirit in their homes, celebrating the more significant ones in ways that have meaning, developing the art of infusing enthusiasm into their children so that they will be moved to join in fully.

The Fourth of July is a good chance for a picnic, but is that enough? When I was young there was always a small American flag at each child's place at breakfast and a larger one that was ceremoniously hoisted on a flagpole besides. Watching it flutter to the top filled me with a pride which has grown, I hope, in depth. Today I would hope to see the flag of the United Nations flown with it. I would also hope that all American children would be told the story of the signing of the Declaration of Independence, Liberty Bell and all, and that parts at least of this great document would be read aloud to them and discussed with them. But I would hope, too, that early in life they would become aware of the goal of peace and brotherhood among nations and the agencies which need our support. We have fallen into the habit of neglecting symbols and ceremonials, but I doubt if we have found better ways of giving dramatic emphasis to great events.

Birthdays

Unless people are very bored with living or have a fundamental distaste for the part they play in life, the chances are that they will want their birthdays noted and celebrated, regardless of age. The particular charm of birthdays is that they do *not* commemorate a great event, but only the fact that our own birthday is great for us and for those who love us. They are deliberately unrealistic. Birthdays pick out an individual from the mass and celebrate his existence, regardless of his achievements or his real significance to the world. They are necessary festivals to any people who believe in their hearts in the dignity and importance of every individual, including themselves, and who are healthy enough to hold to this belief all their lives in the face of all evidence to the contrary. This individualistic, irrational character of birthday parties is their peculiar charm. The wish to celebrate them springs from different sources than the wish that

[213]

prompts the celebration of national or religious festivals, but they serve our needs in equally essential ways.

Christmas

For most people, Christmas is a holiday that goes on being more deeply felt than any other. Because commercial interests advertise it and exploit it almost beyond endurance, many grownups would really prefer to ignore the entire procedure. They find it merely boring and exhausting, something that must be kept up "on account of the children" and sensibly and quietly dropped when they grow up. But even if we never saw gift catalogues, department-store decorations, or public reminders of any kind, even if we had no children, most of us would somehow feel it still at Christmastime and long to recapture something the day once meant to us.

Christmas is a holiday that in its fundamentals offers as much to old as to young. When the day comes, no matter how cruelly the events of the world have seemed to deny its message, the impulse stirs in us again to make it live. We feel the need to yield ourselves to the loveliness of old observances, for it is these things that make Christmas and its meanings come alive again and glow. Too many tired moderns are content to regard the day only as a chance to sleep late in the morning and have a big dinner or cocktail party later. These things may be good, but they will never yield a thrill comparable to that of a Christmas tree laden with colored balls and lights and topped by a shimmering star of Bethlehem, of Christmas carols sung faultily by the familiar voices of our own friends, of the moment when the doorbell rings to tell us that someone we love has come home for Christmas, of stockings by the fireplace, bursting with ridiculous shapes and bulges, of the general profusion and lavishness of gifts tied in gay packages, gifts that do *not* have to be expensive and that, with ingenuity, *can* be made to fit any middle-income budget. But here, too, whether or not we speak of it, there must be some remembrance of what it is all about—possibly, under the tree, some figures of virgin and child in a stable, of shepherds and animals and wise men, bought perhaps at the five-and-ten. Chapter II of the Gospel according to St. Luke is one of the simpler pieces of the world's great literature; it is a pity when children never hear it in their homes and adults have forgotten it. It is the greatest pity of all when human beings lose the will to make merry at their own hearths to celebrate a time that perennially has power to cast its charm so far.

Jewish families have their own beautiful Hanukkah festival, which comes around the same time of year as Christmas, and which, like Christmas, is to be celebrated with joy and knowledge of its ancient significance. My personal hope is that a Christian child may be invited to a Jewish home to see this at first hand—and that the invitation is reciprocated.

These are the experiences that bind human beings in homes and homes in nations. If we lose them as a people we stand in danger of losing our soul, and the road to getting it back again may be a long and tragic journey.

CHAPTER EIGHT

THE FORGOTTEN FATHER

CHILDREN NEED FATHERS as well as mothers; not only that, they need them from the earliest years. Fathers are necessary for the best development of children, not just as providers, but also because they are essential contributors to the child's sound emotional growth. Modern life has so profoundly altered some of the traditional relations between fathers and their households that, without thought and planning, the father threatens to fade out of the picture altogether. In homes where the number of hours a day that the father spends with his children is seriously curtailed, it becomes all the more vital that the quality of his relations to his children be good. What small amount of time he has with them must be made to count.

OLD HOMES AND NEW

In the old-fashioned home the father was usually the head of the household. He made decisions, his wife carried them out. Authority was vested in him; he meted out punishment or approval, and his wishes were paramount. Doubtless the henpecked husband has existed in every age, and in every century and civilization there have been capable or shrewd women who knew how to get what they wanted. But today fact and theory alike have been shifted. Men, it is true, are still in most cases the financial heads of the family; they determine the size of the budget and hold the veto power over expenditures. But in all other respects the wife is likely to rule. It is she who chooses a home, plans the decorations according to her own tastes, and buys the furnishings. In many cases the husband occupies the position of a star boarder, whose wishes are carefully attended to but who is spared much knowledge of the daily ups and downs of the household. Most important of all is the fact that, while a father's affections may be as strong as a mother's and while he may greatly enjoy his children's companionship when he "has time," he has come to regard them primarily as his wife's responsibility rather than his own.

Dominant Women

Today it is apt to be the mother who supervises the children's education, visits the school, attends parent-teacher meetings, and exerts the greatest influence when the choice of school or college is made. She is also disciplinarian in chief. She makes the rules and imposes penalties. Not only are the smaller children her proper domain; she also has the say-so as to whether Mary, aged eight, should be allowed to go to any movie she likes, or how late Mary's sixteen-year-old brother should stay out nights. She is supposed to see that piano practicing is done and that all the thank-you letters for gifts are written. Perhaps it has always been true that the management of daily routines and the task of imposing duties have fallen largely on the mother as the homemaker, but today the ultimate control over children continues to be shifted more and more to her shoulders, with the result that the child's whole moral education tends to be taken over by women. When this happens, the mother rather than the father becomes the source of the child's conscience, and children often grow up believing that women are born to be the world's real bosses. Does such a belief tend to breed passive men and aggressive women? What children think of fathers may be pleasant or unpleasant, as the case may be, but the relationship is too often superficial. It lacks the stuff of which realistic knowledge of another human being can be built.

Obviously many of the reasons for this shift are to be found within the structure of our society. The simple fact is that fathers are away from home most of the day and sometimes in the evening, too. Many never get home for lunch, and contacts with their children are limited to weekends. The principle of the division of labor operates to divide fathers from their families, and each parent has his own separate orbit which rarely overlaps the other's. A man's business is money-making, and this, in modern life, takes him away from home; a woman's business is to bring up children and manage the household. A man expects his wife to be expert with children, and is inclined to hold her responsible when things go wrong. She is like the head of a department or a special consultant whom he may have engaged in his business, responsible for slip-ups in office efficiency.

The trouble is that a home and a business are two entirely different things, and definite dangers lie in trying to model the one after the other. Neither a home nor a child can be regarded as a job to be efficiently administered. In managing both, there is a place for efficiency and a place for expert and specific knowledge, but the purposes are entirely different. In business the object is commercial profit, in the home it is the happiness and spiritual growth of the individuals involved. No matter how well it is managed, a home that does not promote these things is a failure. Success with children does not depend on "efficient methods" or on "good training," although these things have their value, but on the capacity for a warm and living relationship with human beings.

Perhaps the first necessity is to face frankly the real losses imposed on family life and on children especially by modern society and our highly organized industrial development. The father was far less separated from his family in past generations. Even in some smaller individualistic communities today (which we would like to preserve if we knew how) the father remains very much a full-time member of the family. His shop or place of work was often a part of his house or was located near by. Moreover—and this is perhaps even more important—his children ran in and out of his shop; so did his wife. All had a real idea of what a man's work was like. The work itself was far simpler and easier to understand than the job of today. Buying and selling, the handling and the banking of money, and the employment of a few clerks and assistants were highly concrete, and a man, as someone with certain responsibilities in a larger scheme, became a very real and impressive person to children.

"What Does Your Father Do?"

Today many children have never been near their father's place of work, or if they do go there they come away without having gained any idea of what it is all about. Try to explain to a young child, or even an older one, what a broker does, or an insurance salesman, or a bookkeeper for the gas company. This does not mean that the attempt to explain should not be made or that the usefulness of the work is not real. The point is that being a cog in a huge industrial machine is less dramatic and less impressive to a child than running a small shop or being a blacksmith, with skills a child naturally envies, or being a farmer who must plow and plant and fertilize the soil.

Though we must try to help children understand, the modern child has lost more than mere knowledge of actual processes. In the old days growing children could help their fathers at work, and could take more and more part themselves as they matured, thus serving a kind of apprenticeship. Even the very young child could be left to mind the store for a short time while the father went out. Younger children could help empty packing boxes, put goods on shelves, and run necessary errands. But it is one thing to play some part in the solemn business of earning a living, with a man for a boss, and something else to have your share of the work in the family limited to running errands for your mother. These frequent contacts with their fathers in the performance of a man's work had values for children which we cannot match. Through them, children saw specifically the whys and wherefores of hard work, self-control, honesty, and other essential virtues. They learned quickly the good sense behind such secondary virtues as neatness, punctuality, courtesy, and the rest. They saw their fathers practice these things even in the face of fatigue and discouragement and knew that a man's livelihood depended upon his capacity to see things through. Even in the best of schools we have found no substitute for this kind of moral education. It is hard to make the importance of getting a good mark as real to children as the necessity for keeping the good will of a valued customer. Sitting up nights to prepare for an examination may be a responsibility of prime importance, but in terms of meaning to the child it cannot be compared with the need to stay up in order to get goods on the shelves for visitors coming to town for the county fair.

These losses should not be minimized. If these things are gone for good, what can be done to make up for them? Is there justice in the frequent complaint that young people today seem comparatively immature, and can this perhaps be blamed on the fact that they have no chance to share responsibility with a mature person?

ANY WIFE TO ANY HUSBAND— AND VICE VERSA

Fortunately, not all fathers are of the absentee variety. There are plenty who take delight in their children's presence and share eagerly even in the care of the baby. But many postpone it, having the erroneous idea that babies and young children certainly need mothers, but can easily dispense with fathers—having forgotten that it is in the earliest years that foundations for the future are built. The father who wants his school- or college-age son for a companion has a better chance if he begins with his infant. Though there will always be some division of labor between parents, with the major responsibility for physical care and routine management falling on the mother, even the youngest child, if given a chance, will develop a feeling for his father that is quite different from his feeling for his mother. For example, both will know each other better if the father, when he deliberately sets out to cultivate a close acquaintance with an infant's needs, knows how to change a diaper and occasionally *does* change one or gives a bath or sees to the toilet routine or manages a meal. The gains for both are real. Also, he should not have to call for help the moment something out of the ordinary arises or the child gets out of hand. If he develops the ability to see through whatever he undertakes, he and his child will emerge knowing each other better. It is worth while for a child to discover not only that his father is a capable person outside the house, but that he can also assume household authority.

But what often happens is that the young mother, though she thinks she wants help with the children and says that she does, is inclined to be overanxious—especially with her first baby—and begins to interfere the moment her husband shows signs of a quickening parental instinct. For example:

Wife (to her husband): "I'm driving over to Mother's this

evening. She hasn't been feeling well. I'd stay overnight and come back in the morning if I thought you could do without me here."

Husband: "Go ahead, stay. I'll get Tommy to bed."

Wife: "But that means giving him a bath, and tonight's his night for a shampoo. He screams frightfully; could you ever manage?"

Husband: "Let the shampoo wait till tomorrow. I guess I can manage a two-year-old in his bath."

Wife: "The screen at the window has to be arranged a special way before he goes to sleep; otherwise something makes shadows on the ceiling that frighten him. Can you get his diapers smooth? Because he won't sleep if you don't. Oh, and there aren't any more clean pajamas in his drawer. You'll have to fish one out of the machine—Are you listening?"

Husband: "Yes, yes, of course. I tell you I'll manage. Does it really take so much more than common sense to put a child to bed?" (Exasperation and a take-it-or-leave-it manner is beginning to creep in.)

Wife (irritability rising): "Why do you act as though there were nothing to know about a baby? You offer to help but you won't pay any attention to things that are absolutely essential. Do you think I could have a moment's peace while I was away if . . ." (and so on and so on).

By this time the husband is sulking behind his newspaper and his wife has the martyred feeling that she is completely indispensable at all times and must therefore forgo personal pleasures.

Advice to Wives: When your husband makes a proposition like this, take him up with appreciation and expressions of confidence. Don't raise óbstacles and deluge him at once with minute directions. Just before you go he is likely to ask you some questions or accept some *simple* suggestions. Make up your mind that a number of things won't be done just your way and some may not be done at all. They are not as important as you think. Not nearly as important as the fact that father and child have a chance to get acquainted in a new way. Only those who have assumed the actual management of a child's routines can really learn to know him.

Advice to Husbands: Don't be stubborn. Making a child comfortable isn't just a matter of common sense. There are certain things to know, and you shouldn't be too proud to learn them. Your wife's peace of mind while she's away depends on her feeling that you have given these things their just consideration.

Try Getting Together First

A common fault of fathers that mothers especially resent is the habit of suddenly arriving at some momentous decision involving the children, without full knowledge of the facts. For example, a father may come home with tickets for the circus and have his four-year-old round-eyed with excitement over visions of elephants and acrobats before he has learned that the doctor has forbidden the circus because of a particularly virulent flu epidemic. Naturally it is hard for the mother to have to play the role of wet blanket. Or, on the other hand, a father may come impulsively to the conclusion that his three-year-old son is being pampered and needs a stronger hand. He orders that lights must be out and doors must be closed in the child's room after bedtime, regardless of screams, believing that drastic treatment is all that is necessary. He may have forgotten that the three-year-old has been having nightmares, that he has been upset since his former sitter left, that he is having a hard time getting used to the new baby, and that though his wife seems to be overindulging him she may have her reasons.

The mother, however, is not always in the right. Even when she strongly disagrees with her husband she should get over the idea that compromise means having things all her own way. Sometimes she should give in and concede that the father has as much right to rear his children according to his lights as she has, and the child will have to take his chances. No matter how sure she may be that he is all wrong, it may very well turn out that his way has much to recommend it after all. It is surprising, too, how often different people get quite different results with children when they apparently pursue exactly the same course. Sometimes the "wrong" method may work where the "right" method fails, because it is the quality of the relationship rather than the procedure alone that counts. When it comes to getting co-operation from a child, the *method* is always of minor importance; the *relationship* between parent and child is everything. A mother will be in despair because her two-year-old ate all his dinner when his father gave it to him, after doing nothing but dawdle and stall for her.

"But my husband did just the same things I always do," she

protests. "Why will the baby eat for him and not for me?"

There is, of course, some justice in the mother's complaint that the father seldom has to cope with his child in his difficult moments. Many fathers who are absent all day appear in the evening as a treat for their children. It is safe to say that fathers never really know their children until they have enough to do with their daily routines to take them beyond the delightful-stranger stage. An occasional full day with their children, if possible in the absence of the mother, is certainly to be recommended.

Father's Companionship

In spite of the difficulties that modern life places in the way of close relations between fathers and children, there are things to do which may take the place of the older customs, at least to some extent. The father's busyness is seldom the determining factor we think it is. "If you want to get something done, go to the busiest person you know and ask him to do it." This is an old and sound piece of advice, and the busiest fathers are frequently those who have most time for their children. Obstacles are not insurmountable when the father really cares, but this caring must go beyond mere financial anxiety about the welfare and future of his family; it means enjoying the society of his children as they are today and spontaneously seeking them out. This capacity for enjoyment, as has already been intimated, can grow by what it feeds on. Many fathers, like mothers, discover their children slowly. In the early stages they will need to make a conscious effort to find work and play which they can share.

Here are a few suggestions for the busy father, for use with either a son or daughter:

1. Breakfast together as soon as the child can sit in a high-chair. Even if the baby has already finished his breakfast, he can have another piece of bread or some milk at the family table.

2. Some time together in the evening if schedules can possibly be arranged. Quiet activity—not too much rough play and shouting. Bedtime stories can be a father's specialty.

3. Child in and out of bedroom while father is dressing. Conversation while he is shaving.

4. For part of Sundays or other holidays it is to be hoped that a father can find time to play with his child in his own room or wherever he feels most free and easy. This does not mean merely watching the child at play, but actually taking part. Indoors this may mean trying a hand at block building, playing with automobiles, playing dolls and "house," drawing pictures, doing cutouts, looking at, reading, and talking about books. Making something that lasts and that develops from day to day has special value; for example, a scrapbook, or a block structure that is left intact for a week or so and on which both father and child have worked. Activities, of course, must be related to the child's age, development, and interests. The father's own hobby, if he has one, comes to mean much to the child. Carpentry, photography, automobile mechanics, books, pictures, and

collections of all kinds can usually be made interesting to both boys and girls.

From the earliest years, when they can just watch or pass a tool or hold a light, children can be made to feel that they are welcome when their father is at work so long as they observe the rules and do not spoil things. Fathers must realize, however, that patience is an absolute essential in helping their children develop skills. Progress will be slow, interest will fluctuate, carelessness will be evident, rules will be "forgotten"—children, in short, will act like children. The father who requires the utmost order and precision in his shop will find it difficult to tolerate a four- or five-year-old with his incessant questions and inevitable clumsiness. Standards that are too high or a determination to have things done just so or not at all will discourage or frighten a child into a sense of inadequacy. There must be a spirit of compromise with childish weaknesses whenever parents and children do anything together. In helping a child to improve, be careful not to gear your demands so high or to let your attitude become so full of tension and disapproval that you spoil his incentive and pleasure.

5. Outdoor activities: All the good old skills of running, jumping, catching, and throwing; kicking, climbing, and handicap races. If the father was once a member of the old team, let him show his skill. If parents like one particular sport, the children may first enjoy watching and then may be given an opportunity to try their own powers.

Trips to water fronts, airports, fire stations, factories, and all the *ordinary* sights of the town may offer as much as museums. (Calls on adult relatives or parents' friends are not much fun for children unless the relative is one who knows what interests children. Don't think you are doing something for your child when you take him along on a solemn walk, or to visit friends of *your* choice on whom you want him to make a good impression. He is likely to be whiny and irritable, and both your spirits and your ego will suffer.)

6. A trip to his father's office or place of work is almost an essential for a child. Let him see where you spend your day, and explain what you do as clearly as possible. Let him touch machinery or use a typewriter. Be simple. Don't make it a compulsory all-inclusive tour—watch to see what interests him. It is better for the child to learn a lot about one small side issue than to come home all mixed up about everything. Introduce him to other workers. Tell him about them and their homes, so the place seems human.

7. After the child is about five or six his father may take him to lunch in a restaurant, preferably one where he goes often to meet business friends and knows the waiters and where things are quite different from home—a man's world. Let the child indulge his fancy and his appetite very freely. Forget the balanced diet.

8. For the six- or seven-year-old, one of life's greatest treats can be to attend a ball game with his father and have his father act really young again—take sides violently, stamp, cheer, and cry for annihilation of the umpire. Explain as much of the game as a child can grasp and indulge all your

impulses to be reminiscent about a particular game when you were a boy. Be generous with peanuts and pop.

9. Another important and private bond between father and child may be the comics or certain T.V. characters. A capacity for real appreciation of this form of entertainment is left out of the constitution of most women. They simply aren't interested in "slapstick" or the antics of clowns or the troubles of Dick Tracy. They are likely to regard these characters as vulgar and a bore. Fathers know better, however, for the good reason that their own enjoyment of them usually goes right on. What more suitable than a little innocent ganging up of father and child against mother in this matter?

THE IMPORTANCE OF BEING FATHER

Does all this put too heavy a burden on fathers? Is it too much to expect a man to pitch in and entertain the youngsters when he has just come home tired after a day of hard work or is genuinely anxious about his special responsibilities? The answer, of course, depends to some extent on the temperament of the father. For some men—and their families are fortunate —children are actually a relaxation. These fathers get as much satisfaction out of their relationship with their children as some men get from bridge, or golf, or conversation. Some of the best of fathers also live under conditions of nervous strain and business worry without letting it interfere with what they give their children.

The Tired Businessman

This does not mean that children should be permitted to be quite oblivious of the special wear and tear of their fathers' lives. Of course, fathers need rest and privacy (so do mothers), and children should learn when to respect the closed door and to be sensitive to signs or warnings of unusual fatigue. They should understand that there are some evenings when their father would rather not be bothered; he wants to be quiet and do just what he feels like. It is up to mothers to drop hints of this kind to their children on special occasions and to influence the child's behavior by their own attitude of extra consideration. But the job will be more successful if such fatigue is not apparent every evening or every Sunday. Certainly nobody wants a father whose arrival is the signal to stop the fun. A father who is interested in his children only when they are washed, dressed, and well behaved, and who retires whenever a problem arises, is likely to lose any real voice when it comes to the more general and important issues of their education. This is unfortunate, because a masculine voice is needed not only about schooling, vacations, and friendships, but also in the smaller matters of day-to-day living.

How much responsibility can a child be expected to take? Which of life's hard knocks should he have to face by himself? Where should these be eased by his parents? Which should he be spared altogether if possible? It is proverbial that fathers and mothers disagree on these points, and out of their disagreements and discussions comes mutual education. Each modifies the point of view of the other, and their children benefit by the process.

The Maternal Instinct in Fathers

Yet, as we see again and again, the success of any authority depends on what else is offered with it. Children, though they may not understand their own feelings, resist discipline when it comes from someone who merely complains when things go wrong or imposes hardships (even necessary ones) without also offering the satisfaction of friendly companionship. Anyone who imposes restraints on a child and makes demands on his maturity must also be an affectionate friend. Interest must be active at all times, not just when things go smoothly. That is the only way for children to profit by criticism or accept authority without resentment. Fathers, therefore, must be more than either playfellows or disciplinarians. They must also be able on occasion to take over the mothers' role of tenderness and sympathy and give themselves with patience and understanding to a child in trouble.

A little girl of five woke from a bad dream, screaming in the night and calling loudly for her mother. To her surprise and momentary disappointment, it was not her mother who came, but her father—wearing pajamas, bathrobe, and slippers and looking strange with his hair tousled. For a moment the surprise was so great that it knocked the screams right out of her. Then she took up her complaint:

"I want my mother to come. I'm afraid. I'm afraid the house might catch fire."

The father sat down beside her and settled himself comfortably. For a while he just sat and let her talk, nodding his head; then he told her about the fireproof shingles on the roof and the nearness of the fire station. Then he told her something funny that had happened in his office that day. She became interested and asked him questions, and soon he got up to tuck her in and say good night. She began to whimper.

"I had a dream and the house was all on fire," she began.

"You did?" said her father. "Well, the dream must have been a mistake, because houses with green shutters *never* catch fire!"

The child stared round-eyed.

"Never?" she asked eagerly.

"Never," said her father, with great solemnity.

The child thought about that for a moment and then began to giggle and buried her face in the pillow.

"You're teasing," she said, "you know that's silly."

"But they don't," her father said. "Have you ever *known* a house with green shutters to catch fire?"

By this time they were both laughing.

"Get up and go to the toilet and get that glass of water *now*," he went on, "because I'm tucking you in to stay. And in the morning when you get up I want you to count the houses on our street with green shutters and come in and tell me how many there are that can't catch fire. Promise? Seven-thirty sharp."

This same child, now grown up, counts this incident among her earliest memories of a dearly loved father whose care for her seemed to have the certain quality of magic. And there has always been a joke between them that is built on it. Whenever they hear of a disaster, a cruel act of fate that could not have been averted, they look at each other and say, "I guess there just weren't any green shutters."

"A Man About the House"

Today, when the father's intimate and inevitable contacts with his children are in danger of shrinking to the vanishing point, we are just beginning to appreciate how important a part he plays. Father and mother both make a distinctive and indispensable contribution to the personality development of both boys and girls, and the father's indispensability is bound up with far more than the passing pleasures he can give and has more far-reaching consequences even than the important values that come from his masculine approach to daily problems. When he really counts, he contributes indirectly to his children's sexual development and, by his presence and companionship and the emotional ties growing out of them, is one of the essential forces that determine whether their characters assume the necessary maleness or femaleness. The view that a boy "needs a man in his life" has always had common-sense support. We shrink from letting him grow up in a house which has lost a father, through death or divorce, and where as a consequence mother, grandmother, and sisters set the tone. All children need contact with the masculine world, and if there is no man in the house it is a help if there is an uncle, a male cousin, a teacher, or physician, who is close enough to be a near substitute. There is also much to be said for boarding school or other special arrangements for a boy in a fatherless home.

Building Masculine Men

From the time when he first discovers that he is destined to grow up into a man, the smallest boy looks at his father with an envious eye. How big he is, how strong, what a deep, almost frightening voice! Moreover, his mother loves his father as much as she loves him, perhaps even more. Jealousy and admiration go hand in hand, and the feelings they evoke are a very large part of the child's inner life for a long and important period. Normally this jealousy and fear are resolved or eased by the child's growing realization that someday he too can grow up and be *like* his father. He too can be big and strong and can earn money and have a wife of his own.

"Look, Daddy, I'm *nearly* as big as you," says the hopeful four-year-old, with the top of his head just reaching his father's belt.

From this time on, unless the father neglects his son's need of him or other forces intervene, the boy will begin to imitate his father, both consciously and unconsciously. This trend may appear at first in such trivial things as throwing a ball, wearing a necktie, or tending the furnace. Later on it is to be hoped that a boy will strive also for truthfulness, bravery, and responsible behavior of all kinds—whatever his association with his father makes him feel are manly virtues. In doing so, he inevitably envies and strives for masculinity itself. He becomes proud and eager to be a man.

[235]

It is of first importance for a boy's normal development that his father's personality should be strong and manly, so that to envy him and to strive to be like him accords with the boy's developing conscience and emerging sense of what is "good." It may prove disastrous for a son to identify himself with a father of inferior moral character or with one who is habitually soft and overindulgent with his children. It is also disastrous when the father, no matter how upright his character, is habitually severe or, by taking no part in the ordinary daily matters of family life, consequently appears to the child as a remote and somehow terrifying figure. If this happens, a son is likely to conclude that the struggle to be like his father is hopeless. He retreats for safety to his mother and tends to model himself along feminine rather than masculine lines, and his sound psychosexual development is thereby seriously threatened.

In much the same way girls need mothers as well as fathers. It is most important that the smallest daughter should discover in her mother someone who is strong and womanly, who loves young children and knows how to mother them and give to them. When a mother is at war with herself about her own destiny as woman and as mother there is danger that the daughter will grow up resentful also that she is a woman and will be permanently envious of men.

And Womanly Women

But the little girl also needs her father. For her, too, it is essential that he should be strong and loving and that his love for her be of the kind that pays tribute to her as a *girl*. To be

sure, he can romp with her and teach her carpentry or baseball just as he does her brothers, but there should also be
recognition and a special appreciation of her feminine qualities. Let us hope that he finds her pretty and that she is not
unaware of the fact, that he is intimately acquainted with her
doll family, that he notices a new dress, that he is obviously
pleased when she invites him to a tea party in her room. It is
important that these attitudes in the father should be free
from a mushy and exaggerated chivalry and that they should
represent a part and not the whole of his approach to his
daughters. Fundamentally, of course, both his sons and daughters need to feel that he appreciates them as human beings
with individual needs which, irrespective of sex, entitle them
to his consideration and respect.

It is fortunate that being womanly, as we understand it today, need not mean curtailment of strenuous activity in any
chosen field. A girl can play as roughly as her brother if she
likes and can get just as dirty; she may, when she is older,
study and practice a profession, own a business, or be active
in public life. None of these things will threaten her femininity if she also maintains her pleasure in being a woman
and keeps a deeply grounded contentment in the thought of
herself as a mother. Her case, though in certain ways it is different from a boy's, is similar in that she too needs both parents. She needs a father who is more than merely attracted
by women; he must actually value them as equals, and his
attitude toward both his wife and his daughters should leave
no doubt of this. Yet a normal father's love for his daughter
inevitably has a slightly different color than his love for his

sons. If he makes it clear that he appreciates a woman's distinctive femininity, he thereby encourages these qualities, admits how he depends on them, and acknowledges the extent to which they enrich all living.

For both boys and girls the mother is the first human being to be loved. To both, she figures for the rest of their lives as the source and symbol of all that is good and nourishing, tender and forgiving. It is easy for the boy to love his mother; if things are normal he envies and admires and finally loves his father too, though in a different way. But if the girl's normal development is to be assured she must early in life find in her father a love object who, in a different way, is as satisfying as her mother. If her father disappoints her, if he neglects her for her brothers or regards her as unimportant or unattractive, her relation to men will always be colored by bitterness and suspicion. Because her father has disappointed her she unconsciously expects other men to disappoint her too and to reject her love. Even when they seem to find her attractive as she grows older, she can never quite believe the evidence and tends to be on her guard and when she wins them she is likely to use her power to punish them and to take revenge for childhood suffering. Distrust and competitiveness develop between her and the men who enter her life, in place of the mutual acceptance that is the only sound basis for marriage.

Much—perhaps too much—has been said about the dangers of excessive parental love. It is true that it exists, or rather that it can come in a form so possessive that the growing boy or girl is crippled in the process of achieving emotional independence. But we have also learned much about the dangers of indifference or rejection in the relation of parents toward children. A child is handicapped in finding the strength to go forward toward emancipation if he has never known the comfort and security that come from having two parents who have not disappointed him in his need for warmth and approval. Emotional undernourishment in the early years probably gives rise to more crippled personalities than over-indulgence and overprotection at that period. Love itself is never a handicap to a child; only its counterfeits in selfish-ness, weakness, and silliness are handicaps. Both parents must give freely to their children, both must make demands on them as well. But the ultimate test of success will not come until, as adults, these children meet life and its manifold de-mands—or fail to meet it—with self-reliance untainted by hardness and with the capacity to live among their fellows without continuous distrust.

CHAPTER NINE

PSYCHOLOGICAL
GROWING PAINS

FACED WITH the continuous necessity of adjusting themselves to living, children, like adults, are bound to have problems. Not, let us hope, that they are bound to be problem children, but at some time in their development practically all show evidences of some disturbance in greater or less degree.

As we already know, they may be rebellious and unreasonable, they may quarrel with other children, they may refuse to eat, or they may develop fears, become overly preoccupied with sex, or they may show many other behavior "symptoms" that are disturbing while they last; but if the parents' attitude is helpful they usually succeed in emerging with fair success. A problem child, however, is typically a young person who is chronically unhappy and who has arrived at an impasse in his encounters with the manifold problems that living presents. His ability to learn and mature becomes blocked. He may have developed so many symptoms of behavior difficulties that they crowd nearly everything else out of the picture. Or he may have some one form of maladjustment so intensely that by itself it is enough to cripple his personality. Such children make everyone unhappy, but no one more than themselves.

FOUNDATIONS OF MENTAL HEALTH

It is not within the scope of this book to discuss in detail the *treatment* of children with deep-seated maladjustments. Each is an individual problem for the psychiatrist. What all parents need are some criteria for distinguishing serious problems from transient ones. If they are coping with those that are likely to prove transient, they need help in deciding what course they should pursue to help the child through his difficulties. If, however, the problem is deep-seated, they need guidance as to where to turn for professional counsel. There *are* "problem children," and the seriousness of their plight should not be minimized. Not all children "grow out of" their troubles. Parents use this phrase too freely, as though there were a certain inevitability about it. By means of it they avoid full responsibility in facing genuinely serious matters. Sometimes children grow out of personality handicaps and sometimes they do not. Or they may merely exchange one symptom for another. A child may become docile and well behaved and yet develop night terrors. He may stop sucking his thumb and take to nail biting; he may suppress his jealousy of the new baby and start to wet his bed. Later, he may quit being overaggressive but lose interest in the outside world, absorbed in daydreams. Parents must watch and see what is actually happening before making up their minds.

"Will He Outgrow It?"

When a child is really "outgrowing" a difficulty, however, there is likely to be an improvement on all fronts. Sometimes outer circumstances conspire to help. A child who has been under great strain because he was jealous of a younger brother or sister may be greatly relieved if still-another baby arrives to alter the family picture and bring about realignments in emotional ties. But it doesn't always work that way. Another new baby may merely revive the pain he felt at the arrival of the first one. As children grow older, however, their sense of proportion is likely to improve. For example, they no longer interpret every affectionate move that their parents make toward someone else as a slight to themselves. They learn what social give-and-take consists of and what they can and cannot get away with. Just growing older helps in a great many ways, provided always that the child's growth has not been handicapped by accumulations of guilt and a sense of anxiety and shame about sexuality or about his early hates, hostilities, and aggressive acts. It is at these points that parents help or hinder, and they have therefore been discussed at length throughout the course of this book. The problem involved in striking just the right balance between complete indulgence, on the one hand, and loading the child with a sense of inferiority, on the other, is a difficult one; but it is an essential one and must be worked out experimentally with each child. There are no formulas for how to proceed.

Take It Easy

In an effort to help young parents arrive at such a balance it may be wise to warn them that they are likely to be perfectionists. They are intent on finding a way to make everything about their child and his routines proceed with absolute smoothness. Instead they need to know what older parents have been taught by experience—that for all children, even wholly normal ones, life is harder at some times than at others, and they show it in a wide variety of ways. Young parents are too likely to feel that the difficult periods that are sure to come are due to serious mistakes on their part or to some perhaps fatal weakness in their child; they become overalarmed, and this very attitude increases the problem. To add to the strain, a great many books on child training give the impression that if only we do everything right from the very beginning and never let a "bad habit" put in an appearance without smiting it, it is possible to prevent most of the mental attitudes that hamper and hinder us. This is simply not true. Character is not formed by specific training, but develops in a highly complex fashion influenced by the interrelations of family life. Though growing up, by its very nature, means a certain amount of inner stress for the child, parents can do much to help a recovery of normal equilibrium by their understanding of these relationships, even when they cannot wholly prevent such stresses from arising.

In certain children these difficult periods are far more apparent than in others. There are some who seem able to meet every new demand made on them quickly and easily, whether it is a new baby in the family, or contacts with other children, or separation from their parents. For them, living is clearly a delightful experience, and everyone connected with it is a friend. In the same family, however, there may be another child who tends to be generally anxious and uncertain of himself and of others. The great majority of children, however, even those who are well adjusted in most respects, are likely to go in and out of "difficult" periods. At these times, in spite of good health, they may be irritable or anxious and behave in ways calculated to try the patience of even very patient adults. Then, just as parents have resigned themselves to the melancholy fact that even though they tried "to do everything the book says" they have produced a child who is evidently going to grow up thoroughly unpleasant, they discover that there has been a change. He is no longer quite as difficult as he used to be. Other people speak well of him. At a friend's house, when his parents were not there, he is reported to have behaved like an angel. Another year or so makes an even greater difference, and one day they arrive at the conclusion that he is actually quite a nice child. What was it they worried so about? Did they dream it all? How was such a child helped to achieve this better equilibrium and how can we endow children in general with this important capacity for growing out of their difficulties?

Two Important Principles

Two principles apply: give the infant and small child comfort, pleasure, loving, and physiological satisfactions. Let him enjoy eating, eliminating, sleeping, and playing *in his own way*. The enjoyment of living is the best "habit" he can have. Don't push too hard to make him conform. Don't rush him into accepting something new before he himself shows readiness. It has already been emphasized that this principle should be followed as soon as the baby is born. Never mind if the book or the doctor prescribes eight ounces of milk at a feeding and the baby takes only five, or if solids at first are rejected in favor of milk and milk only, or if the child wants his vegetables puréed instead of chopped. Be guided by what *he* wants. Take time. A child's progress toward maturity, like his weight chart, is not a steady upward curve; it proceeds in jumps and plateaus, interspersed with backslidings. Console yourself with the fact that though your child may seem slow, he is sure to take his solids eventually. Other important applications of the don't-hurry, don't-press principle have already been discussed in connection with weaning, with bladder and bowel training, and with the eating habits of somewhat older children, and they are restated here because of their later bearings on behavior problems. Certainly parents should always be ready to help a child take the next forward step, but they should also be able to accept the child's own indications of readiness, not to enforce their own preconceptions. This means offering the child a new food or a new way of doing something knowing that he may not be ready yet to accept your plan for him. You can always try again in a few weeks. If you have a contented infant, unharried by rigid schedules, you have laid firm foundations for his mental health.

Another point of great importance is for parents to know the general significance of various kinds of behavior and to recognize the time when professional help should be called for. The same behavior that is normal and proper for a child at one age may be definitely indicative of something wrong at another. When this is the case, it may also be true that the trouble is relatively superficial and likely to prove transient, so that the parent should be able to handle it alone or with a little help. On the other hand, it may be more deep-seated or of such nature that the parent is helpless by himself and should call expert counsel.

This can best be made clear if we examine some of the commonest difficulties of early childhood.

SOME COMMON PROBLEMS

When Thumb Sucking Persists

The discussion in Chapter I, for example, tried to make clear the view that all infants need to suck, not only because it is useful but also because it is pleasurable, and that for various reasons not all of which are clearly understood they may turn for solace to their thumbs or fingers. Wise parents accept this as part of infancy. But as a child gets older they should indicate gently that they think he's about ready to do without. When extreme thumb sucking persists after the age of four or five, especially if the habit shows no signs of decreasing, we must then face the problem of what has caused the child to retain the need for pleasures that are characteristic of infancy and that normally have almost disappeared before these ages. The answer is *not* that some careless adult has failed to break the habit when the child was an infant. It must be sought in the child's experiences during this early sucking phase of his existence and also in the current problems he faces. Thumb sucking does not *cause* nervousness and neurotic symptoms, but in older children is itself a symptom of the child's inability to relinquish a part of his infancy and look for his satisfactions instead in the activities suitable to his age. Failing these, he clings more tenaciously to whatever earlier ones have proved quick and easy. Of course, the problems of the older thumb sucker are further increased when other children make fun of him and he becomes aware that he is babyish. Actually he is eager to get over the habit and welcomes help if it is offered with sympathy and an absence of nagging and humiliation. Much, therefore, will depend on winning co-operation instead of arousing resistance and antagonism.

It often helps to give such children substitutes. Lollypops, chewing gum, a pacifier, or a string of beads to suck may mark an intermediate state on the way to complete emancipation. The child's own suggestions about what might help should always be adopted if possible, and no device should be forced on him against his will. Mild mechanical restraints, such as closing up the sleeves of a nightgown, are permissible *only if the child himself, when he is old enough to express himself, agrees that he wants them,* and if you are therefore certain that they do not mean further humiliation.

Such devices may be helpful in many cases, but they must always be regarded as of secondary importance. They merely alleviate a symptom (thumb sucking) instead of treating the causes and are likely to be ineffectual unless the child is all but ready to give up the habit anyway and can therefore respond favorably to this type of intervention. No matter what simple restraining devices are used, children who suck their thumbs will also need help in their general adjustments to living, and here the parent can play an important part. Thumb-sucking children are often shy and unable to hold their own with others their own age; or they may be dissatisfied at home, struggling with an unsatisfactory relation to one or both parents or with jealousy of a new baby. Sex curiosity and sex conflicts may be present. At school age, inability to meet school requirements may play a part. If the child is in poor health physically this may further complicate the problem, though this is not the powerful factor it is frequently supposed to be. The more we observe the thumb-sucking child as a whole, the more it is evident that the thumb sucking is merely one of many ways in which he needs help. It need not be reiterated how futile the traditional methods are—the aluminum mitts, cardboard cuffs, splints, thumb guards, and other such devices, and also the scolding, shaming, nagging, and "reasoning." Only by studying the child's emotional needs and helping him find a genuinely better readjustment to the whole problem of growing up can any headway be made. This is no easy task. It always requires patience on the part of the parent and sometimes even professional advice as well.

The Bitten Nail

These same principles apply to most of the other nervous and emotional disturbances of childhood. Nail biting, for example, is closely related to thumb sucking; it is extremely difficult to cure on a basis of restraints, bribes, or threats. It has its origins in nervous tensions and dissatisfactions of which the child himself may scarcely be aware, but from which he finds temporary relief in this way. It is one of the commonest of the "bad habits" that distress parents, and, although it is most often found in those children who are unhappy and insecure, it is also found in children who are apparently well adjusted to living. Like thumb sucking, it can only be successfully overcome by securing the co-operation of the child himself, by avoiding all measures that antagonize and humiliate, and by treating the child as a whole, not just the symptom. The incentive to give up the practice becomes greater as children grow older and care more for their personal appearance and attractiveness, especially if at the same time they are getting along quite well in their own world among their own friends. When nail biting continues well on into adolescence, however, some consideration should be given to the possibility of treatment through a more thorough evaluation of the deeper causes.

"Physical" Ailments

There are a great many apparently physical ills of early childhood that have their origins in emotional disturbances. Nausea and vomiting should, of course, always be a signal for consulting the doctor, and on most occasions it is successfully handled through ordinary medical treatment. But there are cases where emotional factors play the major role and the symptom cannot be traced to digestive irregularities alone.

Emotional disturbances may also lie at the root of fatigue, headaches, disturbances of vision, and dozens of other more or less serious symptoms that may come and *go* or may hang on stubbornly. The child described on page 107, who developed "heart attacks" and night terrors as a result of conflicts centering around unrecognized hostility toward a baby brother, is an example of a more serious case. It is necessary to repeat, however, that no parent or other layman should ever assume alone the responsibility of concluding that any illness is of emotional origin. This is a matter for expert medical diagnosis, without which grave harm may result.

Frequently an illness exists as a combination of both physical and emotional factors and therefore, if persistent, requires both medical and psychological treatment. We are not referring to the half-conscious malingering many children indulge in, that can usually be minimized if the parents consistently refuse to fall a victim to that particular game. We are referring to those illnesses caused by emotional conflicts that are wholly unconscious. Children who suffer from them are in no way dishonest. Help should be given in consultation with a psychiatrist; scoldings, bribes, or "paying no attention" will be futile. There are also illnesses that start for definitely physical reasons but continue because they serve a purpose in the child's life long after the illness itself is over. Continued coughing after infection is over is common enough on this basis; every parent knows that. Convalescence after a real illness is often prolonged more or less consciously by anyone who dreads giving up the privileges of that period for the stern realities of health. In fact, the more medical science advances, the more the evidence accumulates that so-called mind and body are one and that neither can be wholly understood until the purposes of the total personality become clear.

The Wet Bed

When regular bed-wetting persists in children past five or six, we are no longer justified in regarding it as something that will surely be outgrown. Most children are fairly dry at night by the time they are three, and bowel control is usually established before this. There are always exceptions, and many young children respond to strains of illness, change of nurses, the birth of a new baby, or any other upset by a temporary loss of control; but the matter should never be ignored if a child of school age is still wholly unable to keep dry and clean, or if he reverts again to wetting after having been dry for a long period. A physician should be consulted first to see whether there is any physical basis for the symptom, though this is rare. Once in a great while a child is helped by medication, by withholding liquids before bedtime, by a system of rewards for good behavior, or by other methods which gain his co-operation. But when cases have been long and persistent these things are likely to be unavailing, and only an exploration of the emotional origins of the symptom are of any use in effecting a cure. These children need treatment by an adequately trained person, and it is important not to delay too long.

Speech Defects

Speech difficulties of various kinds often come and go during the period of early childhood. While the average child acquires an enormous vocabulary and proficiency with language between the ages of two and three, it is true that speech in some normal children may be delayed longer. It is not uncommon for a child to be almost silent until he is past two or even three and then suddenly begin to speak in quite a mature fashion, rapidly making up for lost time. It is possible that the child who knows how to get what he wants without using words, takes longer to learn. The development of speech is a complex matter. Baby talk, lisping, and faulty pronunciations of all kinds are common and in many instances are evidently not attributable to anatomical peculiarities or to faulty training, but rather to other factors calling for consideration. A child who craves the special privileges of a baby in the family may imitate a baby in many ways, including speech; and the attitude of the adults in his life, and the measures they take to help him find satisfaction in being the age he actually is, will be crucial.

Stuttering probably troubles parents more than any other form of speech difficulty, since they quite naturally fear that this symptom heralds the beginning of a habit that will persist as a major handicap through life. It is very hard for them to keep from embarking at once on a drastic course of training and correction "while there is still time." Yet the first thing for them to understand is that by far the greatest amount of stuttering in children from two to five years old is of a transient nature; it comes and goes, though it is often hard to say why, and gradually disappears as the child matures. The "stuttering" of a two- or three-year-old is usually a normal phase of speech development. At these ages it should be ignored completely and grownups should simply listen patiently as the child tries to talk, without supplying a word or urging him to speak slowly. Many cases of genuine stuttering can be prevented by this early acceptance. But if it persists into the later years, we cannot be complacent. Then, every step should be taken to eliminate emotional strains or seek guidance from experts. These strains may occur in apparently unrelated phases of life, and are worth considering even in very young children.

A child of two and a half, who had spoken quite clearly, suddenly began to stutter. This seemed hard to explain as she was not a nervous child and led an apparently healthy existence. Inquiry, however, revealed that her mother was trying to train her to be dry at night by awakening the child and forcing her to sit on the toilet, to which the child protested violently. When the training was halted temporarily as advised, the stuttering cleared up almost at once. This suggests that though stuttering *may* be simply a phase, it may also be related to an underlying strain.

The arrival of a new baby, tense or angry encounters with adults about eating, feelings of guilt due to sex interests and anxieties about sex differences, difficulties with other children or encounters with the neighborhood bully, dissatisfactions in the relationship to parents, anxiety about the parents' relation to each other or about illness and death—all these things are possible sources for a variety of symptoms, and stuttering may well be one of them. But the causes of such troubles may be very deep-seated. Parents should be wary of "a little knowledge" and should make their guesses tentatively, concentrating their attention always on improving a child's general satisfaction in life, rather than on tinkering with psychotherapy in an amateur fashion. This is definitely dangerous except in the hands of experts.

The Stuttering Child

Here, then, are a few dos and don'ts for parents of a stuttering child:

1. Don't scold or shame the child about his speech or force him to go back and repeat correctly a sentence in which he has stuttered.

2. When he struggles with a word or phrase, do *not* supply it for him. Let him go ahead and express himself in his own way without feeling there is anything wrong.

3. Don't emphasize his whole verbal development by trying to teach him nursery rhymes, or by being pleased when he uses big words, or by questioning him before grownups to get him to show off.

4. Give him plenty of manual and physical activities and emotional satisfactions. Discourage precociousness; let him relax and enjoy life wherever possible. Your standards for him may be too high in many respects.

5. Get an hour or so of added rest into his day if you easily can. Let him loaf through the afternoon instead of going outdoors again. Give him supper in bed if he enjoys it. But arrange it so that he has many active, interesting hours during the day. Boredom and forced inaction are bad.

6. Most important—follow the oft-reiterated plan of treating the child, not the symptom, looking for sources of strain in all of his life relationships, and trying to help him discover as many satisfactions as possible.

Remember also that the above recommendations do not apply merely to treatment for stutterers. In spirit, they are also a guide to our approach to children at all times. The appearance of general irritability or a nervous "symptom" should always be the signal for us to review our whole attitude as parents, in order to discover where our procedures are pressing excessively on the child, causing upsets of various kinds.

For example, the first and second suggestions, if rephrased, are a warning that our attitude toward young children should be helpful and encouraging; excessive criticism or demands for standards of behavior still beyond their powers is mentally unhygienic. Suggestions three and four are good advice at all times, and suggestion five often works wonders with any child who is momentarily "difficult." Of course, the change in routine—supper in bed, and so on—should never come as a threat or punishment; rather it should be felt by the child to be a welcome change in routine and a chance for a cosy time alone in his own room or with his parents. Suggestion number six should by this time stand out in the reader's mind as the very core and substance of what parents should constantly strive to do for their children. It is the fundamental condition both for a child's happiness and for the successful building of the foundations for eventual self-discipline.

Negativism

Between the ages of two and four comes a period that is characterized, among other things, by what is called negativism. Before this time the child is largely dependent on adults. He has probably been pretty successfully routinized and has been willing on the whole to comply. When he begins to get about under his own steam, however, he also makes the important discovery that he possesses powers of many kinds. If he wants something, he can go and get it. He learns to say "no" and usually says it with great vehemence and frequency long before he learns to say "yes" or even, so it appears, before he knows the meaning of it. He discovers that he can throw a whole household of people three times his size into violent distress and confusion and he takes delight in doing so. Clearly he is trying his wings and attempting flights into realms of independence which far outrun his judgment but which, as the signs of the growth of a highly necessary tendency, are to be welcomed. This does not mean that he should be allowed to do anything he wants and to acquire, so to speak, delusions of omnipotence; it does mean that his parents, even while dealing firmly with him, should recognize this phase as a legitimate part of development.

Since the management of this drive for power has already

been discussed in the chapter on discipline, we need only repeat here that what a parent needs during this time is good
humor, plus firmness and a large admixture of understanding
how the child himself feels.

For example: A child comes home from his afternoon out-
ing. There are signs of a certain irritability and a look that
should warn his mother that he is waiting for an opportunity
to annoy all comers. She starts to help him remove his wraps;
he pulls angrily away.

"Very well," she says reasonably, "Donald take his own
coat off."

"Won't take it off," says Donald.

"Come," says his mother, with impeccable logic, "your
coat is for outdoors where it's cold. You'll be all hot and uncomfortable if you wear it in the house."

"Won't," says Donald, who is playing quite a different
game.

At this point the inexperienced or unskillful mother begins
to argue, to threaten, to try to coerce, or shows various other
signs of weakness. Or she may use brute force, spank him, and
get her way—leaving resentment and a you-wait-till-I'm-
older feeling in the child, which makes him long all the
more for power for power's sake. The skillful mother, on the
other hand, may have seen what was coming before she ever
brought Donald into the house. She starts a friendly conversation, game, or stunt, and possibly jollies him out of his antagonism. Once home, she does not insist on the removal of hat
and coat.

"Let's see how the turtles are," she says, and runs off to see them herself while Donald follows, at first reluctantly. After a while, though, the care and feeding of turtles begins to seem more interesting than the game of annoying grownups.

With his hat and coat still on he makes various changes in the aquarium. This process takes perhaps five or ten minutes, but at the end of it Donald's hat and coat are off without his even knowing it, and he himself is on the floor peeling off ski pants. The conversation, however, is still about turtles, not hygienic living for little boys.

There is no need to pretend that this sort of thing always works; it doesn't. However, it usually works if—and this is a big "if"—the mother can manage in approximately this way. When it fails and there is a genuine impasse, it is true that the hat and coat do have to be removed anyway, and perhaps by force. The important thing is that the mother should be able to deal quietly with it and just go ahead and take them off. The child may then shriek and call names. Never mind. Forget it. Do something else as soon as possible. Let the child discover that his mother meant what she said and that there are things that *have to be done;* but once it is over don't make a further issue of it or go about looking scandalized that a child should behave this way. Keep your temper and your sense of humor and find ways for the child to "save face." Face saving for children is as important as it is for a nation. While the child is learning that certain things have to be done it is far better to let him believe that he does them himself instead of making him feel defeated and dominated by grownups at every turn. After all, what we want is to preserve the child's drive for independence and still make it possible for him to realize that independence carries certain conditions with it.

Parents had best prepare their minds for a certain amount of this sort of negativism in children, in later years as well as in these early ones. It is well known that during adolescence there is a new outcropping of it, on a different level. Recognition of some of it as legitimate, and the tactfulness and skill with which it is met, will have a great deal to do with its severity and duration. Sometimes, however, there are children who are chronically so aggressive, so unmanageable, so continuously animated by a desire to hurt others and to get themselves into trouble that we are forced to admit that common-sense methods have failed to meet their problems and that the roots of the trouble lie deeply buried. Expert advice should be sought in these cases, for both child and parent are ignorant of what drives him so continuously into a course that brings only pain. Punishments are ineffective; help must come in another form and must be adapted to the individual case.

Anger and Aggression

Displays of anger and even violent tantrums in young children are not at all uncommon. Expressions of hate and acts of aggression are part of all human nature, and, before the child has learned control or developed a conscience which will not even let him *feel* such impulses, he frequently displays them just as he feels them. The child of two or three who says, "I hate you," and acts upon it, striking, spitting, and often biting, is not bad—he is merely young. His parents certainly cannot sanction such behavior, but they can take it quietly and help the child to find other ways of meeting disappointment or frustration. Some children will go into a rage and strike and kick their toys when, for example, a mechanical rabbit refuses to hop or a block building persists in toppling over.

"Look," we may say, when the storm has abated for a moment, "we have to wind the rabbit with the key *this* way." Or, "Watch how I'm going to put the blocks on each other so that the edges always meet. Now you do it."

In other words, ignore the anger and offer a constructive suggestion. Be firm, be gentle, and *do something*. Don't stand around deploring the anger or merely issuing instructions. As for the I-hate-you and the I-wish-so-and-so-were-dead kind of thing, there is often a great deal more of it in our nurseries than the idealistic young parent expects. Its very sincerity, of course, is what we cannot bear. It is not necessary to protest violently, however. Verbal outlets for children have their uses, and anger is a common human emotion that should not shock us in children even if it is directed against ourselves. Children must learn that there are certain things they may not *do,* and adults will help to restrain them, but they should know that they are at liberty to *feel* as they please. Nobody can love everybody all the time, and in the young at any rate anger is neither a sin nor a mental aberration. Yet parents constantly rush forward with moral disapprobation and with Pollyanna efforts to argue their children into a state of love. Clinical experience shows that children are far more likely to get over these feelings in their own time and in their own way if they are not burdened with too great a sense of guilt about them in the very nursery. We may say nothing at all to the angry child and just set about helping him find something to do to forget about it, or we may tell him, quite as a matter of course, that children often hate people part of the time anyway, and now which would he rather take outdoors, his tricycle or his roller skates?

Prolonged rages, especially those with defiance and an absolute deadlock between parent and child, are certainly emotionally exhausting, particularly for the parent. Most mothers realize that it is folly to give in to the child once things have got to this point and that children must learn that rages will accomplish nothing. The mother of an angry child should stand her ground with all the self-assurance she can muster, but she should avoid meeting defiance with defiance. An angry child is an anxious child. He fears retaliations from his mother. He is in trouble and wants help in extricating himself. Sometimes it is possible for the mother to pick him up and rock him quietly in her lap, letting him rage, and saying nothing, and continuing to soothe him. Sometimes this is impossible. I have seen a mother sit down quietly with her knitting in the room where her child was thrashing furiously about, kicking furniture, and occasionally hurling objects. Once in a while she moved an object to a safer place and occasionally she got up to hold the child from kicking in the door panels. She was firm, she was serious, she left no doubt in the child's mind that she disapproved of such behavior, but she was not agitated—or at least she managed not to show it.

"Of course you are angry at me," she said quietly in the momentary lulls. "You are angry because I can't let you do what you want. Mothers sometimes have to stop their children from doing what they want."

She listened quietly to a whole avalanche of unjust accusations until gradually the storm abated and she was able to lead him back into a friendly conversation about quite different matters. The cause of the original tantrum was never referred to, no apologies were demanded, no moral lessons pointed, no penalties imposed. The routine of the day went on in a friendly fashion. The child had made the discovery that his mother had things under control and, as has frequently been pointed out, this discovery, though temporarily enraging, is profoundly reassuring in the long run. He had also discovered that his mother's interest and helpfulness went on just the same, which is equally important, for if a child's fundamental peace and feeling of security are to be established he must realize always that his parents' affection has no strings to it.

Destructiveness

Angry children, like all angry creatures, are often very destructive while their tempers last. Yet there is a kind of chronic destructiveness to which some children are subject that is associated more with general discontent and pent-up sullenness. Though the anger is there, it may not be of the explosive type. Some youngsters seem to derive special satisfaction from tearing books apart, smashing toys, marking up walls, hammering furniture to bits, and other acts of wanton destruction. Parents find this very hard to put up with, because it seems to them to be morally undesirable as well as hard to handle from a purely practical point of view. This destructiveness is not to be confused with the small child's quite normal desire to explore and to find out for himself what makes things tick. Nor does it exist purely because someone has failed to train the child to be constructive. Certainly everything should be done to help such children find plenty of legitimate outlets for their energies and to induce them to use chalk on the blackboard rather than crayons on the wall and to become interested in the contents of the book rather than tearing it. But when all this has been tried and has failed, we must suspect that the child's inner problems centering around his aggressive and angry impulses are leaving him no peace and that he is trying desperately to discharge them in any way he can find.

Fears—Their Meaning and Management

Fears and night terrors are another extremely common phase of childhood, especially between the ages of two and six. It is hard to explain why a child who has been accustomed all his life to sleeping alone in a dark room with the door closed will not go on casually accepting it as the natural order of things. Whatever the training has been, there seem to be certain children who, as they emerge from babyhood, become restive and anxious when they are left alone or who wake late at night, screaming in genuine terror at imaginary dangers. Children are certainly not born with a fear of the dark. But it is also untrue that fears are built into children solely by the threats of foolish grownups, or as the result of some frightening experience associated with darkness or solitude. Such experiences will of course increase a child's tendency to be fearful. But we must also reckon on the fact that a child becomes more imaginative and more complex as he gets older. His inner life is growing and changing, and these changes can bring discomfort as well as pleasure. A young child is filled with disorderly impulses and angry wishes that are condemned by his own developing conscience, even when he is scarcely aware of it himself. The result is that he fears punishment, and even when it does not come from his parents his fear of it is projected outward in the form of punishing fantasies, lions and wild beasts, thieves, kidnapers.

With such children one proceeds with patience. The presence of such fears is not just a "bad habit" or a "way of getting attention." The fears are real and painful. Often a child can be comforted by simple things: a flashlight under his pillow, a dim light by his bed to turn on and off at will. If leaving his door partly open helps to lessen the feeling of isolation which his mother's departure brings, this is a simple thing to do—provided he understands that someday he will be expected to be big enough and brave enough to have it closed again. It is also important to make the going-to-bed time really pleasant, rather than a hurried and mechanical ending to the day's routines. What is really a difficult transition for the child must be bridged; a few minutes of quiet companionship after lights are out have definite value.

Often, of course, a child who calls his parents or insists on getting out of bed when he should be asleep is not really frightened, he is merely unwilling to accept the inevitable. Usually it will not be difficult to tell the difference between this unwillingness to give up what he wants and the presence of acute anxiety; a mother who knows her own child will be pretty well aware of what is going on, especially if she is discriminating enough to realize that not all inconvenient behavior can be lumped together as simple naughtiness. A child's bluff, when it is bluff, must be called. Parents should do what they can to ease the discomfort of the stiff dose that going to bed always seems to be for the young, but in the end the child should learn that he must accept it. In either case, however—whether the child is genuinely frightened or merely stalling—the parent should always consider the child's life as a whole. Far more important than the things we do when emergencies arise are the measures we take to help children find life so satisfying and constructive in the course of their daily existence that they derive strength enough to meet both inner conflicts and external frustrations. This is always the most promising point of attack.

No matter what the problem, it is useful for parents to know that children sometimes "outgrow" it before they show outward signs of having done so. They have recovered as it were, yet persist in demanding the same privileges as when the disability still existed. Like an invalid cured of his lameness, they persist in clinging to a crutch after the need for it has passed.

This was illustrated in the case of a child of six, who still seemed afraid to sleep without a light in her room all night. Since the age of two she had suffered from very acute and very painful night terrors and fears of being alone in the dark. Everything had been done to reassure her, but she still insisted on having a light. When she was four her mother had made a strenuous attempt to put an end to this and had let the child scream in the dark for several nights, until vomiting and general exhaustion warned her that such treatment was more than the child could stand and she went back to leaving the light on again. One day when the child was six, however, she surprised her mother by saying:

"Mummy, if I tell you something, you must *promise* you won't do it to me. Well, Dick always had to have his light on too, and his father said if he didn't let it be off he wouldn't get one single Christmas present—not one, just think. Mummy, you wouldn't say that to me, would you?"

In the child's face there was fear—but there was hope too, and the mother saw it and knew her chance had come.

"Just the same, that might be a pretty good idea," she said. "What do you think? No, I don't think I'd stop *every* Christmas present, but I *might* say there won't be any bicycle for you until you let your light be out and the door closed."

"Oh no, no," cried the child, but her face was wreathed in smiles and belied her words.

"I do believe I *might* say it," her mother went on, feeling like a culprit, for the bicycle had been talked of as a Christmas gift for a long time. "Yes, I do believe I *am* saying it. Mary—no bicycle until the light is out and stays out every night!"

"Oh," said Mary, "then if I do keep it out, I can really have a two-wheeler?"

"But not until then, Mary."

"Oh, goody, goody, turn the lights out tonight."

This procedure was no simple attempt at bribery. Nor does

[266]

it prove that a child may be cured of deep-seated fears by such special incentives and simple common-sense measures. Two years earlier, far more strenuous efforts had failed completely. The truth was that during the last two years the child had been building up more and more satisfactions in daily living and by means of these had been ridding herself in her own time and way of a need which had once been extraordinarily urgent. We cannot know exactly how this was accomplished, but we can suspect that the child continued to demand the light long after she really needed it. Then one day, by the conversation already described, she effectively informed her mother that she could give up the light if her mother would see to it that she did. She was literally asking for a push in the right direction. This does not mean that the same tactics would have worked years before. They would not. What it does mean is that the mother was quick to seize a moment when a neurotic symptom was genuinely outgrown to secure and consolidate the gain.

The Timid Child

The child who suffers from fears of specific things and places is not necessarily the same as the child who has a generally timid and anxious disposition. Indeed, he may ordinarily be very brave. There are others, however, who early in life are dubbed "coward" or "sissy" and who are a source of concern because their parents realize that each day brings moments of unnecessary suffering. Such a child may be afraid of the water when others plunge eagerly into it; he may refuse to climb the ladder to the top of the slide; he may be frightened by rough games, by dogs, by thunderstorms, by vacuum cleaners, or by fire engines. With such a child the commonest mistake parents make is to insist that he must take his chances with the rest, that he must be tossed into the hurly-burly, come what may. (Many fathers make this mistake if a son is concerned.) Or a parent may get into the habit (this error is more typical of mothers) of protecting, sparing, and excusing to such an extent that the child is never required to face his problems or to learn to take hardship. When each parent assumes the extremes of one of these attitudes, the results are especially disastrous. The child sees only two possibilities—the threat of extreme danger, on the one hand, or the chance for complete escape, on the other. Neither is helpful in working out a solution of what is, for him, a genuine dilemma. There may be some children whose fears are quite superficial, and the "treat-'em-rough" method may work with them. They may learn to swim, actually or metaphorically, by being ruthlessly pushed into the water to take their chances in spite of terror. But we should beware of generalizing. If this method is employed indiscriminately, too many children emerge with their fears increased and anger and resentment in their souls. On each parent rests the obligation of sizing up his own child.

It is especially difficult to be of help when such fears are based on a fundamental physical ineptitude. Children vary greatly in their capacity for motor co-ordination and in the skill and the pleasure they have in using their bodies. These differences are less the result of direct training than of native neuromuscular endowment. Some children are very active while still in their crib; they take bumps with unconcern and seem to delight in physical adventures. Others are cautious or timid and slower to try something new. They hate to be pushed and avoid doing anything where they might fall. These differences persist as they grow older. The child who runs slowly, who has trouble catching a ball, and who shies away from physical encounters with other children is definitely at a disadvantage.

This disadvantage is far greater if such a child is a boy. In a boy's world physical skills and courage count heavily in establishing social standing. If he is awkward, and especially if timidity results as it so often does, he may be ignored or ridiculed and will therefore tend to avoid mixing with other children and exposing himself to situations where he is handicapped from the very start. He withdraws instead into a solitary world of his own and gives up the fight.

Helping such a child to overcome these tendencies is bound to be a slow matter. Hurrying him into competitive encounters with other children in the vain hope of stimulating him to "take more interest" and "try harder" is likely merely to increase his feeling of inferiority.

Help must be given in two ways. Much as a child who has fallen behind in school may have a period of personal tutoring, some special training in bodily skills often leads to genuine improvements that eventually make him more willing to try himself out among others. Sometimes, too, in spite of general awkwardness, ability in some one sport can be fostered, and this serves to build self-confidence and self-respect. Swimming, for example, is a sport that nonathletic children often do well, and a summer near the water and associations with other children who go in and out freely may result in progress of many kinds. An ingenious older person who is willing to take such a child in hand can build confidence. He can demonstrate ways by which certain dreaded experiences may be stripped of some of their fearful aspects and skills acquired instead.

Every effort should be made to develop and give credit for whatever nonathletic abilities such a child has: mental or artistic gifts, mechanical aptitudes and hobbies. He should have a chance to mingle with other children while doing what he can do well, instead of only on occasions when he is outclassed. Hobby clubs, making collections, carpentry groups —anything that serves as a get-together where he can compete on an equal footing with other children his age is an essential need.

Labeling such a child as coward or sissy only increases his hopelessness and leads to greater inactivity. He needs his parents' moral support; he should know that there have been other children like him, that there are ways to surmount this handicap, and that, although he will have to find them in large measure for himself, his parents understand his special needs and can be counted on to help him in any way they can.

HOW SERIOUS IS A CHILD'S PROBLEM?

All parents hope that their children will work out their difficulties in their own individual ways and that time will cure all. If mothers tend to be overanxious about behavior which is perhaps only a growing pain, fathers as a class tend to be oversanguine. "You worry too much," they say to their wives. "Let the child alone—he'll come out of it." Unfortunately, most parents regard behavior problems in their children as a reflection on themselves. "Ask anyone else to tell me how to manage my own child? I should say not!" is the common reaction. They become panicky at the mere notion that *their* children might have problems and will go to any lengths to blind themselves to what is often a genuine distress signal. This feeling has been increased by the insistence from some quarters that "back of every problem child is a problem parent." There is, of course, much truth in this. To a large extent children are a product of their home relationships. Yet it is by no means always true. It is possible for wise and well-balanced parents to have children who develop neurotic disturbances despite good management. There are differences in native constitution, as well as accidental experiences that cannot be predicted or controlled, that predispose one child more than another to find life hard.

Common Sense Can Be Overrated

It is also important to repeat that not all behavior difficulties in children can be successfully treated, as some would have us believe, just by a combination of sympathy and common sense. These things are of fundamental importance to the sound growth of the child, but they are no more a guarantee against occasional personality disturbances than against physical illness. Sometimes things go wrong with our children that could not possibly be predicted or controlled, and when this happens only expert study and treatment can cope with the condition. Sympathy and common sense can go a long way, and many so-called problem children are not problem children at all—they are merely children whose parents have failed to employ these things in daily living. But parents, especially young ones, often find that neither sympathy nor common sense comes as naturally as they had expected and must be developed as they themselves mature. For this reason, the major portion of this book has been devoted to suggesting attitudes and procedures which may help to develop them.

By themselves, however, sympathy and common sense are not effective in the treatment of genuine neuroses, as parents of a disturbed child finally discover; they are not even wholly effective in connection with the transient disturbances that mark development of many normal children. Parents learn that there are times when their most gallant efforts come to a standstill and when the best they can do is bide their time in patience, letting a child struggle in his own way—and, if time does not bring a change, eventually calling for professional help.

How to Tell a Passing Problem from a Serious One

The Child Study Association of America has published a pamphlet: *When Children Need Special Help with Emotional Problems* by Greta Mayer and Mary Hoover. Before listing "danger signals," they offer a special caution: "One symptom by itself does not necessarily spell trouble. Many healthy youngsters may at some time in their lives develop one of the symptoms listed below. . . . A symptom only *warns* us that a child *may* be—*but is not necessarily*—in need of professional help."

Since behavior must always be considered in relation to age, symptoms are listed chronologically, followed by some guidance as to when expert help should be seriously considered. The pamphlet may be ordered for 40¢ from The Child Study Association of America at 9 East 89th Street, New York City.

The following is a condensation from this pamphlet:*

Danger Signals

From birth to two years:

During this period difficulties can show themselves in unusually slow physical development, excessive passivity, lack of responsiveness, excessive restlessness, or constant severe difficulties in sleeping or eating. Your pediatrician or well-baby clinic can help you decide whether what seems a real problem to you is just one of those things "he'll grow out of."

*Included by permission of the Child Study Association of America.

From two to four years:

Occasional nightmares are normal, but frequent night terrors may need to be looked into. Expect some fussiness about food, but a child who constantly refuses to eat anything except a few relatively unwholesome foods may need help.

Other warning signals:

1. refusal ever to drink out of a glass or cup; insistence on having a bottle constantly.

2. refusal to begin toilet training.

3. refusal to accept any limits whatever on his behavior.

4. marked lack of interest in other children especially toward the end of this period.

5. inability to let his mother out of his sight without panic.

6. panic (not just shyness) whenever anyone other than his parents approaches him.

From four to six years:

1. inability to get along with other children—either *constant* fighting with or anxious withdrawal from them.

2. repeated and intentional cruelty to animals.

3. constant overt destructiveness.

4. intense frequent temper tantrums for which there seems no obvious provocation.

5. continuing unwillingness to be separated from his mother—inability to stay at nursery school or kindergarten or to be left at home with a sitter.

6. *intense* fears of not one but *many* things encountered in everyday living—doctors, dogs, fire engines, etc.
7. consistent day or night wetting or soiling.
8. poor speech—stuttering and the like.
9. tics—frequent involuntary movements of the face or other parts of the body.
10. inability to fall asleep unless a parent sits with him.
11. inability or unwillingness to do anything for himself.

From six to eight years:

1. absorption in fantasies *which he treats as if they were real.*
2. real fears about (not just dislike of) going to school—which show up in frequent anxiety attacks in the morning: vomiting, stomach-ache, etc., for which no physical cause can be found.
3. continuous bedwetting and thumb sucking; frequent genital manipulation in public (*not* just when alone).
4. inability to follow directions in school; failure to show a beginning interest in learning.
5. intense worry about becoming ill or fears of bodily injury; recurrent physical symptoms which have no direct physical cause—vomiting; stomach-ache, diarrhea, head-ache, etc.
6. pronounced fear of elevators, crossing the street, being alone in a room; constant intense fear of the dark.

When Does a Signal Need Further Attention?

No quick off-hand answer to this question is ever possible.

Parents must consider their child's *whole adjustment pattern,* past and present, before they can decide whether professional help is needed. But how long can you afford to wait? Here are five test questions to help you decide:

1. Is the child's behavior generally appropriate to the circumstances in which he finds himself? If Johnny is constantly out of tune with his world, seems unable to tell what pleases people and what makes them angry, there is reason to worry.

2. Is the child's behavior generally in keeping with his age? Does he continue in most ways to progress at the same rate as other children his age? Or does he seem to become more babyish?

3. Are there real difficulties in the child's environment that may be to blame for the problem? A symptom produced by outside pressures is likely to be less serious than one due to internal conflict and usually far easier to deal with.

4. Has there been a radical change in the child's behavior? If a youngster suddenly seems to undergo a complete change of personality, that's a different matter. When a symptom is accompanied or followed by this kind of radical change, look for help.

5. How long has the symptom lasted? If it is obvious that nothing you do seems to improve matters, and the symptom greatly troubles your youngster as well as you, at this point it's wise to seek help.

To these five key questions, a supplemental query should be added: Is there some special situation which makes preventive help advisable? There are times when it may be wise to get some professional advice . . . if there is something "different" or special about one's family.

Parents nowadays are far less touchy about seeking expert advice with a knotty problem than they used to be. Word has gone round that a child guidance counsellor is not one who "blames the parents" for everything. On the contrary, he or she is likely to be extremely understanding of the parents' predicament. But it is important to find someone who is trained and qualified for this work. A Family Service Agency in your town can tell you where to go and sometimes offers treatment. Your physician may know the right person or clinic. Failing these, ask your local United Fund or Community Chest or your State Commissioner for Mental Health.

CHAPTER TEN

PROBLEM PARENTS

BY THIS TIME it should be clear that the best thing a child can do for himself is select his parents wisely. To be sure, not all of the faults of childhood and not all of the more serious neurotic disturbances of this period can be blamed exclusively on parents. Growing up means learning to face certain inevitable disappointments, and, though parents can help, in the end the child himself must find his own way. Nevertheless, it is true on the whole that children who are perpetually unadjusted to the demands of living, and whose behavior continuously makes trouble for everybody, are found with far-greater frequency in homes where there is adult maladjustment and unhappiness than in homes where the prevailing atmosphere reflects a reasonable amount of inner harmony in the parents' own lives.

This does not mean that in order to bring up healthy-minded children everything in life must always run smoothly. On the contrary, parents are far too likely to overprotect their children from unpleasant realities and shelter them effectively from painful experiences, in spite of the fact that genuine growth can only come from learning to meet these things responsibly. There is no way by which we, as adults, can keep some experience of illness, sorrows, death, anxiety, financial upheavals, and often actual physical deprivations out of our own lives. We are living in a deeply troubled world, and there is little chance that its violence and conflicts will not press upon our homes along with millions of others. It is worse than futile to try to exclude children from at least some share of whatever comes. The important thing is the spirit in which parents themselves are able to meet these things, for it is this spirit that sets the pace for the whole home. Moreover—and this is important because it is so seldom understood—it is rarely the disasters imposed by the outside world that produce warped and ineffectual personalities. The world is full of countless people who have been more powerful than fate. Far more destructive are the assaults on character that arise from within, caused by those vestiges of early frustrations, of childish attitudes and nursery conflicts, which many so-called adults carry with them to their graves.

Just as there is no clear line between problem children and neurotic children, so there is no clear line between normal and neurotic parents. All adults carry some measure of childish dependence, of incomprehensible depressions, of the habit of evading issues, of unreasonable irritability, of disproportionate anxieties and fears—and all these things prevent them to some degree from being calm, good-humored, and sensible, as they know they should be. Nevertheless, in any attempt to take stock of what they want for their children, parents must also clarify their goals for themselves. Knowing their own shortcomings is by no means the same as mastering them. But though it may not be the whole battle, it is at least an important part.

Teamwork Is Fundamental

First of all, perhaps, they should consider the effectiveness of their own teamwork and the consistency of whatever policy they decide to adopt toward their children. This policy needs thinking over and talking over from time to time, in an effort to come to an agreement about the essential needs of each child. In addition, each parent needs to take stock of his own temperamental weaknesses and to be clear in his own mind about how these are likely to be reflected in his relation to his children and how he may best stand guard. The parents' own relation to each other is of fundamental importance, for it is difficult to keep a united front before the children if friction and discord are deep-seated. Even happily married couples are bound to disagree with each other about many things, including the best way of bringing up their children. Children discover this as they learn to know their parents and usually are quite aware, for example, which parent can be counted on to be more lenient and on what occasions. Some of this is inevitable and also wholesome; it adds variety to children's experiences and puts increased demands on their abilities to adapt themselves. Yet parents must also find ways of compromising and co-operating, even at moments of real disagreement. Continuous bickering or complete failure to find a working agreement when a situation must be met is impractical in the ordinary conduct of daily life and—even more important—it robs children of the valuable experience of discovering a genuine partnership in their parents. This can only be accomplished when husband and wife understand and tolerate differences in each other and when they know about where these differences are likely to arise and agree on a compromise before their children are too aware of the differences. In this way children will be spared the widely inconsistent treatment which confuses them and destroys the possibilities of adequate control.

If parents find themselves continually defeated in their efforts to work out such a policy, they must be warned that few children can healthily survive being used as a battleground for their parents' quarrels. When such conflicts are deep-seated, they are certain to be reflected in every aspect of family life.

GETTING AWAY FROM MOTHER

Immaturity in one or both parties is always a serious threat to success in marriage. One of the first ways in which the underlying childishness of husband and wife may show itself is their failure in becoming emotionally independent of their own parents. Unless an individual has learned during adolescence to rely increasingly on a mode of life and standards of his own rather than his parents' choosing, he can never really grow up. He will be hampered in giving full allegiance to his marriage partner, because his real love, like a child's, is attached to his parents. In addition, even this older affection may become warped and angry because, as an adult, he knows in his heart that it hampers his best development.

Apron Strings Cause Trouble

A certain man, for example, up to the time of his marriage had always let his mother care for his clothes, cater to his wishes, make his decisions, and determine his views on all but the more superficial matters of life. In effect, she acted as his conscience. In spite of some mild objections he had once or twice registered about the way she had bulldozed his sister and hampered her development, he had never actually allowed himself to question that in all things his mother knew what was best. Just as a child, no matter how angry he may be, feels that his mother is bound to be infallible just because she is his mother, so even as an adult this man continued to feel that to oppose her was tantamount to being bad. He had, in other words, never learned to do anything but acquiesce in a wholly childish way, and when he grew up and married he expected his wife to perform the same function as his mother. He demanded the same kind of care and devotion and seemed quite loving and responsive when she gave it to him.

Difficulties arose, however, when his wife turned out to be quite a different type of person, with needs and aspirations taking different directions. She was much less clever than his mother at managing the house but was much more clever at conversation and social relations and was in quick sympathy with a wide range of people whom she found interesting and he did not. With the instinctive hostility that narrow people feel for persons who are radically different from themselves, the mother looked upon her daughter-in-law with disfavor. She expressed disapproval, openly or otherwise, because her son's wife bought the children's clothes at shops that were considered expensive and because she had on several occasions gone away for pleasure, leaving the children and her husband in the care of a maid. Soon the wife discovered that her husband shared his mother's dislike of ways of life which seemed wholly natural to her. Even when his mother was not there in person to influence his feelings the pattern she had set continued to dominate him and prevented him from accepting or even becoming acquainted with a woman whose character had been formed along quite different lines.

One Way or Another

A husband of another type showed a different variation on the same theme. He was not and never had been on very good terms with his mother. She scolded him whenever she got the chance, and he sat like a small boy and accepted it in silence, with at least the appearance of indifference. He left home at an early age and went back as little as possible; he neglected his mother, often unkindly, and had developed a shell of indifference to her needs. It was as though somewhere in his early childhood she had hurt him in a way that made it impossible for him to forgive her, and his lack of forgiveness had prevented him from ever knowing her as one adult can know another.

When he married, his mother felt that here was a fresh chance to win her way back to her son. She could perhaps gain lost ground by establishing an intimacy with her daughter-in-law. She telephoned daily, was lavish with attention, and full of favors for her grandchildren. But the attentions were the kind that demanded returns and the favors had strings to them. The daughter-in-law, no matter how she tried, could not give satisfaction because she could never fulfill the real hope of her mother-in-law and bring her son back to her. Complaints came in the wake of the favors, and the husband found himself besieged by his mother's criticisms of his wife's management of his home and of his children's behavior; he found a whole array of his mother's worries now laid at his wife's door. Caught between the two women, he was unwilling to meet the problem squarely because he had never in his life met squarely any problem that involved his mother.

Naturally, his reaction was to be extremely annoyed. Somehow he too, like the first husband described, held his wife responsible for his discomfort. His attitude toward her said, "I can't be bothered. You fix it." It is clear that, though he did not know it, he had assumed from the day of his marriage that his wife could bring about a peace between him and his mother which he himself had never succeeded in achieving. He wondered angrily why his wife could not do things the way his mother wanted them done, since it meant so much to her. Why hadn't she made the children more polite? Why hadn't she arranged for them to visit his mother more often? There were numerous other things, too, that he himself would not think of doing and never had done, but now believed his wife should do in his place.

They Must Be Cut

No prescription can be given for a way out of either of these dilemmas. There may be a kind of wisdom in the wife who is willing to accept even a childish husband just as he is and play the part he requires. But this is a partial solution and will not really satisfy either of the parties concerned, though it may keep an external kind of peace. In the soundest marriages the years tend to build fuller allegiance between husband and wife, keeping each truly first in the life of the other. Their affection is based on what the other one actually is; it does not depend on conformity to a special pattern which dates from the unsatisfied childish needs of the other. In marriages where affection does depend on such conformity there are frequent disasters, and it is inevitable that the children should suffer from repercussions of the stresses and strains between the parents. There will be disaster also in the relationship between the two older generations; for genuine affection, unmixed with resentments, can flourish between grown-up children and their parents only if their relationship has finally been freed of the domination-and-dependence phase which should belong only to the nursery years. If parents would keep the love of their adult children, the first step they must take is to help them to be free.

Actually, the two husbands just described do not differ from each other in essentials. Superficially it may appear that the first one loved his mother too much and that the other was selfishly indifferent. Neither the love nor the indifference, however, was real. Both of these men, in the deeper levels of their feelings, were controlled by their mothers and depended on their good graces and approval. Neither of them was yet free to see either his mother or himself in adult terms—with separate needs and separate paths in life, perhaps, but with a bond between them which should have become one of deep appreciation and affection, if infantile dependence had not prevented it from flowering. Both of these husbands were hampered in all their relationships because they were children who had never grown up, in spite of the fact that each had a home and children of his own.

Are You a "Strong Personality"?

Even without selfishness it is difficult for some parents to avoid taking too strong a hand in the affairs of their families. Certain energetic natures, with the best of intentions and with real love for their children, are often pushed into an over-prolonged position of leadership which they do not know how to relinquish. Often this does not appear to be resented; their children may submit quite voluntarily to such leadership, feeling it to be strong rather than dictatorial and therefore without the graver dangers of attempted tyranny. Nevertheless, a growing child, whose powers are ill-matched against such a parent, can be handicapped in his own growth and beneath the surface he knows and resents it. How is he to find his own opinions, his own wisdom, his own self-chosen experiences? How is he ever to learn to think for himself when his parents so obviously think better and more promptly at every turn?

When such a personality is the mother it is doubtless better if she has many children, so that her power does not concentrate on any one child. If such a mother has only one or two children she should have larger worlds to conquer than her home and family. Her energies need deflection if she is not to overwhelm less aggressive natures who happen to be close to her or if there are not to be endless clashes with a child who happens to be endowed with a similar capacity and will. A mother of this type, if she has the insight to recognize the dangers, should take particular pains to help her children get away from her at critical points. Nursery school may offer a beginning. Visits in the homes of friends or relatives, even while they are still young, may help; and still-wider opportunities for being on their own, later on, often furnish the initial impulse to expanding personalities. Children must have breathing space; they need a chance to proceed at their own pace and under their own steam. Instead of being eternally saved from the consequences of their own acts by being compelled to accept their parents' superior wisdom, they need actually to make some mistakes and find their own solutions.

Leave Them—Sometimes

All these things are likely to be accomplished better if parents get away from children from time to time and mix with other adults. They need friends shared in common; even friends whom one of them likes and the other doesn't. They need intimate friends, as well as a fringe of acquaintances who keep their social group fluid and changing to some extent. Parents of even young children should go to some pains to preserve old interests, even if they are not domestic at all. It always adds to the children's development in the end if a mother keeps other activities alive. Women begin to forget that there is anything else in life if they let themselves become submerged in details of their children's lives—first in tonsillectomies and inoculations, later in motoring the children to their dates, then finally in over-involvement in each move the children make.

One woman to whom this happened tells the following story: An old friend, with whom she had once shared a studio when they were studying art together, came back to town. The mother looked at her friend's recent paintings, which reflected a radical change in her style and ideas, and suddenly found herself in a state of inner turmoil that was only quieted when she took a brush in hand and started painting again herself. The first results were: bad pictures, a deskful of neglected correspondence, curtains in need of repair, no more afternoon dates at the club, surprised husband and children. Gradually the pictures became more intelligible, and just as gradually the household slipped into new grooves. This woman had always kept one maid, who now began to assume more responsibility for marketing and the keeping of simple accounts. She tried to arrange life so that she painted when the children were out or napping or busy with friends, but her work was often interrupted, and there were plenty of times when for weeks on end their needs were such that she had to drop the painting entirely and take it up again later. It all took planning and there were plenty of hitches, but she felt so much happier and her sense of proportion about her relation to her household and children was so much saner that her husband commented on the difference. "Of course, there were readjustments," he said, "but it's a more peaceful home now than it was. Perhaps the furniture needs new slip covers. My wife says it does; I haven't noticed. Whether or not she's a good painter, she gets a great kick out of trying; it's a real need for her. I think the children are better off because she's less nervous and fussy, and though she does more she's less tired. She seems to have more fun with the children. Somehow, I believe she actually likes them better, and they know it."

Although only a few women may want to paint, this is not a special case. Whether their interest is in art, gardening, household skills, or, like one woman, making dollhouse furniture, every mother is better off if she does something that makes her forget now and then that she is either wife or mother. In the end, she is better as both because she is a more developed human being.

Families need also a working relation to the community in which they live. In finding how best to be a citizen there will always be wide temperamental differences and preferences. Some people are natural-born joiners. Others, no less public-spirited, are paralyzed by large public gatherings and are acutely unhappy serving on a committee. Nevertheless, it is worth while to try to develop powers that are not purely self-interested. Children are proud to have their parents take a place in public affairs. It may take time, but there are usually enough varied ways of serving so that every individual and every temperament may find his own niche.

WHEN PARENTS FAIL—AND WHY

The problem of getting along with children is complicated all along the line by special weaknesses within the parents' own personalities. Discipline fails sometimes because one or both parents understand neither its true purposes nor the child's deep need of it. Even when they can think and articulate clearly about it, however, discipline can also fail because, when faced with a situation where it is clearly called for, all thought is useless; certain personalities *cannot* assume an authoritative role. They either go off half cocked and put the screws on in the wrong place or they become anxious, vacillating, and unable to take action in behalf of a good strong "must" or "must not." Such parents are likely to be the type who are overwilling to accept the short end of the horn, whether at work or in personal relationships and are consequently submissive toward their children as toward everyone else. High-spirited, power-loving youngsters ride roughshod over their lives. Parental demands, parental standards, parental authority itself—experiences all children must have if they are ever to develop their own standards and learn to make demands upon themselves—are dangerously absent when this situation prevails.

If, from his earliest memory, a child finds himself in a position of easy dominance, where any sort of ruthlessness is tolerated and selfishness accepted with an amused shrug, if he never experiences those spontaneous and hearty resentments hot off the griddle of real feeling which should exist wherever the rights of others are violated, if the parent never censures, the child himself is deprived of the means of self-censure. Conscience has its beginnings in the voice of the parent, internalized and finally made one with ourselves; if that voice is never raised, the inner voice fails to be born.

The deeper causes for such continued inability of a mother to manage her children must be sought then, not in her methods and procedures, but in the relationship existing between herself and them.

Mixed Feelings

Sooner or later parents make the discovery that their feelings toward their children are often mixed. They are delighted with a child at times; at others they find themselves caught in a mood of genuine dislike for something about him, whether it be appearance, mannerisms, or a character trait they fancy may be permanent. Or their feelings vary toward their different children. One child they find altogether satisfactory—"just what we ordered." Another, despite weaknesses, has such a strong appeal for one or both parents, on the basis of some quality of personality to which they warm instinctively, that this child cannot help but grow up nourished by an awareness of the satisfaction he gives. With still another, parents find that a barrier exists between him and them, in the face of which they are helpless. Time after time in their relations to this child they find themselves unable "to get close to him." Or anger surges up that is anger at the whole child and everything about him, not merely the passing anger anyone may feel because of some special action, which can quickly be forgotten.

These mixed emotions and hostile impulses are terrifying to parents. It is at sharp variance with their ideals to find such feelings in themselves; their standard of what makes a good parent demands someone who is bound to love all his children continuously and equally. There is likely to arise, therefore, a moral self-censuring so strong that frequently parents are unable to admit the facts or face what is going on in themselves. They develop a system of pretenses unconsciously designed to throw sand in their own eyes, so that they may continue to believe that they feel only love and affection for the child in question, and they often succeed in putting up a very plausible appearance of these things. In this way they deceive themselves, each other, and perhaps their best friends, but they never deceive the child. The child always knows when such a barrier exists, though as he gets older he too may learn to deceive himself about it and find himself, in consequence, as helpless and troubled in his relation to his mother as she is toward him.

There is no denying that these variations and blockings of parental affection are not only painful but can also leave permanent marks on a child. And they are far from rare; to a certain extent they are even inevitable. In calling attention to their existence, our last intention is to give parents the feeling that when such blockings exist they are behaving reprehensibly and ought to know better. On the contrary, the more deeply the study of human nature proceeds, the more apparent it becomes that these mixed feelings and jumbled motives exist in all of us and are operating constantly in every home and in all human relationships. To love everyone fully and equally, or even to love our children fully and equally, is possibly a useful ideal but it is also one that is impossible to realize completely. While some approximate it better than others, there is no love, not even mother love, wholly uncomplicated by conflicting feelings. These contradictory feelings, even toward people we love, are so integral a part of human living and human loving that perhaps no adult can be said truly to have come of age either in marriage or as a parent until he or she has acquired some measure of insight into them and can use this knowledge constructively.

Personal vanity, for example, and competitiveness from which none of us escape, clearly play their part. We want our children to shine before our friends and later before the world, knowing that we will share the reflected light. We begin by feeling humiliated when, in the nursery, they reject the friendly advances of relatives or perhaps put on a shocking display of temper when our old college friend comes to call. Later, in the school years, we watch sharply to see if our child's performances equal those of our sister's child, if he is as bright, as popular, as athletic. Or perhaps we compare him with our own secret hopes fashioned only to fit the dream child we have yearned for. If he refuses to deliver what we expect of him, we are confronted with the constant temptation to try to remold him and to make him over to suit our needs, not his. When another of our children has turned out according to specifications we are especially prone to press and to prod the one who lags behind. We may allow far too little for individual differences and blindly refuse to make use of a truth we flatter ourselves we have accepted—that children differ in physical attributes, in temperament and mental capacities, that our role is to help them realize the best in themselves rather than use them as a means of self-gratification or, as is also common, to fulfill our own frustrated ambitions.

Some of these attitudes, especially those like the foregoing which cloak selfish demands for ourselves, can be recognized and checked if we honestly focus attention on ourselves rather than on the child. Most parents, as their own development proceeds, gain increasing ability to help themselves toward a clearer view of what they are feeling and doing in relation to each of their children. But such attitudes cannot always be disposed of this way. There are sometimes other and subtler barriers which may grow up between parents and their children that are persistently baffling, even when every ounce of effort has been brought to bear to fathom the meaning of such barriers and to alter them.

The Intangible Barrier

"No matter how I try," one mother said, "I cannot get close to my only son. I would like to show him more affection, but he always holds me off. The only demands I make on him, so far as I know, are that he be just moderately co-operative and reasonable about the things that have to get done in a day. I give him all sorts of leeway and try to limit my demands to the minimum essentials. But it troubles me that he apparently isn't interested in all the things that delighted my other children and seems to glory in just being an obstructionist. This bad spirit is growing in him. How can I help being irritated and showing it? He exasperates other people, too, and he is growing up to be generally disliked. Does the fault lie in the child or in me and, if in me, what mistakes am I making?"

This is a fair question and it is regrettable that there is no simple answer to it. The explanation can only be revealed if the mother gains a detailed knowledge of all that has gone into building her feelings about this child, and such knowledge comes only through an understanding of the *unconscious* forces that have caused it. Until she understands these things she is literally helpless. Honesty and the habit of searching our motives may take us far, but they are often powerless to reveal to us the deeper sources and origins of attitudes continuously affecting our daily living. Without a discovery of these origins, the attitude persists in spite of all we may do to try to change it.

This mother, who was a woman of good sense and integrity, had two older daughters with whom she was on the happiest of terms. Everything in their development had gone forward easily, with only minor upsets and passing problems. But her son proved to be another matter. "I don't believe it ever occurred to me that my third child might be a boy," she said. "Of course, we wanted one, but after my girls came I gave up thinking there would ever be a boy, and when Ted came he seemed almost a stranger. That feeling of strangeness has gone right on. I just can't seem ever to get in touch with him. This is so unlike my relation to the girls. They have always seemed a real part of myself, and we understand each other."

To account for this feeling of strangeness it was necessary to go back into this woman's early life and to learn something of the way she felt toward her own older brother when they were still in the nursery. He was clearly the privileged member of the family—the father's pride in him was frankly expressed, and the feelings of both parents for their daughter were tepid in comparison. She envied her brother; in fact, she remembered hating him, because he seemed to have everything she wanted. Also, she could scarcely help being angry at her father and deeply hurt by his lack of interest in her. As she grew older she drew closer to her mother and to other women friends. Evidently she discovered that in their society she need not fear her own antagonism toward men, which had developed in retaliation for their having regarded her as unimportant during her earliest years. It is significant, too, that in her marriage she chose a kindly, colorless man whose business took him away from home a large part of every year. When he was at home she lived with him harmoniously, but at a great psychological distance. In view of these facts it became clear why her daughters brought her nothing but happiness and a sense of safety, though her son aroused in her—entirely without her knowledge—memories of her own painful nursery years. Here, reincarnated, was the small brother who had been her enemy and whose return revived in her a feeling of anger and desire for revenge so dangerous that she could not even give it recognition. All that remained was the shadowy reminder of the past expressed in her feeling that somehow this child was a "stranger." Only by a fuller understanding of all that had built up her relation to the male sex in general could she fully understand and alter her relation to her son. Such understanding was possible only under psychoanalytic therapy.

When Parents Need Psychiatrists

This brief account of one woman's problem is not offered as a pattern to use to explain the origins of all similar difficulties. Each case is entirely separate, and guesses made by untrained amateurs are useless and dangerous. It is offered only as one example of the fact that many of the most troublesome and insoluble problems we have to face have a long history and, without professional help, we cannot hope to disentangle them.

It should further suggest that if we find ourselves in trouble in our relations to our children and cannot change the picture by hard-headed, unequivocal self-scrutiny, it might be wise to seek the help of a psychiatrist—with ourselves, not the child, as patient. This, of course, in no way implies that we are "mental cases" or "failures." On the contrary, it shows that we are strong enough to ask for specialized help when we need it. It is usually the weak, uncertain person who is afraid to ask for help. Fortunately, psychiatric counsel for both adults and children no longer has the terrors it used to have. It is increasingly regarded as another form of medical counsel to which we turn freely—not because we are desperately ill, but because we want to get full value for our potentialities and also to become free to give our children the best that we have.

The mother who is conscious of barriers in relation to her children is not the only one who may do harm; the one who admits no such barriers, yet always hovers over them anxiously, may do quite as much. A great deal has already been said about the dangers of chronic maternal fussing, overprotection, worry about health, and the feeling of being indispensable twenty-four hours a day. When this is carried to excess we must suspect that the mother is driven to use this attitude as a mask to save herself from seeing how mixed her feelings for her children really are. By such anxious hovering or by overindulgence and the inability to meet common disciplinary situations, she safeguards herself from seeing beneath the surface of her feelings. In contrast, we see that parents whose relationship to their children is soundest somehow just naturally arrange to dispose easily of a multitude of nonessentials in domestic life. They manage to be on hand a great deal of the time and always when they are really needed, but they are free to give attention to many other things as well.

In Chapter IX of this book we mentioned sources of information about professional guidance for children. These agencies can furnish the same information regarding adults also.

CHILDREN AND DIVORCE

But the most threatening of all situations for children, the one in which parents are most urgently counseled to seek psychiatric advice, is the one which occurs when the marriage relationship itself has become unbearable. Usually the true state of affairs is apparent to the children no matter how hard parents may try to conceal it, and they suffer in many ways. Among these are bound to be divided loyalties and the fear that such disharmony will end in separation and divorce. Unhappiness in marriage is not new, but the widespread prevalence of divorce is. When divorce comes, it is a further and final blow to children. Some marriages cannot and should not be saved. Others might be. This is especially true if husband and wife have, first, the will to save their homes, and, second, the courage to accept professional help in discovering the causes for the breakdown that lie deep within each of them.

For children, divorce means the disruption of the foundations on which their lives rest and the confusing realization that the parents on whom they depend have failed. It is futile to attempt to trace to the full conclusion either the consequences of divorce itself or of the conditions which lead to it or to say which is the greater disrupting force. Certainly the children's development is influenced in many ways by the irresponsible or immature personality make-up of one or both parents, which has made them unable to choose wisely or to live successfully in marriage. Although many children seem, at first, to take the breakdown of their home in their stride and to adopt a sensible, matter-of-fact attitude toward it, they are likely to be concealing far more complicated feelings. Others cannot understand why their parents, both of whom they may love and admire, cannot live together in friendship and harmony and they say so frankly. When they are older and have learned the meaning of responsibility, many are indignant to the point of bitterness to think that their parents have subjected them to all the consequences of their own personal failures, after contracting to make a home for them and assuming the obligation of supplying them to the best of their ability with the stuff out of which peace and happiness may be made. "They had no business to fail," says intolerant youth.

Helping Them Know the Truth

Yet adults are human, as their children discover, and sometimes the best must be made of what is irrevocably a tragedy. Though it may have been a necessary step to avoid more serious consequences, divorce, like the amputation of a limb, comes to all members of the family as a permanent mutilation. A certain amount of damage is irreparable, even though there is nothing to do but go on trying to patch it up as best one can and help the children to meet it. To this end there is no use trying to conceal the truth; as usual, the wisest course is to help children to face it. They will need encouragement toward a realistic, thoughtful consideration of the matter, one which is neither cynical nor sentimental. When a home is broken we can do best for our children by acknowledging our own mistakes, our regrets, and our realization that we have made life harder for them than we would have wished, and our hopes that when their turn comes they will do better. The worst parents can do for children is draw them into their own conflicts and bitterness, use them as the butt of their hate for each other, and let them grow up with the feeling that marriage is worthless. This is often apparent in the attitudes of people whose marriages have failed, and it is bound to be conveyed to children in a multitude of ways.

There are some marriages so irreparably bad that even for the children's sake alone they are better broken. Studies of children growing up in homes where there is chronic tension between parents show that they are more emotionally disturbed than those where such a marriage has been broken. Yet some seemingly hopeless marriages may be saved, especially if both parties accept professional help. For there is very little that can mean as much to a child as a home with his own father and mother in it and the chance to grow up with parents who are loyal and affectionate and who, despite odds—often great odds—foster each other's potentialities for growth instead of contriving to destroy them. It might be argued that children reared in a home with unhappily married parents might well learn what *not* to do by the force, as it were, of negative example; or, similarly, that living in constant contact with "too happy" a marriage might set standards of perfection rarely attainable. Studies of children from all kinds of homes, however, prove the case to be otherwise. On the whole, unsuccessful marriages breed more unsuccessful marriages in the next generation, and homes where parents have lived together harmoniously tend, by their very nature, to rear young people who have assimilated at least the necessary foundations of the same art.

Mental Hygiene of the Broken Home

If a divorce must finally take place, however, both parents should avoid the martyr role. Their lives should be as full of interests outside their homes and of friendships and family life within as they possibly can. A happy solution in the life of either parent, whether through another marriage or not, is likely to be an asset for the children, for it will go far to assuage those resentments in the parents themselves which otherwise exist and which inevitably leave their mark on those with whom they live closely.

Unless there are exceptional reasons against it, children are better off after a divorce if they can continue their relations with both parents. This is still their best chance to gain a realistic notion of what grownups of both sexes are like at close range. Otherwise the child of a broken marriage seems to have an unfortunate tendency to idealize whichever parent he has been deprived of and to form romantic notions of the one who does *not* have control of his immediate life. "If only I had my father"—thinks the child whose father in actuality may be a reprobate of the first order or perhaps just a very ordinary human being no more able to set everything to rights than the child's mother is. Yet without the experience of a flesh-and-blood person, this father can quickly assume magic qualities that hamper the child in coming to grips with his real problems and with his own inescapable responsibilities toward them. A parent who exists only in dreams is too ready an alibi for anything and everything.

No doubt a divorce that preserves the semblance of friendliness and reasonableness, where the parties are able to put the welfare of the children to some extent above their private bitterness, is infinitely to be preferred to one in which the full brunt of adult hate falls upon the children's heads. Unfortunately, however, the same personality defects that led to the failure of the marriage continue in most instances to operate against harmony between the parents after the divorce has taken place; the children therefore continue to be victimized. Jealousies are dominant. The absentee father is often accused of buying his children's love with material favors that the mother cannot afford. One home or the other, especially if there has been remarriage, is considered a "bad influence," and each parent may suspect the other of misrepresenting the true facts and prejudicing the children against him. Here again is a situation where a professional counselor or family-guidance agency, such as can now be found in many cities in the United States, may act as an impartial third party and by a kind of mediation and adjustment help divorced parents to adopt the course that is really best for the children.

WOMEN IN CONFLICT

It is hard to escape the conclusion that women have a special responsibility for the success or failure of marriage. In spite of all that a man can gain or lose by it, women usually gain or lose much more; their emotional investment in it is greater. At the same time their relation to marriage, along with all their other relations, is complicated because they are today living in a transition period, a period during which they have been steadily evicted from their traditional position in society and have not yet established a new one. Industrial developments have removed from the home most of the clothing and much of the food industry. Mechanical inventions and neighborhood transportation facilities simplify housekeeping at every point. In an age of specialization a woman is no longer a household jack-of-all-trades. With essential work removed from her hands, she is all too likely to becomes too busy with nonessentials as her children get older.

Out of a Job

Most important of all, and for whatever reasons, women do not bear anything like the number of children they used to and they do not educate them at home for nearly as many years. The average number of children per married couple in America today, in spite of the increased birth rate of recent years is no where near as high as it was a hundred years ago. The "population explosion" is the result of a reduced death rate. Although a woman's work is tremendous while her three or four children are young, it suddenly dwindles at a time of life when she herself is more fit than ever before for an active life, not only physically, but mentally and emotionally. The figures show that today women are actually healthier than men. At every point, from birth to old age, it is evident that the female of the species has more resistance to disease and better chances of survival than the male.

Modern women of forty are by no means on the shelf. Their own physical attractiveness is still as important to them as their daughters', and they have not relinquished their expectation of sexual happiness. In addition, they take their intellectual development seriously. Many of them have had a good education, often as good as their husband's or even better. Education for women is now the rule; culture is positively the fashion. Restless—partly because everyone is unsettled nowadays—energetic, realistic, capable, and for a long span out of a job, the American middle-class woman of today is almost certain to be a problem to herself and to her family.

All of this doubtless seems remote to the young matron who is busy rearing her two or three children on a small budget.

"But there is so much more to be done for children today," she protests. "Teeth and tonsils and inoculations and a much more elaborate education to prepare them for heaven knows what, and besides all that we now have their psychological problems that books like this make us conscious of. Our ancestors let their ten children grow up as best they could and half of them died young. People didn't demand so much of life. Now we feel that we've failed if in addition to bringing up healthy children we don't also bring up happy children!"

And with this protest we are forced to sympathize. Beyond question the life a *young* middle-class mother today is just as active as her energies can manage. For a few years she has a full-time job cut out for her just as surely as her forebears did.

Complications

Yet the fact remains that all this ends, and sometimes quite abruptly, when her youngest child, perhaps aged ten, is in school all morning and busy with the gang most of the afternoon. The older ones have even more pressing appointments, sometimes at home, more often elsewhere, and respectfully request their mother's absence. Nevertheless, there continue to be demands on the mother's time and attention which, when they come, are altogether imperative. Children must be taken here or there for special appointments of many kinds. There are parties to be planned, lots of conversations and shared enjoyments—let us hope—as well as the unexpected from every quarter. Illness does occur. In a multitude of ways there are things that the growing child's mother, and only his mother, can do for him. Even adolescents need parents, not in the same way that younger children do, but quite as urgently.

Mothers must remain on call, but there are nevertheless a great many hours a day when they are not required to care for their children and when housekeeping, reduced as it is by the use of modern conveniences, does not keep them busy. What, then, is the answer for the woman in her forties or fifties whose children are grown up or nearly so, who is still young herself and energetic and eager to go in the direction, whether she knows it or not, of work that is commensurate with her abilities?

One of the troubles is that women's technical training for work has been neglected. While most young men get their training and early work experiences, most young women become wives and mothers. It is hard to start from the beginning in the forties when others started in the twenties, and even a woman who has worked before her marriage will have become decidedly rusty if she has let her work lapse for twenty years. The married woman with children has to compete not only with men, but with unmarried women whose home claims are usually not as complex or absorbing as hers.

Already movements are afoot to try to meet this problem. Radcliffe College is leading the way with special opportunities and aids to enable its gifted graduates to resume work. Other colleges are following suit. But the problem is not simple. Men are traditionally the breadwinners and are, moreover, psychologically oriented toward careers and the achievement of success in the world at large. Women by the very nature of their biological make-up have other paramount claims. They are the childbearers, and this very fact seems to make it incumbent on them to be child rearers as well. Some do it better than others and find more pleasure in the job, but it is a rare mother who can actually turn this task over altogether to a substitute, no matter how capable the substitute may be, without feeling that she is cheating and being cheated. Mothers feel strongly tied to their children's physical lives. Children have a strange way of wanting their mothering from their mothers. If they are disappointed in this respect, no matter how warm the attentions of a substitute, children feel in their souls that they have been deprived of something vital and may nourish an angry resentment that is none the healthier because it is so often unconscious.

It would indeed be rash to try to say what men want of women and what husbands want from wives. The needs of human beings in the sex relation are so complex, so individual, and so profoundly affected by the culture in which they live that almost any generalization breaks down. Two generations ago the prospect of women voting implied for men that women would be wholly robbed of their feminine charms and that their homes would promptly be reduced to a wilderness of unrocked cradles and undarned socks. Today many men feel personally threatened by the idea of a wife who has a job outside the home, who works for pay or pursues a profession that claims her time and attention. Their interests and energies, they feel, should be for their homes alone, and they are resentful if their wives do not think so too. At the same time there are more and more husbands whose wives have jobs outside their homes and who genuinely prefer it that way. They feel that the deeper values of home life need not suffer by certain minor sacrifices and rearrangements of traditional routines; that, in fact, each member of the family gains by the enrichment of life which comes through the woman's widening activities.

Conflicts—External and Internal

We are still in a transition period, and women have by no means found themselves, either emotionally or in purely practical ways, in relation to the social revolution which has robbed them of much of their work. For their own happiness and their families', they need to be put back to work, not given the rest or vacation they often think they need. They are facing a genuine dilemma, however, in their struggle to find themselves in a dual role. They must meet the demands of love and family life, on the one hand, and, on the other, the demands of intellectual hunger and need for purposeful and significant activity in the larger world. Sometimes this dilemma is real, sometimes it exists almost wholly in the mind of husband, wife, or both. But it is usually the inner rather than the external problems that create the impasse. It is because of these that women have committed many follies in trying to renounce one course altogether in favor of the other, as well as in trying to meet both claims at once. A great deal of nonsense has been talked about this whole matter, both by those who insist on innate and eternal differences in the psychological make-up of men and women, by which their "spheres" are inevitably marked out, and by those who insist that there are no such differences. Marriages which have started favorably, entered into by young people who in all reason seemed well mated, have gone on the rocks as a result of a lack of clarity in this whole matter and therefore the feverish pursuit of one or the other extreme.

PERSONAL OPINIONS

At the risk of adding to the confusion through which every woman—and every man too, for that matter—must in the end find her own way unaided, the author cannot resist the temptation of hazarding some opinions and reflections based on personal experience, urging that these views should in no way be regarded as a prescription for living. There is always more than one path through the wilderness, and each person must find his own way according to his special needs and requirements.

1. In our society today there is an alarming tendency for women of the well-educated classes to engage in mere busy-work or spasmodic community jobs which do not command their full powers. It is true that women are found with increasing frequency in gainful occupations outside their homes—a trend which is likely to continue. But the *choice* is up to them. Even childbearing is optional. Women do not lose caste, as a man does, if they do *no* regular work. Society today, as always, safeguards its women in order to ensure the functions of childbearing, homemaking, and child care. But in the modern world these duties are soon discharged. Women are restless and often feel deprived of a sense of meaning in their lives. This makes for resentments between men and women, whether they know it or not, which threaten healthy home life. This is a dangerous state of affairs. Would women be happier and everyone better off if there were a few more "have-tos" in their lives? Are we wise enough actually to make sound choices now that we have won all this freedom?

2. Three or four children, a normal husband, and a modern home are *not* enough work to make a wholesome life for a well-educated, spirited woman between the ages of thirty-

five and sixty-five. When her last child goes off to school, she begins to have time on her hands. As commentator James Reston remarked: "Educated women . . . are the greatest unused natural resource in this country today."

3. It *is* possible for women who are clearheaded to combine work in and outside their homes without sacrificing the social graces and their femininity. It has, in fact, been done again and again. It *is* possible to have a happy husband and a family atmosphere where there is fun and gaiety and children who are warmly mothered, even if the mother does regular work, gainful or otherwise, outside the home. It will take planning, the plans will sometimes go wrong, and there will be upsets, difficulties, and occasional conflicts of interest. However, women today must face these no matter what choice they make. Any success in a plan which combines home and outside work will also require the kind of not-impossible husband who is sympathetic to his wife's wider interests and is willing to make certain adjustments. These adjustments need not be a threat to his masculine role in life and they need not interfere with his work.

4. Success in doing justice to both undertakings will depend, I believe, on women's realizing and accepting the fact that in performing a dual role their role as wife and mother will have paramount claims. Women who fail to realize that they stand in a special relationship of responsibility to their children, to the whole emotional climate of their homes, to the success of their marriage itself, are likely to be in for grievous failure. If there is an irreconcilable conflict, as

there sometimes is, and it comes to a showdown between work claims and home claims, not just their sense of duty, but the dictates of their heart, force them to choose their homes. They had better be clear about this in the first place, rather than discover it later at great cost. Whatever outside work they do should be undertaken in the full realization that personal relations claim them first.

5. If this is true—and it is a view which is admittedly colored by personal experience—it will mean that so long as women bear children and continue to want to rear them the main responsibility for breadwinning will rest with the men. The work women can do outside the home is likely to be irregular and their energies subject to deflection. These facts will put them at a competitive disadvantage and will lower the wage scale. They should be able, however, to accept the fact that they have two jobs in life, not one; and they should understand that the returns on neither of them can ever be measured in terms of money alone. This is, of course, hard on the woman who has been forced by circumstances to be the main breadwinner of the family.

6. From this much it is clear that I would further venture the guess that men and women besides differing physically differ also in their psychological constitutions. Yet as soon as one begins to say just what these differences are one gets into deep water. Briefly, it seems to me that these differences have to do with the amount and intensity of "drive" in women toward goals other than love goals. Women put

intense energy and aggression into the matter of ensuring their love life, finding husbands, caring for their children. Usually they put less into the pursuit of their other talents or intellectual endowments.

7. Though there are distinguished women in all fields, most seem to do the best work in fields related to personal relationships and the home, and at the present time they are found in greatest numbers in these occupations. As social workers, office workers, trained nurses, and in certain branches of the retail trades they are indispensable and are better at these jobs than most men just *because* they are women. The medical profession, especially where child welfare and public health are concerned, offers special scope for their talents and interests. Women have always contributed greatly to the arts, especially literature, and it is futile to speculate on why they nevertheless appear so rarely in the first ranks of artists and whether the explanation lies in cultural or in biological forces.

Meanwhile, both industries and the professions have been finding more and more places for women and, if we succeed in preserving our democracy, seem likely to continue to do so. There are numerous signs also of a demand that working conditions for women will be adjusted to the needs of women themselves, not merely to the needs of the job. Already maternity leave is granted in most of the public-school systems. Employers in all fields increasingly prefer to hire normally attractive women for all kinds of jobs, not just in department stores and offices, even knowing that they will probably marry and have children and end their work in industry altogether or at least put it on an irregular basis for many years. If industry really needs women, it will find ways of making the terms of their employment possible. Part-time jobs, irregular jobs, special conditions making it possible for women to get absences when emergencies arise at home, more day care centers and other provisions for adequate, part-time care of children—all these are possible adaptations to this end. These things will cost money. They are not "efficient" in the narrow sense of the term. But viewing them at longer range we see that they need not be socially wasteful if they make it possible for women to bring to the world outside their homes their own unique talents and special approach to living.

Nowadays, more than ever before, it should be unnecessary to point out that women's age-old task of producing new human beings and guiding them to maturity takes on new meaning, and that homes are among the few spots left on earth where civilization is a reality and where ideals of human kindness, simple decency, and justice can still be maintained. If these ideals are ever to be extended beyond the walls of the home and into society at large, women must do their share. They may, perhaps, never have "power" in the commonest sense of the word, but as they learn to know themselves better they will cease to want it because they will have ample confidence in the enduring value of what they have.

"I am done," says William James, "with great things and big things, great institutions and big successes, and I am for those tiny, invisible, molecular forces that work from individual to individual, creeping through crannies of the world like so many rootlets, or like the capillary oozing of water, yet which, if you give them time, will rend the hardest monuments of man's pride."

CHAPTER ELEVEN

WHAT IS CHARACTER EDUCATION?

WHAT CAN WE give our children today that can possibly serve them in a world where the finer human aspirations seem to have been defeated and where perhaps for the duration of their lives they may have to live in a nation which, at best, has become an armed camp? How can we educate them so that they understand the meaning and value of justice, tolerance, culture, truth, freedom, and at the same time put enough iron into their souls to enable them to find ways to preserve these things? To many it looks as though we had been educating youth to appreciate and to enjoy civilization at the very moment when mere survival is threatened. Young people are likely to discover, too, that life will be led through a type of collective action that is alien to the individualistic habits of us all, and through a course of austerity which has all but gone out of fashion. For the nation today the primary problem is how we can both survive and defend the values that make life for ourselves and our children worth living and without building a machine which by its very nature will destroy these values. The same applies to youth. How can they be helped to become strong and yet know what they are to be strong in behalf of?

The problem is not altogether new. Events throughout the world have sharpened our sense of a need which has long been felt. In this "unbelieving world," perhaps just because it is an unbelieving world, parents have for many years been demanding new guideposts for the character training of their

children. Though church *membership* increases, there are many for whom the church fails to meet spiritual needs and seems out of accord with contemporary knowledge. In this age of science we must learn to live with hypothesis and partial truth without losing those moral convictions needed for action. This is the dilemma.

So great is our bewilderment that we sometimes yield to the temptation to cast longing glances backward to what at this safe distance looks like the simple faith of our forefathers and the definite moral codes by which right was right and wrong was wrong; back to the era when men and women, instead of expecting happiness, prayed only for the strength to perform their duties. Many have asked if it would not be better to do a rightabout-face and, for the sake of infusing new vigor into us all, strive to recapture what seem in retrospect the moral simplicities of the past.

It is only too apparent, however, that there is no going back even if we would and that many of us would not even if we could. Solutions do not come through mere reaction or through attempts to revive a way of life that died perhaps, for the fundamental reason that it failed to meet human needs. We must, therefore, face the fact that we are committed to work our way as best we can through the dilemmas confronting us today, searching for our own solutions and believing, too, that despite our weaknesses we have some real achievements to our credit. If we must be reproached with lost idealism, and some of us with cynicism, at least we need not sigh for a recent past where cruelty and hypocrisy could so easily conceal themselves in sanctimonious clothing. Whatever our faults, we perhaps possess a more penetrating eye. The world of the average man or woman today encompasses a larger number of facts; their minds are more tutored, their insights keener. Yet it is this very realism, informed and rational though it is, which often seems to be exactly what has robbed this generation of the habit of feeling strongly and simply, accepting the possibility of personal deprivation, of giving themselves zestfully to the experience of living. We emerge clear-eyed perhaps, yet also—if many were to make their confession—feeling impotent and empty.

For parents for whom the church and religion have been vital and satisfying forces, the answer is relatively simple. They will inevitably want to give to their children what has proved valid and substantial *for them*. They will introduce their children early to both the observances and the teachings of their particular creed, seeing to it that they are taught not only in church but at home also. But parents who have found no such answer for themselves within any religious group also continue to raise the question of what it is that they owe their children in spiritual nourishment. Should children be **encouraged to attend church or Sunday school even when** their parents have become indifferent? Does religious belief give added weight to the demands of morality? Does a firm belief in an ever-present God infuse into those who have it a sense of peace and inner security which they are likely to need sorely?

These are the questions parents ask and the answers will differ widely. Many have seized desperately on religion as though it were some sort of patent medicine. They take it or recommend it as a dose for spiritual sickness and feel justified if it makes them feel a little better. The truth or falsity of the view of life offered by the religion in question is quite evidently of secondary importance. They do not seem to need to know whether this or that set of doctrines will stand scrutiny by a mature and honest mind; they only want to know whether it gives a rosier view of things. Devoid of the kind of pride which forces them to demand reality first and foremost, they make their choices without intellectual conscience. If illusions taste sweet in the mouth, they seem to say, then let us have illusions.

I confess that to me, at least, there seems something dangerously weakening in this approach to religion. It by no means includes all of religion's adherents; even today there are a few hardier mentalities who strive to bring all the intellectual forces at their disposal to the position which they hold to on religious matters. But I would venture the guess that we are not again likely to have a religion that plays a vital and imperative role in our lives unless a movement is born which widely enlists, as it has in past centuries, the most vigorous minds of our times. Today there are evidences in some quarters of renewed religious interest. It is questionable how deep this goes for the majority of Americans. I would venture to guess that if religion is ever to recover from its present doldrums and live again, its teachings must achieve an accord with modern knowledge, modern social problems, and the requirements of the modern world, which it lacks today.

For these reasons, then, I would prefer to see parents ask whether religion offers truths that *they themselves* believe are fundamental and applicable before they set out to present religious teachings or encourage church affiliations for their children. Children are quick to find us out, and a child can hardly be expected to regard as essential what his parents are lukewarm about. Every Sunday school knows that the home's attitude counts incalculably and that it is the hardest task in the world to make religious teachings live unless they are backed up and sincerely practiced by parents at home.

Whatever our religious beliefs, or lack of them, all of us are descendants of some great religious tradition that has had an enormous effect on the culture in which we live. Whether we accept or definitely reject religion in our own homes, religion as a force is something that should be understood. We impoverish our children's cultural heritage if we limit their connection with these things to purely formal observance or if we let them grow up in ignorance of the meanings and practices of religions, holy days as celebrated through the ages. Whatever their failure, religions at their best have expressed man's highest hopes and should be understood both in expression and belief. It is of value, too, to know something of the religions of other peoples and races, though this can never take the place of a fuller understanding of the traditions of one's own people. To understand, however, involves more than intellectual "knowing"; it involves feelings and senses and firsthand emotional experience of the festivals and rituals as they have been practiced in home and church for centuries.

Such knowledge by no means need involve us in a return to treligious *belief*, to a church connection, or to systematic religious education; each home must make that choice for itself. It does mean that everyone needs not only clearly held inner convictions concerning spiritual values but perhaps also dramatic forms to give them expression. And further it is a reminder that parents cannot hope to give their children a sense of the importance of non-material values if they themselves do not show that they regard them as important in all their relationships. If parents are spiritually empty, the chances are that their children will be too, and this emptiness will be handed from generation to generation until some great human calamity wakes us all from our troubled sleep.

Children do not necessarily need parents who are church members or who instill them with religious beliefs; they do need parents who themselves hold strong and passionate moral convictions. If these convictions are honestly thought out and sincerely felt, it will not matter whether they are religious, unreligious, or definitely antireligious. It will not matter whether children at first only half understand them or whether as they grow older they seem to repudiate them. The important thing is that children should grow up with parents who believe that there are some ways of life which for us today are better than others and that these ways are worth defending with every ounce of our strength. Tolerance, the moment it becomes nothing but perpetual indecision and an inability to prefer and to call "good" one way of life rather than another, is mere indifference. There are many "good" ways, it is true, but in recognizing this we must know also that some ways are bad, and we must take care that we do not lose the power to distinguish between them. A child's spiritual education begins as soon as he becomes aware that his parents feel intensely concerning these distinctions.

All these things may seem far removed from matters properly belonging in a practical manual on child development, but perhaps it accords with the writer's fundamental belief that if we are to help our children develop we must develop ourselves; that to awaken them to the possibilities for a good life we must possess some understanding of it ourselves and some small measure of ability to live it or at least to pursue it sincerely. Whoever has children to rear dares not be a coward or a pessimist or to be indifferent to everything which gives life nobility or beauty. This is our responsibility, since whether these things will be present or absent in the world depends wholly on whether or not man develops the will to put them there.

Children, even small ones, are sensitive to what their parents hold most dear. If truth, honor, kindness, and responsible living have values for their fathers and mothers far beyond questions of immediate personal profit, these values are very likely to become theirs. But children must also have a chance to subject themselves to tests. They will not only need to honor responsibility; they will need to take responsibilities—not only to know that it is good to be kind, but to give and receive kindnesses; not only to honor bravery in heroes, but to feel compelled to practice it themselves in the face of disappointment, sickness, or death itself, when it enters, as it may, the life of even a young child. It is true that the parents must lead the way by their own courage, but children too must face realities.

The best help that can be offered parents in bringing up their children is help in their own personal, emotional development. Parents need to be free and alive enough themselves so that they can do things actively with their children— so that they can have good times together, laugh, talk, work, and play together, get angry at each other without excessive guilt, and love each other without dependence. If the way is clear for these things and if parents are able at the same time to confront their sons and daughters with their own mature standards in living, children will learn—not all at once, perhaps, but gradually as they develop and with many backslidings. Sound and responsible character in children does not come because they have been caught young and trained that way, but because they have been enabled, of their own free wills, to give up their early egoistic and primitive wishes through affectionate contacts with parents who themselves love and practice civilized living.

What makes a good home? First let us be clear that there are some things that can never, by themselves, make a home a good one and that will always remain of secondary importance. We have all been inclined to set too much store by them. These things can be grouped under what are commonly termed advantages. "Giving children every advantage," however, is hardly any advantage at all, and may even prove a handicap. Music, good books, private schools, summers in the country, travel, and all the other goods that money brings have been vastly overrated. When it comes to helping children acquire a toughness of fiber and the sense of reality they are likely to need, none of these things are comparable to taking responsibilities and looking success and failure squarely in the eye. We would all do everything in our power to give our children good health, but we must broaden our concept to include good mental health as well, and we must take thought both of what is meant by this and how it may be achieved. Children have never thrived because their parents had some remarkable educational "system" and stuck to it; they thrive, when it comes right down to it, because there is something in the spirit or atmosphere of a home which causes them to thrive. This spirit rests basically on what kind of people their parents are, on their vision of what is worth while in life, and on their steadfastness in giving this vision some reality.

If we look closely at the good homes we know, homes where children are fairly happy, natural, active, and responsible, where quarrels are not too bitter and children's faults not too deep-seated—what will we find? We will probably find that in these homes punishments are used sparingly and always fairly; moral lectures are scarce. And if we ask the parents we envy to tell the secret of their success with their children, they will probably not be able to, but will laugh and say, "Well, you see, we think an awful lot of them. We have lots of good times together."

A remark not without significance, and one which brings us back where we started: success with children depends on enjoyment of them and sympathy with them at all ages and stages—in sickness and in health, when they are difficult and when they are delightful. Even when we ache with discouragement we must see their need as well as ours and know beyond any doubt that the task of helping them to grow strong is a task that can never be abandoned. Raising a family is the hardest of all jobs, but in the end it is also the most rewarding.

SUGGESTED READING

The following titles were selected from lists issued by the Book Review Committee of the Child Study Association of America.

On Parenthood and Family

BROTHERS AND SISTERS. *Edith G. Neisser.* Harper, 1951. 241 pp., $3.00. Warm, simple, and competent discussion of the friction and jealousy to be found in normal children in the same family and of constructive ways of handling the problem. Has a chapter on twins.

CHILDHOOD AND ADOLESCENCE: A Psychology of the Growing Person. *L. Joseph Stone* and *Joseph Church.* Random House, 1957. 456 pp. $7.75. Two members of the Vassar College Department of Child Study who have studied, lived with, and enjoyed children describe how children grow, learn, feel, think, and react, giving a living picture of growth toward maturity.

CHILDREN . . . THEIR WAYS AND WANTS. *Katherine Reeves.* Educational Publishing, 1959. 192 pp. $2.95. In this sensitively written volume, the author describes children's emotional needs from nursery age to later school years, in the light of what growing seems to mean to the child and what it might feel like to him. Combines mind and heart in the understanding of childhood. For parents and teachers.

DR. SPOCK TALKS WITH MOTHERS: Growth and Guidance. *Benjamin M. Spock, M.D.* Houghton Mifflin, 1961. 306 pp. $5.00. Dr. Spock combines his unique ability to help parents understand themselves and their children with warm, nonauthoritarian, but specific advice on coping with the problems of growing up. The various chapters cover such areas as health, jealousy, discipline, bedwetting, dawdling and whining, fears, sex, and the strains of adolescence.

THE ENCYCLOPEDIA OF CHILD CARE AND GUIDANCE. *Sidonie M. Gruenberg.* Doubleday, 1954. 1016 pp. $7.50. In nontechnical language, this book covers every imaginable topic on the child's physical, mental, and emotional growth, from birth through adolescence, and on family relationships. Alphabetically arranged; chapters by outstanding authorities; illustrations and charts; extensive bibliographies; sources for further materials and services for families and children.

EXPECTANT MOTHERHOOD. *Nicholson J. Eastman, M.D.* Little, Brown, 1957. Rev. ed. 198 pp. $2.00. A practical handbook which gives a simple, clear picture of various aspects of pregnancy, labor, delivery, and the postpartum period. This revised edition of a little book that has already been widely used incorporates the principal advances in maternity care of the last decade.

THE HAPPY FAMILY. *John Levy, M.D.,* and *Ruth Monroe.* Alfred A. Knopf, 1956. 16th printing. 328 pp. $4.00. First published in 1938, this sane and wise discussion of marriage and family life remains one of the best in the field.

MARRIAGE IN THE MODERN WORLD. *Phillip Polatin, M.D.,* and *Ellen C. Philtine.* J. B. Lippincott, 1956. 313 pp. $3.95. Provides a constructive treatment of marriage as a personal relationship involving unique individuals. It covers sexual attitudes and behavior, parent-child relationships, economic and emotional considerations, preparation for marriage, as well as an analysis of difficulties and a discussion of divorce. An unusually well presented and understanding volume.

MATERNITY: A Guide to Prospective Motherhood. *Frederick W. Goodrich, Jr., M.D.* Prentice-Hall, 1959. 130 pp. $1.75. A simple, reassuring presentation by a prominent obstetrician of the facts a pregnant woman wants to know. Breast feeding and bottle feeding are discussed in a way which leaves the mother free to choose the method which will suit her best.

PARENTS WITHOUT PARTNERS: A Guide for Divorced, Widowed, or Separated Parents. *Jim Egleson* and *Janet Frank Egleson.* Dutton, 1961. 249 pp. $4.50. This sympathetic book offers much down-to-earth guidance in the many problems which one-parent families face. Includes a fine chapter on the divorced father and many helpful suggestions for ways to improve parent-child relationships as well as relationships between ex-mates.

WHAT TO TELL YOUR CHILDREN ABOUT SEX. *Child Study Association of America.* Arco, 1961. 92 pp. $1.50. Paperbound ed., Pocket Books, 35c. A book to help parents impart the facts of life to their children. The book contains many concrete, practical suggestions for answering children's questions, along with helpful guides to understanding children's sexual development from early childhood through adolescence. Includes a good reading list.

On Infants and Preschool Children

A COMMON SENSE BOOK OF BABY AND CHILD CARE. *Benjamin Spock, M.D.* Duell, Sloan & Pearce, 1957. Rev. & enl. ed. 627 pp. $5.00. Paperbound ed., *Baby and Child Care,* Pocket Books, 50c. A comprehensive handbook on baby and child care by a pediatrician who understands the physical and emotional needs of babies and their families. This recent edition has a fine chapter on discipline and a deeper insight into behavior problems.

THE MAGIC YEARS. *Selma Fraiberg.* Scribner's, 1959. 305 pp. $3.95. This nearly perfect book about the child's development in the first five years is a truly scientific work written for parents. Writing simply, yet profoundly—and with humor—the author discusses feeding, talking, sex education, self-control, fears, fantasy, and other areas. An important addition to the classic literature on early childhood.

THE NURSERY SCHOOL: A Human Relationship Laboratory. *Katherine H. Read.* W. B. Saunders, 1955. 264 pp. $4.25. A revealing book for parents and teachers, which describes the role of the nursery school in the life of the growing child, and stresses its use as a laboratory for the study of human behavior.

THE WONDERFUL STORY OF HOW YOU WERE BORN. *Sidonie M. Gruenberg.* Hanover House, 1959. 39 pp. $2.50. A simple story, beautifully told, to be read aloud to a young child, yet for older children, too. A "Guide to Parents" inside the jacket helps parents to put this book to the best possible use.

YOUR CHILD STEPS OUT. *Edgar S. Bley.* Rev. ed. of *Launching Your Preschooler.* Sterling, 1961. 124 pp. $1.00. A useful small book chock full of wise and happy suggestions for introducing preschoolers to such varied "first experiences" as a zoo trip, doctor's visit, and nursery school.

On School-Age Children and Adolescents

EMOTIONAL PROBLEMS OF ADOLESCENTS. *J. Roswell Gallagher, M.D.,* and *Herbert I. Harris, M.D.* Oxford, 1958. 174 pp. $3.50. A straightforward, reassuring book by a pediatrician and a psychiatrist to help parents and others foster sound emotional development in adolescents. Emphasizing the malleability of this age, the authors explore the basis of emotional difficulties and ways in which the understanding adult can alleviate them.

FACTS OF LIFE AND LOVE FOR TEENAGERS. *Evelyn Millis Duvall.* Association Press, 1956. Rev. ed. 426 pp. $3.50. Paperbound ed., Popular Library, 25c. A useful book for both the teenager and his parents. The author has a lively understanding of young people's need to know how to behave with each other in a variety of situations. The first section deals clearly and accurately with the physiology of sex.

HOW TO LIVE THROUGH JUNIOR HIGH SCHOOL. *Eric W. Johnson.* Lippincott, 1959. 288 pp. $3.95. A schoolmaster with a firm sense of values describes with humor and wisdom the seventh-, eighth-, and ninth-grade children he knows so well. Adding their thoughts to his own, he discusses schoolwork, social life in and out of school, sex education, and life at home. His book will help parents keep their own sense of humor and perspective during these difficult early adolescent years.

ON BECOMING A WOMAN. *Mary McGee Williams* and *Irene Kane.* Dell, 1959. Paperbound, 159 pp. 25c. A sympathetic, practical, straightforward book intended to help the teenage girl understand the physical and emotional pressures she is experiencing. Parents who read it should gain new insight into the problems and feelings of their adolescent daughters.

THE PARENTS' GUIDE TO EVERYDAY PROBLEMS OF BOYS AND GIRLS: Helping Your Child from Five to Twelve. *Sidonie M. Gruenberg.* Random House, 1958. 384 pp. $4.95. An eminently wise and sane book dealing with the often overlooked school age child. The author is always aware of the many changes in the world today which make the lives of children different from the past generation. The book is rich in suggestions for daily life and better family relationships; also for the child's development in the arts.

THE WONDER OF LIFE. *Milton I. Levine, M.D.* and *Jean H. Seligmann.* The Golden Press, 1952. Rev., illus. ed. 116 pp. $2.95. Parents will welcome this book of sex information for the 7- to 11-year-old, presented simply and without sentimentality by authors experienced in dealing with children.

YOUR ADOLESCENT AT HOME AND IN SCHOOL. *Mary* and *Lawrence K. Frank.* Viking, 1956. 336 pp. $3.95. A Signet Key Book, New American Library, 1959. 287 pp. 50c. A useful distillate of the best of previous knowledge of adolescence, plus the authors' clarifying point of view. It is addressed to parents and teachers, who will find it of daily practical value and appreciate its fairness in ensuring the individuality of both adolescent and adult.

On Special Topics

ADOPTION AND AFTER. *Louise Raymond.* Harper, 1955. 238 pp. $3.00. A thorough, thoughtful, and sympathetic treatment of the emotional experiences of the adopted child and his parents. Discusses the need for the parents' emotional preparation, the ways whereby the usual parent-child tensions and emotional strains may become accentuated by the fact of the adoption, and what to do about them. Procedures for adopting a child are also explained.

THE COMPLETE BOOK OF CHILDREN'S PLAY. *Ruth E. Hartley* and *Robert M. Goldenson.* Crowell, 1957. 462 pp. $5.95. A description of children and their play from birth to adolescence, showing how their development affects their interests and skills and how appropriate play at each level can stimulate growth. Included are hobbies, pets, travel games, television, convalescent activities, and lists of books, records, and pictures. Though classifications by age of children's interests and characteristics may seem too scheduled, the book gives a balance of psychological and practical information.

HELPING YOUR GIFTED CHILD. *Ruth Strang.* Dutton, 1960. 270 pp. $4.50. A sensible, thorough discussion of gifted children: how to identify them, how to rear them, how to educate them. The author's concern for gifted children as individuals rather than as sources of potential brainpower is always refreshing and helpful.

PREJUDICE AND YOUR CHILD. *Kenneth B. Clark.* Beacon, 1955. 151 pp. $2.50. A clear, dispassionate analysis of factors which contribute to prejudice, along with helpful suggestions as to what school, community agencies, churches, and parents can do to reduce and prevent feelings of prejudice in children.

TODAY'S CHILDREN AND YESTERDAY'S HERITAGE: A Philosophy of Creative Religious Development. *Sophia L. Fahs.* Beacon, 1952. 224 pp. $3.50. An appealing and useful book about children and their religious development. Nonsectarian in approach, it stresses the role of the parent and teacher in helping the child to develop his own beliefs about himself and the nature of the universe.

YOU AND YOUR CHILD'S HEALTH. *Paulette Kahn Hartrich.* Harper, 1955. 208 pp. $3.00. The sick or convalescent child, the child who must undergo an operation, even the healthy child about to meet his first dentist—all present problems that call for wise handling. This book should help parents to meet such situations with sympathy for the child and understanding for his anxieties.

YOUR CHILD'S READING TODAY. *Josette Frank.* Doubleday, 1960. Rev. ed. 408 pp. $3.95. Thoughtful discussion of the place of reading and the mass media in the child's life, with suggested lists of books for various ages and interests. An understanding, warm, and helpful book, addressed to parents but useful also to teachers, librarians, and everyone concerned with children and their books.

INDEX

Adjustment pattern, 276 ff.
Aggressiveness, 79, 132 ff., 259 ff.
Anger, 259 ff.
Anxiety, 163 ff., 173, 253, 265 (see also Fears)
Apron strings, 581 ff.

Bed wetting, 21, 251, 275 (see also Bladder and bowel training)
Birthdays, 213 ff.
Bladder and bowel training, 47 ff., 156
Blanket sucking, 20
Bodily differences between sexes, 159 ff.
Books, 207 ff.
Bottle feeding, 7 ff., 274
Breast feeding (see Nursing)
Brothers, 96 ff.
Bullying, 132 ff.

Character training, 69, 90 ff., 316 ff.
Child Study Association of America, 273, 327
Cleanliness, 54 ff., 67
Common sense, xv ff., 271 ff.
Concentration, 198 ff.
Conflicts, 308 ff.
Conscience, 67, 80, 291

Counseling, 277
Counterfeit love, 81 ff.
Crying, 28 ff.

Dawdling (see Punctuality)
Dental malocclusion, 27 ff.
Destructiveness, 262 ff.
Discipline, 18 ff., 29 ff., 70 ff.
Distractibility, 200 ff.
Divorce, 299 ff.

Eating, 37 ff., 274
Emotional danger signals, 273 ff.
Excrements, 52 ff.

Face picking, 23
Family Service Agencies, 277
Fantasies, 200, 275
Fathers, 31 ff., 169 ff., 216 ff.
Fears, 263 ff., 275
Fighting, 274 ff.
Friendships, 126 ff., 151 ff.

Habits, x, xii, 20 ff.
Head bumping, 20 ff.
Hobbies, 203 ff., 227 ff., 288 ff.
Holidays, 212 ff.
Honesty, 62 ff.
Hostility, 79, 259 ff.

Imagination, 65 ff., 275
Immaturity, 274 ff., 281 ff.

Jealousy, 100 ff., 109 ff., 119

Lying (*See* Honesty)

Manners, 59 ff.
Masturbation, 178 ff.
Mealtime, 37 ff.
Medical care, 5, 249 ff.
Mental health, 240 ff.
Middle children, 114
Movies, 209 ff.

Nail biting, 248 ff.
Neatness, 56 ff.
Negativism, 256 ff.
Nervous system, 10 ff.
Nightmares, 107 ff., 274
Night terrors, 12, 107, 250, 263 ff., 274
Nudity, 167 ff.
Nursery schools, 145 ff.
Nurses, 30 ff.
Nursing, 6 ff.

Only boy, 115 ff.
Only child, 117 ff.
Only girl, 115 ff.
Optimism, 128 ff.
"Outgrowing it," xiii, 242 ff., 265

Pamphlets, 5, 273
Pets, 211 ff.
Play, 130 ff., 186 ff.
Playing alone, 196 ff.
Problem child, 240 ff., 271 ff.
Problem parents, 278 ff.
Psychiatrists, 277, 297 ff.
Punctuality, 58
Punishments, 84 ff.

Quarreling, 96 ff., 110
Questions about sex, 159 ff., 165, 169 ff., 175 ff.

Reading (*See* Books)
Religion, 317 ff.
Restlessness, 273
Rewards, 84 ff.
Rocking, 20 ff., 261

Schedule, 16 ff.
Second baby, 98 ff., 253
Sex play, 172 ff.
Sexuality, 154 ff., 234 ff., 253
Shyness, 60 ff., 142 ff.
Siblings, 96 ff.
Sisters, 96 ff.
Sleep, 35 ff., 210
Sleeping with parents, 6, 166
Social development, 126 ff.
Spanking, 21, 87 ff.
Speech defects, 252 ff.
Stealing, 66 ff.
Stuttering, 254 ff.

Television, 210, 230, 273
Thumb sucking, 23 ff., 155, 246 ff., 275
Timidity, 66, 267 ff.
Toys, 188 ff.

Unhappiness, xv, 274

Weaning, 9 ff., 25 ff.
Women, 217 ff., 303 ff.
Wool picking, 20
Working mothers, 309 ff.
Worry, 163 ff., 275

Youngest children, 114